Contents

INTRODUCTION

Reading *Richard II*

I: Overview

RICHARD II is a fascinating play with a fascinating critical history. The purpose of this volume is to collect together and discuss some of the criticism that the play has inspired over nearly four hundred years. Running through the volume are five main themes: history, theatre, politics, language and criticism itself. To these five areas we should add the category of character; it is an unfashionable approach today, but in the past a great deal of the debate focused on Richard's character and its significance. Not all these themes appear in every chapter, but they provide the basic framework of ideas connecting the different extracts and under-lying their choice. The volume does not cover every twist and turn of the play's critical history since that would clearly be impossible – the 1988 bibliography by Josephine Roberts, for example, lists over 800 articles on the play since 1944.[1] Rather, it is concerned with some of the major figures who have written about the play, with the critical positions and ideas that have informed their writing, and with the aspects of the text that seem important to foreground.

One of the obvious advantages of examining a range of criticism from different periods is the different perspective this provides on the text and on how to read it. In turn this can change or challenge our usual critical practice and open up new ideas to think about. The question of reading – why we do it, what we read and how we read – is something touched on below, but first it is worthwhile summing up very quickly the major shifts in criticism that the play has undergone. Such a brief overview is bound to be inadequate given the complex argument which has surrounded the play, but it does offer a kind of map of that discussion and its features, together with an outline of the chapters that follow. The argument can perhaps best be sum-marised by combining a chapter summary with a short series of quotations from the sixteenth through to the twentieth century; three of these are about the figure of Richard II and one about modern critical theory.

The first is a remark made by Elizabeth I in 1601 to William Lambarde, the Keeper of the Records at the Tower of London, in which she appears to identify herself both with the historical figure of the king and also with the hero of Shakespeare's play:

■ I am Richard II. know ye not that?[2] □

Elizabeth's remark needs to be seen in context, but even in this simple form it gives a sense of the potential political implications of *Richard II* and its possible contemporary relevance to Elizabethan England. These are aspects taken up in Chapter One. What will emerge there is a sense of the richness of the play's historical contexts, and of the difficult and awkward questions it raises about rebellion and the deposition of a legitimate monarch who breaks the law. These are questions that later criticism will return to time and again.

Included in Chapter One is a substantial essay by David Norbrook which acts as preparation for much of that later criticism. In the essay, Norbrook refers, for example, both to Walter Pater and his influential nineteenth-century view of Richard as a poet-king figure, as well as to such central twentieth-century critics as E. M. W. Tillyard and Ernst Kantorowicz. The essay itself thus serves as a map of the book and the arguments that have shaped modern approaches to *Richard II*. It also provides a further introduction to the critical debate about the play, but focused through its relation to contemporary history. Norbrook's own approach is essentially that of traditional historical criticism which sets the text in its immediate context of specific events and persons.

The second chapter moves on from the early contexts of the play, and examines the critical discussion of Shakespeare during the eighteenth century and the adaptation of *Richard II* by Nahum Tate in 1712. This was one of a considerable number of adaptations of Shakespeare's plays after the Restoration of Charles II in 1660. Criticism at this time was dominated by Neo-Classical thinking, which found faults with Shakespeare's writing and did not hesitate to correct or rewrite the plays. At the same time the eighteenth century sees the beginning of the serious editing and discussion of Shakespeare. The chapter includes excerpts from Tate's version, as well as from the major critic of the age, John Dryden, on the question of tragedy. As will become apparent, the eighteenth century had little time for Shakespeare's history plays, largely because they lay outside Neo-Classical rules, but also because of their potentially subversive nature.

Chapter Three is concerned with the response of Romantic writers to Shakespeare and to the play. In particular, it looks at how Schlegel, Coleridge and Hazlitt (all writing at the end of the eighteenth century and start of the nineteenth century, after the French Revolution of 1798) forged a new critical understanding of Shakespeare as a great artist, developing new critical ideas, in particular about character, language and the organic unity of works of art, on which to build that understanding. Thus, for example, the following by Coleridge in his Lectures on Shakespeare and Milton (1812):

■ I will now advert to the character of the King. He is represented as a man not deficient in immediate courage, which displays itself at his assassination; or in powers of mind, as appears by the foresight he exhibits throughout the play: still, he is weak, variable, and woman-ish, and possesses feelings, which, amiable in a female, are misplaced in a man, and altogether unfit for a king.[3] □

Essentially, Coleridge here suggests that Richard is lacking in manliness. Such remarks may seem out of tune with modern sensibilities and ideas about gender, but, like Elizabeth's comment, this view needs to be set in context, in particular the context of nineteenth-century Romantic criticism and its reaction against the Neo-Classical views of the eighteenth century. Paradoxically, Coleridge seems to echo eighteenth-century criticism by suggesting that Richard's 'womanish . . . feelings' are 'unfit for a king', as one of the tenets of Neo-Classicism was a concern with appropriate behaviour.

Nevertheless, in many ways Coleridge's writings mark a turning point toward modern criticism and its concern with the human subject. Indeed, Coleridge's interest in, and analysis of, character is perhaps the most important legacy of Romantic criticism, though it would be mis-leading to see it simply as that. As Chapter Three seeks to show, what Romantic criticism also creates is not only a new attitude towards Shakespeare's history plays, especially *Richard II*, but also a new kind of close attention to the details of the text – in a word, critical analysis.

Coleridge was to exert a powerful influence on succeeding genera-tions of critics, especially on Walter Pater at the end of the nineteenth century. The idea of Richard as a weak king prone to poetic dreaming is central to Pater's essay in Chapter Four. The chapter itself deals with the criticism from 1880 through to the beginning of the twentieth century, specifically the stress seen in the writings of Pater and W.B. Yeats on the value of feelings as against the harsh materialism represented by Bolingbroke. In this emphasis both Pater and Yeats were reacting against the excesses of the Victorian economy and its values of wealth and masculinity.

If Coleridge marks a radical change in direction of criticism in the early nineteenth century towards character and feeling, the next and probably the most influential change is that brought about by the critic E.M.W. Tillyard in the 1940s. Indeed, in absolute terms, Tillyard is the major critical figure as far as Shakespeare's histories are concerned, and much recent criticism has been absorbed with either rejecting or contesting his ideas about the plays. These are a few brief comments from his work on *Richard II*:

■ Thus *Richard II*, although reputed so simple and homogenous a play, is built on a contrast. The world of medieval refinement is indeed the main object of presentation but it is threatened and in the end superseded by the more familiar world of the present.

    . . . In doctrine the play is entirely orthodox. Shakespeare knows that Richard's crimes never amounted to tyranny and hence that outright rebellion against him was a crime.[4] □

The language here is very evidently different from that of Coleridge: in place of the language of feeling and character is that of politics and history. With Tillyard we seem to be back with historical criticism again, as in the case of Norbrook above. There are, however, important differences between the kind of critical thesis Tillyard puts forward about the history plays and their intention, and looking at the play's immediate historical context and reception. Those differences lie in the extent to which Tillyard articulates a political position for the plays, locating them in a conservative philosophy or set of ideas. This kind of political/historical approach has had a huge impact on the study not simply of *Richard II* but also of the whole of Shakespeare and Renaissance literature. This, in part, explains why the critical history of the play is important: the critical argument about the play is an argument about the sort of value attached to Shakespeare and literary studies more generally, and also about the place of literature in culture and cultural history.

Similar issues come up, as might be expected, in relation to Shakespeare's other history plays. At one level it is misleading to cut *Richard II* off from these, and there is, indeed, much to be said for the argument that *Richard II* is designed as the first play in the sequence of plays known as the second tetralogy or group of four plays. This group, also sometimes called the Henriad, includes *Richard II*, the two parts of *Henry IV*, and *Henry V*. Tillyard was not the first critic to focus on the histories as a group, but he did thrust the plays into sharper political focus by his reading of them.

The three quotations above – from Elizabeth I, Coleridge and Tillyard – provide a series of pointers that take us from the beginning of the seventeenth century through to the end of the Second World War, from the initial circumstances of the play through the profound changes brought about by Romantic criticism to mid-twentieth-century criticism's reinterpretation of the history plays. While there are large gaps to be filled in between these positions, they do offer a fair picture of the critical fortunes of *Richard II*. Never quite as popular as the major tragedies

(*Hamlet, King Lear, Macbeth* and *Othello*), the play nevertheless has been the subject of fierce critical argument. That argument was renewed almost as soon as Tillyard published his books on the histories, and is evident in Chapter Six. This deals with New Criticism, with those critics who looked closely at the play's imagery and its themes, but also with those critics who challenged Tillyard' s reading of both *Richard II* and Elizabethan ideology. It could be argued that such critics reflect a further stage in the development of criticism of the play, and it is the case that they have many new ideas and insights to offer. But they do not quite mark the kind of decisive break with the past that Coleridge or Tillyard do. For that we need to turn to the impact of modern critical theory on the study of English literature.

A sense of that break with the past can be found in the following quotation from the French structuralist critic Roland Barthes's essay 'The Death of the Author':

■ The reader is the space on which all the quotations that make up a writing are inscribed without any of them being lost; a text's unity lies not in its origin but in its destination. . . . Classic criticism has never paid any attention to the reader; for it, the writer is the only person in literature.[5] □

By 'classic criticism' Barthes means both the sort of criticism written by Coleridge and by Tillyard and the New Critics. For such critics, Barthes argues, the meaning of a text lies with its author, in the author's intentions. In turn this implies that the meaning of the text remains singular, the job of the critic being that of trying to search out the author's original, lost intention. Barthes's essay contests this idea and replaces the notion of the writer as central with that of the reader as central. The point of this change might not, today, be all that startling, but in the context of the critical revolution of the late 1960s, with the introduction of structuralism and poststructuralism, and with the impact of feminism as well as other strands of radical and political criticism, Barthes's words marked a striking challenge to all that had gone before.

'The Death of the Author' is a highly significant essay: it signals the break-up of the old assumptions about the job of the critic and also the break-up of the boundaries between literary studies and other disciplines, including history, politics and psychoanalysis. Barthes signals the age of the postmodern, the world we inhabit where there no longer seems the same sense of old certainties, old values and old ideas. The change is one of epic proportions in the study of almost all humanities subjects in the universities, but especially English Literature. There are, of course, still traditional critics writing, but almost everybody commenting on Shakespeare today has been influenced by these changes. Chapter Seven gives a sample of recent essays written from different theoretical positions, but without any attempt to cover the full range of poststructuralist criticism on Shakespeare. What should be evident in them, however, is the extent to which critics today deliberately confront many of the assumptions and values of previous generations of critics.

Implicit in the current critical debate is one answer to the question of why we read criticism from a different age and what we get out of it. Criticism is not about finding answers to problems or solutions to puzzles. It is about questions and questioning, including questions about the nature, extent and limits of literature and criticism.[6] To achieve these aims we need a historical perspective, an engagement with the past and of the possibilities of the past. As Regenia Gagnier puts it:

■ Most social scientists, like scientists generally, are presentists. They think entirely in linear, progressive terms. They believe that the history of their discipline is the history of error and that the current state of knowledge is all the knowledge that has survived. . . . Most literary scholars, on the other hand, believe that history can provide possibilities, roads not taken, gardens of forking paths.[7] □

Put another way, reading gives us the chance to reflect upon other interpretations, to think about what we make of a text, to see how we might have been influenced to think otherwise. Reading in this sense is about seeing texts in a larger context as well as about close critical attention to the words on the page and their nuances. Reading is also, as Diane Elam has suggested, about thinking and about opening out thinking. That involves thinking about the past, about past ways of thinking, as well as recognising the limits of present modes of thinking. Only a very narrow kind of literary critic would assume that only today's criticism matters, or has anything valuable to say to us. The logic of this last position would be that only today's literature has any meaning for us, leading to another version of presentism whereby change is neither possible nor recognisable. Looking back enables us to look forward because we gain a sense of difference between times. It also enables us to see more of the text rather than less of it.

II: Which text?

In claiming that criticism of the past is valuable and instructive for our own critical practice, however, I have slid past one of the most troublesome issues of modern criticism. It is the case that several of Shakespeare's plays exist in radically different forms. The reasons for this have to do with the publication history of the texts. Eighteen of Shakespeare's plays were published during his lifetime in Quarto form: a quarto is a small format book roughly seven by nine inches. Some, such as *Richard II*, appeared in several Quarto editions. In 1623 two of Shakespeare's actor-colleagues, John Heminges and Henry Condell, arranged for Shakespeare's complete works to be published in Folio form: a folio is a large book roughly fourteen by nine inches. There are considerable differences between the Quartos and Folio texts, ranging from speech prefixes and punctuation to wholesale additions. In the case of *Richard II* the Folio text includes Richard's actual deposition, his renunciation of his kingship, in Act IV scene i, which had been omitted from some of the early Quarto texts, a point that will be discussed in more detail in the next chapter.

The question of the differences between the various versions of Shakespeare's plays led in the 1980s to a thorough rethinking of the status of the texts we read and what they represent. A growing number of researchers and teachers of Shakespeare now accept that the 1623 Folio edition of the plays contains or reflects revisions by Shakespeare of his earlier work which, though it may have been performed or used for acting, does not represent a final fixed text. In other words, they suggest that it is to the Folio we should look for our version of the plays rather than to the Quarto editions which, traditionally, have been highly regarded.

The argument about the relationship between the Quartos and the Folio is extremely complicated, but it has a relevance for all readers of Shakespeare. Most texts today are composite versions of the plays. In other words, most editions present us with a text that combines words, punctuation and so on from the Quartos and the Folio. There is an obvious objection to such a process, which is that it cannot possibly represent a text the Elizabethans may have seen or read. But the issue has other implications, too. When we look back at the criticism of previous ages, we need to recognise that most critics are working with texts very different from modern editions and indeed from Elizabethan texts. Put simply, we would be naive if we thought that Coleridge based his criticism on a Penguin or Arden edition of the play. The actual material circumstances of earlier criticism, then, need to be kept in mind; as we read back from our position in history we should recognise that the critics we are reading are not working with modern texts but in many cases are contributing to the formation of these texts. Indeed, in some sense the Shakespeare we read is in part a product of the critical debate this and similar volumes trace.

There are two further matters to consider here. As I noted above, most modern editions of the play are composite versions. In some senses this is unavoidable: reprints of the Quarto or Folio versions would have to be edited in some form or other to be readable. But this does raise the question of what we are reading. In what sense is a modern text Shakespeare? In what sense can it ever be Shakespeare?

A more practical question has to do with the use of quotations in the present volume. In most critical guides quotations are harmonised to a single edition for ease of reference. This might seem a sensible course, but it creates difficulties of its own. It will become evident, for example, that a number of critics prefer to use the form 'Bullingbrook' for the name of Richard's opponent rather than the eighteenth-century form 'Bolingbroke'. Almost all editions of the play vary in terms of punctuation and presentation. To regularise quotations to one edition would not only obscure these minor differences, but also flatten out one dimension of the critical debate about Shakespeare. In the end, therefore, I have reprinted the extracts as I found them. In some cases, where they have been taken from reprints, they have already been modernised. My own quotations for the play are from the Arden edition edited by Peter Ure, though I have also consulted the excellent editions by Stanley Wells (New Penguin) and Andrew Gurr (New Cambridge).[8]

III: The critic and the text

If it is necessary to be aware of the provisional status of modern editions of Shakespeare, it is also as well to be aware of the changing role of the critic over the last four hundred years. Many of the critics writing before the twentieth century were not academics but literary figures writing for the public. Their job was not to produce the kind of literary analysis that we are familiar with today but rather to praise and evaluate texts. Thus, for example, Pope talks of 'pointing out an Author's excellencies'.[9] The role was essentially one of appreciation as opposed to analysis or inter-pretation. The concern with analysis – with what the text has to say and how it says it – largely came about in the early twentieth century when English became a university subject, one with its own discourse and con-cerns separate from those of the ordinary reader. On one level this volume records a small part of that process of change. As we read the criticism before the twentieth century we do need to bear these things in mind. Not out of any sense of progress or superiority but rather to see how criticism can change and think about what it is we understand by criticism. It may be that as we look at the critics we find that there are many versions of Shakespeare and many versions of *Richard II* for us to think about, and that perhaps each age and criticism produces its own version of these. If we are aware of earlier constructions of the text and its author, this may help us to see a way of standing outside the one we have produced in our own critical reflection.

As I noted above, there is a vast amount of criticism of *Richard II* which, in the limited space available, it is impossible to reproduce; and even those items that have been selected have had to be cut. What the volume attempts to do is draw together as much material as possible, but also to focus attention on the main lines of critical development and argument. In order to do this nearly all of the footnotes to essays and articles have had to be cut unless they are essential. As far as possible I have tried to avoid 'snippets', preferring to give substantial pieces wherever it seemed desirable. Similarly, wherever possible I have included details of performances and productions of the play, though this would really require a separate book. Fortunately, it is easy to recommend, in this respect, Margaret Shewring's recent study.[10]

The present volume divides into two broad parts, with approximately half being given to earlier criticism and half to that of the twentieth century. This seems right: intensive study of *Richard II* really only takes off in the twentieth century, though, as we will see, that criticism finds itself constantly returning to the play's own history. Equally, it seemed right to concentrate exposition and commentary in the first half of the volume, so as to provide an opportunity to include longer pieces of recent criticism in the second part of the book. In line with this, later chapters provide much less 'background' information, offering instead merely brief pointers about the pieces included.

CHAPTER ONE

Richard II in 1597 and 1601

Introduction

RICHARD II is unique in so far as it is the only play of Shakespeare's that we know was demonstrably subject to some form of censorship. In the first three editions of the play in 1597 and 1598 (two editions) the scene of Richard's deposition as king in Act IV scene i was omitted. The significance of this omission is discussed further below, but here we can note that the scene itself was clearly politically sensitive; indeed, it was first published only after Elizabeth's death in 1603. It appeared, in fact, in the 1608 Quarto which advertises the additional material on its title page as 'With new additions of the Parlia/ment Sceane, and the deposing/of King Richard'.[1]

Richard II is also unique, and this is probably a related point, in that it is the only play by Shakespeare that seems to have been involved directly in contemporary political events. In 1601 Robert Devereux, the Earl of Essex, staged a rebellion against Elizabeth which led to his trial and execution. The day before the fatal attempt Shakespeare's company was paid to put on a performance of *Richard II*. Both of these aspects of the play's history – its being censored and its being acted for Essex's men – are tied up with its central subject matter, the deposition and killing of the monarch. Most critics are agreed that the deposition of Richard had a signal importance for Elizabeth's rule because of the analogy constructed between her reign and that of Richard. As we have seen in the introduction, the Queen identified herself with Richard II in a conversation with her Keeper at the Tower, though the exact meaning she had in mind is not clear. Less ambiguous is the statement by Sir Francis Knollys in a letter of 1578, where he excuses himself 'for giving unwelcome counsel to the queen', writing that he will not 'play the partes of King Richard's the Second's men'. As Chambers notes, what Knollys means is that he will not play the part of a 'courtly and unstatesmanlike flatterer',[2] such as Bushy, Bagot and Green, in Shakespeare's play. The significance of Knollys's remark lies in its assumption that there is an evident comparison between the political situation of the two monarchs, Richard and Elizabeth.

At the heart of these implied parallels between the reign of Richard and Elizabeth lay the problem of succession, of who would follow Elizabeth on the throne. Elizabeth remained unmarried and by the 1590s the question of who would succeed her was being openly debated. This chapter begins by looking at these matters – the censorship of the text and the parallel with Elizabeth – and then at the more complex matter of the play's involvement in the Essex rebellion. The chapter draws both on historical material and also on modern interpretations of that material. As we will see later in the volume, the actual historical circumstances of the play and its connection with events in the 1590s is something criticism returns to time and again.

There is, though, a third feature of the play which distinguishes it and which is worth noting briefly here. As Andrew Gurr points out, 'Richard II is almost alone amongst Shakespeare's plays in being entirely in verse. It has more rhymes, more declamation and more formally structured speeches such as oaths, curses, lamentations and proclamations than any of the tragedies'.[3] In addition, it employs a great many couplets, so that the effect of the play is one that critics have often compared to that of lyric poetry. The stress, that is, seems to falls upon feeling, upon emotions. This is most obvious in the case of Richard's speeches after Act III, but the heightened formality of the play is also a consequence of its highly patterned language. As with the play's historical context, this is an aspect that criticism has paid particular attention to, often seeing in it a self-conscious 'medievalism', as if the play, through its patterned language, is striving to create a sense of a feudal past.

I: The play in 1597

We can start with some factual details. Richard II was first printed in 1597 in Quarto form. On the title page it is described thus:

■ THE/Tragedie of King Ri/chard the se/cond. As it hath beene publikely acted/by the Right Honourable the Lorde/Chamberlaine his Ser/uants.[4] □

The Lord Chamberlain's Men was the acting company to which Shakespeare belonged. The title page tells us that the play had already been acted, but perhaps more importantly it tells us that here the play is to be read as a tragedy rather than as a history. The question of genre is one that will come up both implicitly and explicitly throughout this volume, with critics approaching the play from these two complementary angles. It is worth noting that when the play was published in the 1623 Folio of

Shakespeare's complete works it was put under the heading of the histories, suggesting that the relationship between history and tragedy was much more fluid and ambiguous than has sometimes been suggested.

The 1597 edition of the play lacks one crucial episode, the portrayal of Richard's deposition in Act IV. The cut starts, in modern editions, at IV.i.155, with Bolingbroke's instruction:

■ Fetch hither Richard, that in common view
He may surrender; so we shall proceed
Without suspicion. □

York then fetches Richard who enters ironically questioning why he has been sent for before he has learned to flatter. His resignation of the crown follows, but with Bolingbroke forced to 'seize the crown' and stand opposite Richard as it is handed over. Richard refuses, however, to read out the list of accusations Northumberland offers him which is intended to justify the deposition. Instead he sends for a mirror in which to examine both his face and the sorrow that marks it. After smashing the mirror Richard begs to be removed. The cut in the text ends at IV.i.319:

■ *Bol.* Go some of you, convey him to the Tower.
Rich. O, good! Convey! Conveyors are you all,
That rise thus nimbly by a true king's fall.
                    [*Exeunt* Richard *and* Guard.]
Bol. On Wednesday next we solemnly proclaim
Our coronation. Lords, prepare yourselves. □

The missing text is a substantial passage. In the early texts, Stanley Wells argues, 'a little tinkering was done to bridge the gap but there was no real revision'.[5] This suggests some kind of simple covering-up job done to get over the omission. This, however, might not be so easy to achieve on the stage, or in any sustained critical analysis of the play, given that between these lines come a number of Richard's major speeches in the Act, including his unkinging of himself:

■ Now, mark me how I will undo myself.
I give this heavy weight from off my head,
And this unwieldy sceptre from my hand,
The pride of kingly sway from out my heart;
With mine own tears I wash away my balm,
With mine own hands I give away my crown,
With mine own tongue deny my sacred state,
With mine own breath release all duteous oaths; □
                    (IV.i.203–10)

As I noted above, the cut seems to imply some form of censorship, though nobody knows exactly by whom – it may have been the printer fearing prosecution or the cuts may have been ordered by the authorities. Books and plays were licensed, however, by different bodies, so even if the printed play was cut, this does not mean that the stage play did not contain the censored scene. What is clear is that the cut passage deals with political matters of enormous significance to the play's debate about deposition and succession. One reading of the above lines, for example, might be to argue that even in the moment of deposition Richard retains his kingly power and that the scene recognises the king's exclusive right to depose himself and to appoint his heir. Such a reading leads towards the idea that the act of deposition serves, paradoxically, to inscribe a kind of absolutism within kingly discourse, to turn Richard's words into the sole authority.

Some critics think that the importance of the censored lines as well as the play's connection with contemporary political events have been exaggerated, even given the 'cautious and vigilant watchfulness of the Tudor state's security organs'.[6] But this in turn seems to simplify what was perhaps a more complicated set of circumstances. The matter has been well put by Margaret Shewring in her recent book on *Richard II*, part of the Shakespeare in Performance series which is concerned with the relationship of stage performance to other cultural factors, including historical, political and social elements. In the paragraph immediately before the extract that follows, she examines the ways in which lawyers at the time had sought to resolve the question of succession after Elizabeth:

■ This matter was of crucial and immediate significance in the 1590s. It was a frequent topic of debate among members of the Inns of Courts, both in the context of legal disputation and in the subject matter of their entertainments and Revels, sometimes played in the presence of the Queen herself. Shakespeare was not the only writer to draw parallels with the reign of King Richard II. *The Life and Death of Jack Straw* (1590–93) as well as *1 Richard II; or Thomas of Woodstock* (1591–95) had already given Richard's image a currency on the public stage. Certainly Shakespeare's *Richard II* was regarded as politically sensitive in its earliest performances, which may well have included the deposition scene that was not permitted to appear in print in the first Quarto in 1597. . . . Such censorship may have been all the more necessary because of the play's popularity. It was printed in three quartos in the years 1597 and 1598 and, in 1598, Francis Meres cited *Richard II* in *Palladis Tamia* (his survey of the arts in England) as 'foremost amongst the tragedies on the day'. By 1600 the play's popularity warranted the inclusion of six passages (three from Gaunt's speeches) in the anthology published as

England's Parnassus. But it was not until the fourth Quarto in 1608, five years after Elizabeth's death, that the deposition scene was permitted in print and featured on the title page: . . . By 1608 the moment of 'national crisis' had passed and the throne of state was not in danger of remaining empty.[7] □

Later in her argument Shewring adds further evidence about the political impact of the story of Richard II and the sort of difficulties it raised for authors. In 1599 John Hayward published his *The First Part of the Reign of Henry IV.* This is a history of the deposition of Richard II and the opening of Henry IV's reign. The history was dedicated to Essex and at his trial was brought up in evidence against him. Shewring's account is again worth quoting in full:

■ The topicality of the story of Richard II in the context of the late 1590s is again in evidence in the relationship between the Earl of Essex and . . . Hayward's *The First Part of the Reign of Henry IV* . . . published in 1599. Hayward's history was dedicated to Essex; and at his trial, an accusation repeated on more than one occasion was that the Earl had permitted 'the treasonable book of Henry IV to be printed and published . . . also the Earl himself being so often present *at the playing thereof,* and with great applause giving countenance to it' . . . It is impossible to say what the relationship may be between Hayward's prose history and the performances the Earl is alleged to have attended and endorsed by his applause. Sir Edward Coke, prosecuting Essex, refers to Hayward's book as the source for the play performed on the eve of the Rising. If the play was Shakespeare's, he is of course wrong. And yet the accusation is right in linking the various facets of the complex political climate in which fact and fiction, state and stage seem to merge in the public consciousness. The sensitivity of such 'dangerous matter' is clear in that Hayward was imprisoned for the dedication to Essex in spite of the fact that John Chamberlain, the contemporary letter-writer, could 'find no harm' in the dedication itself. Certainly the Queen thought Hayward's book 'a seditious prelude to put into people's hearts boldness and faction'. In June 1599, just four months after the publication of Hayward's work, the Archbishop of Canterbury and the Bishop of London issued an order forbidding the printing of English history without the express consent of the Privy Council.

This extraordinary sensitivity to historical parallels was further confirmed when, immediately after the Essex Rising, the Privy Council ordered sermons to be preached referring to Richard II's reign, and asserting Hayward's crime 'in cunningly insinuating that the same abuses being now in this realm that were in the days of Richard II the like course might be taken for redress'. In such a context Shakespeare's play found its own special energy, absorbing and refracting dangerous splinters of light in the many-faceted prism of political and cultural history.[8] □

(Shewring, pp. 27–8)

Shewring's analysis brings out the complicated interrelations between text, stage, theatre, history and politics in the years between 1597 and 1601. As she rightly notes, Shakespeare's play is but one of a series of documents that bear upon the question of the meaning or meanings that were constructed around the story of Richard II. In order to grasp the full implications of Shewring's argument, however, two further historical events need to be borne in mind. Both of them have already been referred to in passing several times, but are worth further consideration. One is the rebellion by the Earl of Essex in 1601 and his attempted coup, which we will look at in more detail below. The other concerns a conversation of the Queen, some six months after the coup, with William Lambarde, the Keeper at the Tower, who kept a written record of it. It is in many senses an extraordinary document in the way it shows Elizabeth preoccupied with history. The record takes the form of a memorandum or note with two speakers, as well as some introductory scene setting:

■ That which passed from the Excellent Majestie of Queen ELIZABETH, IN HER Privie Chamber at East Grenwich, 4⁰ Augusti 1601, 43⁰ Reg. sui, towards WILLIAM LAMBARDE

He presented her Majestie with his Pandecta of all her rolls, bundells, membranes, and parcells that be reposed in her Majestie's Tower at London; whereof she had given to him the charge 21st January last past. *Her Majestie* chearfullie received the same into her hands [and] . . . opening the book, said, 'You shall see that I can read;' and so, with an audible voice, read over the epistle, and the title, so readily, and distinctly pointed, that it might perfectly appear, that she well understood, and conceived the same. Then she descended from the beginning of King John, till the end of Richard III, this is 64 pages, serving eleven kings, containing 286 years; in the first page she demanded the meaning of *obltata, caslae, literae clausae* and *literae patentes* . . .

W.L. He likewise expounded these all according to their original diversities, which she took in gratious and full satisfaction; so her Majestie fell upon the reign of King Richard II. saying, 'I am Richard II. know ye not that?'

W.L. 'Such a wicked imagination was determined and attempted by a most unkind Gent. the most adorned creature that ever your Majestie made.'

Her Majestie. 'He that will forget God, will also forget his benefactors; this tragedy was played 40^{tie} times in open streets and houses.'

Her Majestie demanded 'what was *praestita*?'

W.L. He expounded it to be 'monies lent by her Progenitors to her subjects for their good, but with assurance of good bond for repayment.'

Her Majestie. 'So did my good Grandfather King Henry VII. sparing to dissipate his treasure or lands.' Then returning to Richard II. she demanded, 'Whether I had seen any true picture, or lively representation of his countenace and person?'

W.L. 'None but such as be in common hands.'

Her Majestie. 'The Lord Lumley, a lover of antiquities, discovered it fastened on the backside of a door of a base room; which he presented unto me, praying, with my good leave, that I might put it in order with the Ancestors and Successors; I will command Tho. Kneavet, Keeper of my House and Gallery at Westminster, to shew it unto thee.' Then she proceeded to the Rolls . . . □

(Shewring, p. 191)

Shewring comments perceptively on this dialogue and its features, noting, for example, how the image of Richard II seems to haunt Elizabeth's mind 'even to wishing to recover a portrait of him' (p. 26). And she goes on:

■ Both Elizabeth and Lambarde move easily from discussion of recorded history to the current situation . . . and from a painted image to the performance of plays . . ., blurring the distinctions between them as if they were all one in their consciousness. □

(p. 26)

Indeed, the significance of the dialogue may lie in the way it provides a moment when the speakers look back over the series of events we have been tracing and how those events mirror one another without quite fitting into a neat historical allegory. There is a note of puzzlement in the dialogue, as if the speakers cannot quite pin down the links and connections between the reign of Richard and Elizabeth, his picture and the performance of the play. There is something elusive in the tone of the conversation as Elizabeth dwells on the movement and moments of history where the truth is always harder to find than in the papers which record it. In this, the conversation is not unlike Richard's soliloquy in Act V scene v where he seeks to understand the processes of change that have unkinged him. In the soliloquy, Richard, like Elizabeth and Lambarde, confronts a complex world which seems made up of uncertainties about the meaning of events. It is a new kind of world where history does not readily unfold its secrets, a world where we cannot be sure of the relationship between the play of *Richard II* and its immediate political situation.

II: The play in 1601 – the Essex rebellion

Much of the above discussion leads into and out of the so-called 'Essex rebellion', the attempted coup by Robert Devereux. A one-time favourite of the Queen, in 1599 Essex had been sent to Ireland to quell the rebellion there but failed. Instead, he held talks with Tyrone, the Irish leader, who offered to help make him king of England. Essex returned to the mainland and on 27 September 1599 entered London with two hundred followers. The next day he burst into the Queen's bedroom, but she stood her ground and he was placed under arrest. He stayed under house arrest in Essex House in the Strand, building up a rival court to Elizabeth and projecting an image of chivalric heroism amongst his followers. As Mervyn James has pointed out, Essex thus cultivated a popular image of the Protestant champion, a figure of chivalry and romance.[9]

In February 1601 Essex began his attempted coup against Elizabeth. Curiously, the day before, his steward Merrick 'commissioned a special performance of what is usually taken to be Shakespeare's play at the Globe' (Shewring, p. 24). The motivation for the performance, Shewring suggests, 'seems to have been to confirm the resolution of the members of the invited audience' before the next day's attempted rebellion. Certainly there is evidence that *Richard II* was especially staged since one of the Globe's shareholders, Augustine Phillips, answering for the company when it was questioned, said that they had been unwilling to present it because it was 'so old and so long out of use' and so therefore unlikely to attract a sufficient audience.[10] There is one other factor to note here. Essex himself was descended from the Duke of Gloucester whose murder lies behind the action of the play and through him traced a line of descent to the throne.[11] To that extent one might expect the play to have ignited the rebellion into full flame, but it did not. When Essex entered the city the next day it remained unmoved by his entry; there was no sudden rush to support him. The rebellion failed.

History always leaves us with more questions than we started with. What are we to make of the Essex rebellion and its connections with the play? Shakespeare's company, we know, was not punished and within a few weeks was back playing at the court. Perhaps plays were regarded as having no real influence or effect on anything? Perhaps it is only later ages that have come to recognise theatre as potentially dangerous or subversive?

There are, too, other aspects to the problem. In an article in 1980 the historian E. W. Ives suggested that

■ The significance in having *Richard II* performed in 1601 was not only or even primarily the identification of Elizabeth's supposed senile loss of governance with the misgovernment of Richard, nor the inference about deposition (it was never Essex's stated intention to oust the Queen although the same may not have been true of all his followers . . .). The main thrust was against the dominance of Richard by a corrupt faction at Court, paralleling what Essex and his supporters believed was the capitulation of Elizabeth to the Cecil interest [i.e. the Cecil family], and in consequence, the exclusion of true-hearted Englishmen (themselves) from their rightful favour.[12] □

Ives suggests, then, that the staging of the play and the rebellion were not so much about deposition as about the power struggle for dominance at court. It is an attractive theory, but it raises once more the question of how we interpret the relationship between literature and history. Ives's answer starts from outside the text and works in. By contrast David Norbrook, in the extract that follows, starts from the text and works outwards towards historical circumstances. The essay is quoted at some length precisely because it synthesises so much of the preceding discussion.

Norbrook, one of the leading Renaissance scholars of the late twentieth century, draws on much of the recent criticism on the play while placing it in a specific historical context. The essay might thus have been included in the final chapter, especially as it refers to earlier criticism of the play by Tillyard and Kantorowicz, but it is printed here precisely because, as well as looking at the Essex rebellion, it points forward, providing a reference point for much that is to follow in this book. In brief, Norbrook's argument is that the language of the play opens alternative perspectives rather than a simple choice between Richard and Bolingbroke, and how, while the text may lend some comfort to the aristocratic rebellion, it also recognises the wider, growing power of the London populace whose importance both the monarchy and the rebels underestimate:

From David Norbrook, '"A Liberal Tongue": Language and Rebellion in *Richard II*'

■ . . . [F]or all the volume of commentary generated by Shakespeare's plays, there is still a great deal to be done in understanding their initial contexts. *Richard II* is a case in point. It is generally accepted that it is the play of which the Lord Chamberlain's Men staged a special performance on 7 February 1601; the following day, eleven members of that audience took up arms in Essex's rebellion. The interpretation of that evidence, however, is much more problematic. I believe that the play has been widely misinterpreted – or at least very selectively interpreted – by a misunderstanding of its contexts in political and intellectual history. . . . In the limited space available, I shall try to question the validity of some long-current contexts and offer some alternatives, on the basis of which I shall attempt, in a necessarily very tentative way, to reconstruct some of the ways in which the audience of 1601 might have responded to the play.

The play's opening line can put us on the right track. But all too often it has done the reverse. 'Old John of Gaunt, time-honoured Lancaster': the ethos is of age and tradition, looking back to a medieval past. From the nineteenth century onward, the medieval era has conjured up an image of an organic community, of a harmonious hierarchy united by a simple religious faith, with deferential peasants and mystically sanctioned rulers. That image of the middle ages became hardened during the reaction against the French Revolution, and it was in that period that conservative readings of the first tetralogy as expressing nostalgia for a lost social unity became current. E. M. W. Tillyard's reading of the histories, while more historically grounded, drew on similar patterns of analysis.[13]

The nostalgic readings gained a new lease of life with the publication in 1957 of Ernst Kantorowicz's *The King's Two Bodies*. Kantorowicz reads *Richard II* as dramatizing the theory that the monarch has two bodies, one natural and mortal, the other artificial, mystical and immortal. The tragedy of the play lies in the emerging split between these two bodies. Stage by stage Richard's sacramental unity becomes violently severed until in the deposition scene his body becomes 'now void of any metaphysis whatsoever'. This pattern of explanation throws the emphasis firmly on Richard, and Kantorowicz acknowledges a debt to Walter Pater's analysis of the poet-king. His political sympathies are clearly with Richard. One of 'Richard's so-called "tyrannies"', his claim that the laws of the realm were in his head, in fact 'merely referred to a well known maxim of Roman and Canon Laws'.[14] His accusers, then, were merely betraying their provincial ignorance. That emphasis is characteristic of Kantorowicz's strategy in his book, which is to uncover a buried vein of metaphysical mysticism in what had traditionally been seen as the hard-headed empiricism of English common law. . . .

Kantorowicz's reading has exercised a powerful influence on recent new historicist criticism:[15] it brings together favoured themes of the body, power and display, . . . [b]ut the emphasis on mystical bodies has distracted attention from very different aspects of the play and of Elizabethan political discourse in general.

For if the Elizabethans did feel nostalgic for the medieval past, it was not necessarily for mystical bodies that they yearned. 'Old' and 'time-honoured' would not have conjured up unequivocally monarchist associations for the rebel party of 1601. And, indeed, for any reader of Holinshed, the reign of Richard II as there described is no timeless idyll of metaphysical unity, but a period of sharp contestation: popular rebellion, attempts at religious reformation under Wyclif, and struggles to maintain or increase the status of Parliament. In those struggles, London plays a key role: Richard tries as far as possible to hold Parliaments out of that city for fear that they will be swayed by growing extra-parliamentary pressure on the MPs. The House of Commons begins calling for annual Parliaments, to which Richard retorts that he would rather submit himself to the King of France than to his own subjects. A group of lords try to keep Richard under strict control to the point of threatening to depose him.

If the late fourteenth century offered an object lesson for readers of the 1590s, it was not because subjects were nostalgic for absolutism but because they feared its recurrence. Those chivalric spectacles that look so quaint and archaic today had a sharp political edge: . . . Essex and his circle vindicated traditional aristocratic ideas of honour against the monarchy's attempt to centralize honour in loyalty to the monarch. Essex tried to revive feudal offices that had served to restrict monarchical power. An increasingly important body of antiquarian thought was beginning to formulate the concept of feudalism and to heighten public awareness of long-lapsed constitutional precedents for challenges to royal power. The remedies of annual Parliaments and aristocratic councils were to be looked to increasingly under the early Stuarts. When the Civil War broke out, Parliamentarian leaders consciously looked back to the Middle Ages; for them, absolutism was an innovative phenomenon to be resisted by an appeal to deep-rooted constitutionalist traditions. Sir John Hayward's *The Life and Raigne of King Henrie IIII*, which opened with Bullingbrook's challenge to Mowbray, was re-published in 1641, 1642 and 1643. The Parliamentarian leaders saw themselves as offering a comparable trial by battle, and indeed individuals were still ready to engage in trial by combat.

This aristocratic constitutionalism could blend with classical republicanism: Roman history too could be read as a struggle between independent aristocrats and tyrannical sovereigns. Republican discourse was circulating in England in the 1590s: Hayward's history, the first major synthesis of classical Tacitean discourse with English history, appeared two years before the Essex rebellion, with a dedication to the

Earl. The leading republican theorist of the later seventeenth century, Algernon Sidney, was to remember how his ancestors had been betrayed by monarchical deceit:

> Henry the Fourth was made king by the earl of Northumberland, and his brave son Hotspur . . . but [he could not] think himself safe, till his benefactor was dead.

Sidney was proud of his connections with the earls of Northumberland, a traditionally independent aristocratic dynasty. . . .

In this context, it is very interesting to note that two of the three commissioners of the 1601 performance were Charles and Jocelyn Percy, brothers of the ninth Earl of Northumberland. Far from being nostalgic for the loss of sacramental absolutist monarchy, they would have feared its recurrence. . . .

The young Percies . . . would have had a particular interest in seeing their house at a period when it was a kingmaker; and *Richard II* presented their rebellious activities in a somewhat more favourable light than its successors. Shakespeare and his company had close links with Essex's circle in the 1590s, Essex himself being a regular play-goer, and the revival of this by now 'old' play would have been a reassuring evocation of a familiar cultural world. We may still wonder why the Essexians did not choose a more directly and overtly rebellious play like *Woodstock*, which handles resistance to Richard and his favourites in a more starkly critical mode. *Richard II* is more oblique in its handling of the motives for rebellion. Yet insofar as there is a sense of caution, of evading direct statement on such key issues as Richard's implication in Gloucester's death, that sense of blocked communication could have served to heighten the political tension. The rebels had long been urging Essex to overcome his reservations about rebellion and take a stand to redeem the country's honour; here was a play that demonstrated a slow and painful process of formulating opposition. The issue of blocked communication is at once internal and external to the play: the most sensitive moment, Richard's self-deposition, seems to have been omitted for political reasons from the early quartos. The chronicles were full of stories of monarchs who tried to consolidate their power by stifling Parliaments and other outlets for public discussion. The preservation of a guaranteed space for debate and criticism was a major concern of those worried about the growth of royal absolutism, whether in the fourteenth century or the sixteenth. Shakespeare's play embodies that concern, both in the story it tells and in its medium, opening up in a public theatre areas of debate that absolutists wanted to keep veiled as mysteries of state.

———

The opening part of the play involves continual anticlimax, a repression of political and military action which serves only to fuel the underlying conflicts. Bullingbrook's combat with Mowbray, whose political consequences would have been known by an informed audience to be explosive, is deferred in the first scene and again in the third. Actual conflict is sublimated into a war of words: Bullingbrook threatens to bite off his tongue and spit it out at Mowbray (I.i.190). Despite his attack on mere words as womanish (I.i.48), however, Mowbray, like all the protagonists, is an able rhetorician, and he will lament that exile makes it no longer possible for him to use his language. Shakespeare has given this feudal society an anachronistic inflection of civic humanism, a concern with the dignity and political importance of full and open speech. (Modern critics' model of language in the plays as a 'fall' from plenitude into rhetoric suppresses the centrality of language as a mode of action in pragmatically-oriented humanist rhetoric.) Mowbray pleads for 'free speech', which Richard allows him (I.i.55,123). But we are aware of ironies: Richard and Mowbray cannot afford to speak too freely since they are engaged in a cover-up. And the fact that Richard 'allows' free speech is one of the points at issue: how far should such freedom be a grace offered from above, rather than a constitutional right?

For the more Richard tries to stifle dissent, the more he undermines himself. His own position is vulnerable because he increasingly places his own and his favourites' private interests against the common good, his party dwindling to 'some few private friends' (III.iii.4). Only as he is falling from power does he realize that his mystical conception of kingship needs a material foundation, that his role as head of the body politic depends on 'the blood of twenty thousand men' (III.ii.76). By contrast, in the opening scenes his opponents rediscover a threatened sense of corporate identity. The first scene had opened with an address to Gaunt, the second opens with his pondering 'the part I had in Woodstock's blood', which acts with his widow's reproaches to stir him to resistance; and the Duchess loses no opportunity to reinforce the appeal to blood and to a sense of common identity: 'Yet art thou slain in him' (I.ii.25). Gaunt's language registers a struggle to overlay such sentiments with a discourse of patience and submission; to which the Duchess starkly retorts, 'Call it not patience, Gaunt, it is despair' (I.ii.29); her 'old Gaunt' (line 54) rings reproachfully against the play's opening words. Gaunt's struggle continues in the ensuing scene. Bullingbrook celebrates the energy he gains from 'the earthly author of my blood' which gives him 'a twofold vigour' (I.iii.69–71). Gaunt goes along with his banishment, but his language registers the crisis of language and agency into which he has been plunged:

But you gave leave to my unwilling tongue
Against my will to do myself this wrong.   (I.iii.245–6)

Bullingbrook, however, is by now starting to break loose from such restrictions, and there is exhilaration in his concluding self-description as 'a trueborn Englishman' (I.iii.308). His stance is modulating from an exclusively aristocratic to a generally national one; the play's strong sense of nationalism is another anachronism with a strong contemporary resonance. There was a certain appropriateness in eighteenth-century editors' spelling 'Bullingbrook' as 'Bolingbroke', associating Shakespeare's protagonist with the spokesman for a form of monarchism that was deeply influenced by classical republicanism. In the ensuing scene we see the courtiers contemptuously discussing his courting of the people at large. Richard's description of the commoners as 'slaves' (I.iv.27) confirms the opposition's claims that the absolutist faction want to enslave them (II.i.291); contempt for the commons is a consistent characteristic of the court party (cf. II.ii.128ff, III.iii.89, V.i.35).

It is in this context of escalating opposition that the Essexians would have read a speech that has tended to dwindle to a mass of patriotic clichés: Gaunt's 'sceptred isle' speech. The tension between submission and resistance that has so beset him finds a resolution in his determination to make a final appeal to the king through rhetoric rather than arms, and he musters all his rhetorical forces. But York is sceptical: flattery has deafened the king's ear. And though Gaunt feels a prophetic afflatus, there is a certain irony in the fact that it comes before the king has arrived, so that his greatest appeal to a common patriotic spirit serves to vent his own feelings rather than to sway the king. The reference to Eden does conjure up a nostalgic mood, but it should also be noted that greater emphasis is placed on the island's prowess in war, a somewhat un-Edenic activity crucial both to the feudal aristocracy and to the 'war party' around Essex. It is because of their skill in war that Gaunt reveres the kings of the past. As the huge sentence with its suspended verb builds up, we feel the strain of Gaunt's dying powers, as if the very intensity of his rhetoric is serving to destroy him: 'I die pronouncing it' (II.i.59).

Shakespeare has boldly placed this set-piece speech, which he must have known would quickly enter anthologies, at a potentially anticlimactic point: how will Gaunt be able to follow it up when Richard does arrive? Richard's first words apply the 'aged' label, but with a perfunctory insensitivity that graphically registers how the same words can perform widely different speech-acts: 'What comfort, man? How is't with aged Gaunt?' (II.i.72). After parodying Richard's brittle symmetries in skirmish of bitter punning, Gaunt launches into

27

a speech that pushes at last beyond the threshold of obedience: he imagines Edward II as deposing Richard, and indulges at least in imagination in rebellion. As 'landlord', Richard has reduced a political realm, one in which law and public accountability predominate, to a mere household economy where the subjects lack political rights. Richard cuts off his speech, overruling the 'ague's privilege' that transgresses normal rules of speech, and gives Gaunt's words a vivid, self-destructive materiality:

> Wert thou not brother to great Edward's son,
> This tongue that runs so roundly in thy head
> Should run thy head from thy unreverent shoulders.
>
> (II.i.121–3)

Again discourse is brought to the brink of violence but holds back: Richard pays grudging tribute to feudal bonds. But this provokes Gaunt into his climactic charge: at last he holds back no longer and directly accuses him of complicity in Woodstock's murder. The audience have been waiting for this moment since the opening scene. In civic humanist spirit, Gaunt's finest rhetorical hour is not the lyrical meditation of the 'sceptred isle' speech but his last moment of strenuous active engagement.

And it is at this point that Northumberland enters the play, bearing the news of Gaunt's death with a characteristically acerbic irony:

> My liege, old Gaunt commends him to your Majesty.
> What says he?
> Nay nothing, all is said;
> His tongue is now a stringless instrument[.] (II.i.147–8)

This further 'old Gaunt' reminds the audience of Richard's recent irreverence, the Duchess's rebukes, and the play's opening words. The Percies in the audience would have had a special interest in Northumberland's role: would the open opposition now begin? But there is yet another moment of anticlimax: York now takes on the role Gaunt had earlier occupied, struggling desperately not to topple over the verge into rebellion. But for him it is even harder: his often-protested patience (II.i.163, 169, 207) is coming to seem more and more like cowardice. York makes one last appeal to common bonds between Richard and his peers, to the common memory of Edward III: 'His face thou hast' (II.i.176). He engages in a series of sharp antitheses between Edward's patriotism and Richard's absolutism; but the sharpness of those antitheses, undercutting any possible resemblance, itself becomes seditious, and York breaks off:

> Richard! York is too far gone with grief,
> Or else he never would compare between –   (II.i.184–5)

If you continue as you are, he resumes, 'Be not thyself': Richard's personal identity must depend on being bound up with a larger community. Such paradoxes are not enough to contain York's sense of facing a discursive crisis that he does not know how to resolve. His final sentence begins 'Now afore God – God forbid I say true!' (II.i.200): to call on God for him not to speak truly is a desperate recourse. If you continue, says York,

> You lose a thousand well-disposed hearts,
> And prick my tender patience to those thoughts
> Which honour and allegiance cannot think.   (II.i.206–8)

This speech brings out explicitly what the whole opening part of the play has implied: that quite apart from external censorship, absolutism depends for its maintenance on self-censorship, on keeping subversive thoughts away from the threshold of consciousness. In the following scene we have another glimpse of that process, as York momentarily confuses the queen with the Duchess of Gloucester, whose death the servant has forgotten to announce. The audience are reminded that the Duchess had despairingly abandoned an invitation to him as she bowed out of the play (I.ii.62ff). York is troubled by his inability to formulate a response to her fidelity to Gloucester's memory. The Duchess's abandoning of her request to 'commend' her to York has re-echoed in Northumberland's heavily ironic 'old Gaunt commends him to your majesty'.

But Northumberland is by now emerging as the agent of a different policy, crossing the threshold to active resistance. The aristocrats who linger after the king's departure in Act II scene i emphasize the continuity of agency from one generation to another:

> Well, Lords, the Duke of Lancaster is dead.
> And living too, for now his son is duke.   (II.i.224–5)

Northumberland's role is to translate seditious thoughts into effective action. When Ross laments that

> My heart is great, but it must break with silence,
> Ere't be disburdened with a liberal tongue   (II.i.229–30)

it is Northumberland who tells him to 'speak thy mind' (II.i.230). Ross's 'liberal' does not of course have its modern sense, and carries with it rather the pejorative charge that would have been the response to Richard's careless speaking of his 'liberal largess' (I.iv.44); but the play does have an emotional and intellectual pressure toward wishing for more open communication. To encourage his friends, Northumberland remains within a very traditional discourse of obedience: like York, he claims that 'The king is not himself' (II.i.241), that he is merely led by flatterers. We may however suspect disingenuousness at least on the part of Northumberland, who reveals himself as a determined political manipulator; certainly the Richard of the play takes the initiative rather than being manipulated by courtiers, who often find it hard to get a word in edgeways (cf. III.ii.213ff). Northumberland's role is to sharpen the contrast between common feudal bonds and allegiance to the king, and he does so in an economical antithesis: Richard has exiled 'His noble kinsman – most degenerate king!' (II.i.262; cf. York at II.ii.114). Northumberland titillates his fellows by claiming that 'I dare not say' what his hope is; but Ross appeals to the common bonds of aristocratic solidarity:

> We three are but thyself, and, speaking so,
> Thy words are but as thoughts; therefore be bold.   (II.i.276–7)

The transition is about to be made from purely verbal to military opposition.

Northumberland's imagery as he urges decisive action is one of opening out, of bringing the private once more into a public realm:

> If then we shall shake off our slavish yoke,
> Imp out our drooping country's broken wing,
> Redeem from broking pawn the blemish'd crown,
> Wipe off the dust that hides our sceptre's gilt,
> And make high majesty look like itself,
> Away with me in post to Ravenspurgh;
> But if you faint, as fearing to do so,
> Stay, and be secret, and myself will go.   (II.i.291–8)

Northumberland's language negotiates between loyalty to the monarchy and a wider patriotic loyalty, one in which public resistance is preferable to secret compliance. The suppressed pun on 'guilt' at line 294 (to be echoed at V.i.69) associates the king with the dust that hides the monarchical sceptre. But the imagery of shaking off yokes, of opening out wings, points beyond a narrowly monarchical conception of national interest, while leaving the precise constitutional implications tautologically vague ('make high majesty look like itself').

What ensues as the play moves to its climax is certainly not a straightforward celebration of rebellion, and Northumberland does not emerge in a light that would have been unequivocally appealing to his descendants. Though Shakespeare plays down the full extent of his role in the rebellion, he emerges as a cool and ruthless operator, ready to flatter Bullingbrook's nascently regal 'discourse' as 'sugar' (II.iii.6–7), outrageously quick to redefine treason for the new political order (IV.i.150). Nevertheless, it is important that he does offer the audience a perspective on events distinct from any simple dualism between Richard and Bullingbrook. While modern critics tend to concentrate on his personal moral duplicity, an audience of the 1590s would have been equally alert to his role in trying to maintain a discourse of the aristocratic, and occasionally of the common, good, independently of whichever monarch may be in power. When he laments 'civil and uncivil arms' (III.iii.102), the play on words seems to be echoing the opening line of Lucan's Pharsalia ('Bella . . . plus quam civilia'), whose republican sympathies were gaining it interested readers in the 1590s; Marlowe's translation of Book I had been printed the year before the Essexians' performance. Northumberland's discourse thus has a tinge of civic humanism; and in the deposition scene he is more keen than Bullingbrook to keep attention on constitutional issues as opposed to Richard's personal emotions. It is Northumberland who keeps urging Richard to read out the 33 articles – the evidence of what Kantorowicz termed Richard's 'so-called tyranny' – so that the commons 'May deem that you are worthily depos'd' (IV.i.227, cf. 272). Northumberland's language here directly echoes that of Holinshed: the articles were read 'to the end the commons might be persuaded, that he was an vnprofitable prince to the commonwealth, and worthie to be deposed'. The 'and' in that sentence is pregnant with a whole set of decidedly unmetaphysical political assumptions. The play's closing speech is given to Bullingbrook's desire to wash away his guilt; Northumberland has bowed out of the play on a characteristically less emotive note: 'My guilt be on my head, and there an end' (V.i.69). We are made to condemn the harshness of the separation of king and queen, and Northumberland's justification with the conventionally suspect, Machiavellian term 'policy' (V.i.84). That is, appropriately, his last word in the scene. Feudal rebellion has merged with a more modern form of political agency. Even those of the audience who did not approve of Northumberland would have had to acknowledge the dangers of a lack of 'policy'.

———

When Charles and Jocelyn Percy watched *Richard II*, then, they would have found much to fire them in emulation of a medieval past that was far from cravenly monarchical. And they would not necessarily have been daunted by the pathos of Richard's fall . . .

By concentrating on the aristocracy's role in the play, it is possible to see how limited is the perspective that sees it as offering a straight-forward choice between Richard and Bullingbrook, That is not to say, however, that the aristocratic viewpoint is finally endorsed. In *Richard II*, the voices of other social groups are by and large excluded, being reserved for the *Henry IV* plays. The effect is to heighten the sense of an archaic, hieratic political order that has so swayed some critics. But there are hints of alternative perspectives.

It is in the garden scene that members of the lower orders make their only extended appearance. Critics have emphasized this scene's formal, archaic quality. It is indeed particularly dense with sacramen-tal rhetoric. But it is important to note how that rhetoric is placed. It is here associated with the queen; it is consistently the favoured dis-course of the Yorkists. And in this scene it is placed in direct contrast with different conceptions of political order. Of course we are made to sympathize with the queen's grief and shock; but this should not blind us to structural problems in the scene's discourse. The queen initiates the contrast as soon as she sees the gardener and his servants: she decides to hide and eavesdrop, convinced that

> They'll talk of state, for everyone doth so
> Against a change; woe is forerun with woe. (III.iv.27–8)

For the queen, this talk of 'state' by the lower orders is a subversion of order. The gardeners, however, have their own conception of order, which looks back to Gaunt's 'this England' speech, though it lacks his feudal militarism. They insist on the predominance of public over private interest, and on the need for active intervention to remedy abuses even at the cost of violence:

> Go thou, and like an executioner
> Cut off the heads of too fast growing sprays,
> That look too lofty in our commonwealth:
> All must be even in our government.   (III.iv.32–6)

The word 'commonwealth' here, along with the emphasis on evenness, and the reference to decapitation of favourites, carries an oblique tinge of republican discourse. The rhetoric is literally radical: the role of the head gardener is to 'root away' the weeds, a role which he himself compares to Bullingbrook's (37, 52). It is one of the under-gardeners who initiates direct political discussion, converting the literal discus-sion of the garden into a political allegory and asking why they should work while their leaders let the realm go to ruin. The head gardener has enough of a sense of hierarchies of discourse to ask him to 'Hold thy peace'; but he goes on to develop the allegory, contrasting the gardeners' skill with the courtiers' incompetence, and building up to prophesying that the king will be deposed.

At this point the queen angrily intervenes:

> O, I am press'd to death through want of speaking!
> Thou, old Adam's likeness set to dress this garden,
> How dares thy harsh rude tongue sound this unpleasing news?
> What Eve, what serpent, hath suggested thee
> To make a second fall of cursed man?
> Why dost thou say King Richard is depos'd?
> Dar'st thou, thou little better thing than earth,
> Divine his downfall? Say, where, when, and how
> Cam'st thou by this ill tidings?   (72–80)

The queen's opening words return the play yet again to the theme of suppressed discourse; though in this case the queen has imposed the limitation on herself. Her grief at the news is displaced by anger at its bearer for breaking her rigidly hierarchical conceptions of language: it is not for such underlings to meddle with mysteries of state. She finds his tongue 'harsh' and 'rude': understandable though her response is under the circumstances, it does recall Richard's preference for euphemistic harmony over unwelcome truth. The queen lives in a world of absolute oppositions between rulers and people as between good and evil, and she recasts the gardener's horticultural discourse in authoritarian terms. Like all the Yorkists, the queen speaks disparagingly of the lower orders; and she appeals to a theological conception of political order, with any intervention by the commons presented as a fall of man. Her interpretation of the garden thus contrasts sharply with the gardener's less mystical, more interventionist garden/state allegory, and the gardener stands his ground. He describes Richard's fall not in a traditional mode of the Fall of man or *de casibus* tragedy, but in a secular language of balance of power: reinforced by 'all the peers', Bullingbrook is bound to triumph in the end. Richard falls not because God has withdrawn his favour but because he has neglected the proper political means. Let her go to London – the centre of England's public sphere – and she will find the truth. The queen's response is to curse the gardener's plants. The gardener, however, gracefully deflects this destructive speech-act, planting an emblematic bank of rue. If the scene thus ends on a pathetic and organic register, it has arrived there by a far more complex route.

This scene is entirely of Shakespeare's invention, and it bears scrutiny as an allegory not only of political discourse but of the role of

Shakespeare's company in politics, of their disposition of their flowers of rhetoric. Several critics have noted that the gardener's reference to cutting off heads may allude to a story in Livy about Tarquin's sending an execution order through an agricultural code so that the messenger would not understand it. In this case, however, it is the messenger who understands more than the queen. The scene opens on a note of courtly recreation: the queen asks her ladies to divert her, and they offer to engage in whatever activity pleases her. In place of aristocratic festivity, the gardener offers a more didactic form of entertainment, one ultimately too didactic for the queen, who considers that it interferes in mysteries of state and halts the narrative. This scene immediately precedes the deposition scene, which was of course not printed in full in the Elizabethan quartos. *Richard II* contains an oblique prophecy of its own censorship: the play is aware that it is touching on sensitive areas of political discourse, areas that displace a top-down hierarchy. And yet it protests that those above may need that commoners' discourse at least as much as the commoners need them.

In this play, however, the commons remain spectators, not agents. Emphasis is placed on aristocratic agency – the gardener's own analysis of the power structure refers only to the aristocracy, not to the commons. To some degree, that omission reflects changes between Shakespeare's own time and the period he represents, that growth in the public sphere in which the theatre formed a significant part. It might have been better for the aristocratic rebels of 1601 to have taken this point. Though they enjoyed some passive support from the London populace, their coup sought legitimacy from feudal traditions rather than from wider consultation, and was ultimately short on 'policy'. When, on the morning after the play's performance, Essex rode through the city asking for the Londoners' support, counting on their admiration for his aristocratic dash and charisma, he failed to reckon with the fact that they might find him impulsive and irresponsible. In the play the citizens are presented as fickle and politically immature, turning easily from Richard to acclaim Bullingbrook in his passage through London. When Essex and his followers made their entry to the city, in a display of their aristocratic authority, the citizens of 1601 stayed in their houses, and watched, and waited.[16] □

III: History and the history play

Norbrook's argument opens up a good many questions. Not every critic, for example, is persuaded that *Richard II* can be so closely connected with the Essex rebellion,[17] while the issue of how the history play genre might have been perceived in the 1590s is also problematic. The most informed writer on this topic is Phyllis Rackin who suggests that the history play enjoyed the same ambivalent position that the theatre did in the early modern period; that is to say, it could at once incite subversive behaviour but also portray examples of moral virtue and heroic patriotism, making the country's glorious past into a present enacted before an audience.[18] The following short extract from her book *Stages of History* focuses on the way the play reflects the ambivalence surrounding historical reconstructions and historical writings, including plays:

From Phyllis Rackin, *Stages of History*

■ Tudor historical accounts of Richard, in fact, exemplify the difficulty of historical reconstruction at a time when history was being reconceived as a form of secular, scientific inquiry that displaced historical causation from the will of God to the deeds of men. Richard's deposition was interpreted in terms of first causes as a transgression against God for which the entire country would have to suffer until the crime was finally expiated in blood and the land redeemed by Henry Tudor. Nonetheless, Richard's deposition was also explained in terms of second causes – Richard's faults and errors as a ruler, his bad luck, and the enmity of powerful nobles. Moreover, Richard's reign was interesting to the Elizabethans not only because it marked the point of separation from a lost, feudal past but also because of its immediate, present relevance. The teleological reading of history that located the restoration of the royal legitimacy lost in Richard in the union of Henry VII and Elizabeth of York, Queen Elizabeth's grandparents, established a direct line of providential purpose between the long-ago-deposed Plantagenet king and the reigning Tudor queen. Even more to the point, Elizabethan analogies between Richard II and Elizabeth I served as disquieting reminders that the tragic process might yet be re-enacted on the stage of history as well as Shakespeare's theatre. Queen Elizabeth's often-quoted comment, 'I am Richard II, know ye not that?'; the sponsorship by Essex's followers of a performance of an old play about Richard II (probably Shakespeare's) on the afternoon before their rebellion; and the suppression of the deposition scene in Shakespeare's play during the queen's lifetime all indicate that for Shakespeare's audience the play was not simply an exercise in historical recreation or an occasion for nostalgia. Janus-faced, the history of Richard II looks backward to a lost medieval past, but also looks forward to a disquieting Elizabethan present.[19] □

Rackin's underlying thesis is that the Elizabethans were intensely conscious of having developed a form of drama that was political, national and serious. This is worth remembering throughout the next chapter, which is largely concerned with the eighteenth-century's disparagement of Renaissance drama and its failure to observe Neo-Classical rules, and also throughout Chapter Three which is concerned with rediscovery of the history plays in the Romantic period. Both chapters reveal, as we might expect, how the critical fortunes of *Richard II* are never separate from the politics of the culture that reads or stages it.

CHAPTER TWO

Tate's Adaptation of *Richard II* and Neo-Classical Criticism of Shakespeare

Introduction

THE PREVIOUS chapter looked at the debate surrounding the place of *Richard II* in contemporary historical events. This chapter looks at the years approximately 1660–1790, which cover the Restoration and the eighteenth century up to, but not including, the Romantic era. This is a long sweep of time, involving a great deal of material, and it could be argued that it would be more reasonable to give more space to each of the different phases and topics covered, but the critical debate about Shakespeare during these years tends to focus on *Hamlet* and *King Lear*, especially the latter, rather than the histories or *Richard II*. This is not to say that there are not significant issues raised during this long period, but the fact is that very early in criticism *Richard II*, like the other history plays, found itself part of an overwhelming interest in tragedy. It is not until Tillyard in the 1940s that the histories came to occupy a clearly defined critical position of their own.

The plan of the chapter is as follows: it begins with information about Shakespeare's texts and historical dates; it then moves on to the Restoration and the staging of Shakespeare's plays, in particular Nahum Tate's adaptation of *Richard II*. Then follows a brief account of the informing Neo-Classical ideas behind Tate's practice, especially the debate about tragedy and Shakespeare. The chapter ends with a brief look at Dr Johnson's famous *Preface to Shakespeare* and his attack on Neo-Classical criticism. The term Neo-Classical (sometimes 'Neo-Aristotelian' is used) simply means in imitation of the classics. Writers in late seventeenth- and eighteenth-century England looked back to classical literature for intellectual models for their critical and artistic practice, particularly to

Aristotle and Horace. The same had happened earlier in the Renaissance in, for example, Ben Jonson's criticism. The main figure in the debate after 1660 proved to be the poet and dramatist John Dryden, but other writers will be mentioned, especially Thomas Rymer, a detractor of Shakespeare who wrote a long piece ridiculing *Othello*. The overall intention of this chapter is to highlight some of the implications of Neo-Classical criticism so that, subsequently, the Romantic reaction against the eighteenth century can be more readily appreciated.

I: Adaptations

Richard II was first published in 1597. Shakespeare's complete works, in Folio, were published in 1623 for the first time, and then in 1632, 1664 and 1685. The works were then edited by a series of editors: Rowe in 1709, Pope in 1723, Theobald in 1733, Johnson in 1765, Capell in 1767 and Malone in 1790. This reprinting of Shakespeare is evidence of the growing interest in the plays after the restoration of the monarchy in 1660, and also of a transition from just the staging of the plays to both reading and discussion of them, often alongside new adaptations and performances. We might, in fact, argue that the eighteenth century lays down the foundation of modern Shakespeare study. It does so because it begins the debate about the texts of Shakespeare and also about how to interpret them, what they mean and what sort of problems they raise. Modern criticism is radically different from that of the eighteenth century, but it is the late seventeenth and eighteenth century that turns Shakespeare into a text to be studied, a cultural icon central to thinking about literature and society.

Alongside this set of dates to do with the printing and publishing of the plays we can add another set of dates that help contextualise the growth of the critical debate about Shakespeare. Elizabeth died in 1603; she was followed by James I (the first of the Stuarts), and then, in 1625, by Charles I. The Civil War broke out in 1642, with Charles executed in 1649. The theatres were closed between 1642 and 1660, and only reopened with the restoration of the monarchy in 1660. In 1670 Charles II made a secret treaty with the French and joined them in 1672 in attacking Protestant Holland. In 1678 Titus Oates fabricated a popish plot to restore Catholicism, and this led to the attempt to exclude Charles's brother James from the throne as he was a Catholic convert. As we will see, Nahum Tate's adaptation of *Richard II* got caught up in this exclusion debate, surrounding the play with further controversy. In 1685 Charles died and James became king; Charles's illegitimate son Monmouth tried to seize the throne but was defeated. James himself, however, was forced to flee to France in 1688 when William of Orange and James's daughter Mary were invited to become King and Queen. In 1690 William defeated James in Ireland at the battle of the Boyne.

This potted history is intended as no more than an outline to help locate the ensuing extracts within the debate about the place of Shakespeare after the Civil War. It is never easy to work out the correlations between criticism and political events, but most critics seem agreed that the Civil War marks a significant alteration in British history and culture. T.S. Eliot, for example, suggested that with the Civil War came a dissociation of sensibility: that after the year 1660 there is a break with previous habits of thinking and even feeling. The precise meaning of Eliot's phrase is not clear, but it does point to the way in which after 1660 there is a change in cultural perspective.

In support of this idea, there is some concrete evidence we can point to. In 1660 the monarch returned from France, where he had taken refuge, bringing with him a new court manner. The new court (but not just the court) thought of itself as more refined than the previous barbaric age which had executed the king. So, for example, we find a remark such as this by the diarist John Evelyn, writing on 26 November 1661:

■ I saw *Hamlet* Prince of Denmark played: but now the old playe began to disgust this refined age: since his Majestie being so long abroad.[1] □

Evelyn's disgust may well be connected with the fact that *Hamlet*, like *Richard II*, is concerned with the killing of a king; his comment provides a sense of a society seeking to distance itself from the past and to establish its difference. As Terence Hawkes has pointed out, one of the things we use Shakespeare for is to make meaning or to give ourselves a type of identity, and this seems to have been equally true in the Restoration period, Shakespeare acting as a focus for an analysis of particular ideas and values which have more to do with the eighteenth century than with the Renaissance.[2]

As Vickers notes, according to the canons of the new refined court, 'Shakespeare left much to be desired' (I, 4), and this posed particular problems for the theatres. While critics could juggle their praise of Shakespeare at the same time as condemning his 'roughest most unpolish't and antiquated Language' (I, 5), the only ploy left open to the theatres was to adapt. Indeed, the period immediately after 1660 is characterised by a substantial rewriting or adapting of Shakespeare, including *Richard II*. Vickers explains the logic behind this phenomenon:

■ Part of the explanation for the need to adapt is social, to do with the size of the audience and the number of theatres. Whereas in Shakespeare's London there were from five to eight theatres open any one time, and a weekly audience of some 18,000 to 24,000, in November, 1660 only two companies were licensed by the crown: the Duke's men, managed by Sir William D'Avenant, and the King's Men, run by Thomas Killigrew. . . . The theatres were much smaller than the open-air public theatres of Shakespeare's day; they accommodated about four hundred people, at much higher prices, in late afternoon and evening performances . . . by comparison with Shakespeare's this was a more socially select audience, of fashionable or would-be fashionable people, their hangers-on and their servants. Since the available audience was small, a company would get through its repertoire quickly, and . . . would be in constant need of material. It was evidently with this in mind that in the winter of 1660 D'Avenant 'humbly presented . . . a proposition of reformeinge some of the most ancient Playes that were played at Blackfriers and of makeinge them, fitt.' □

(Vickers, I, 5)

By 'fitt' D'Avenant means fit to meet the taste of the Restoration audience rather than Shakespeare's audience at the Globe or the Blackfriars, but also fit to meet the new physical arrangements of the theatre, with sliding scenery and a proscenium arch stage.

The scale of this making fit is considerable. The most famous of the adaptations is that by Nahum Tate of *King Lear*, introduced in 1681, and performed on the stage until 1823 when Shakespeare's tragic ending was restored. Tate had changed Shakespeare's ending, preferring to keep Lear alive; he had also married off two of the main figures (Cordelia and Edgar), cut out Lear's Fool and rewritten much of the dialogue. Adaptation, it should be apparent, is a broad term, going well beyond simple things such as bringing costume up to date or cutting out the occasional small scene. In effect, adaptation was more akin to translation or rewriting (but without the kind of experimental imagination that fires modern adaptations of Shakespeare, such as Stoppard's *Rosencrantz and Guildenstern are Dead* or Edward Bond's *Lear*).

Tate was not the only adapter of Shakespeare: D'Avenant conflated *Measure for Measure* with *Much Ado About Nothing*, Dryden with D'Avenant changed *The Tempest*, Dryden adapted *Troilus and Cressida*, D'Avenant altered *Macbeth*. The adaptation fad wanes towards the end of the period but this is not before *Hamlet, Titus Andronicus* and *Julius Caesar* had also been transformed, all with prefaces explaining and justifying the changes (Vickers, I, 6–10). In a moment we will look at Tate's 1680 adaptation of *Richard II* (Theobald, as well as editing Shakespeare, adapted the play again in 1719), but first it is worth quoting Vickers on the general principle behind the adaptations:

■ The adaptations themselves constitute a unique document: there is no comparable instance of the work of a major artist being altered in such a sweeping fashion to conform to the aesthetic demand or expectations of a new age. In the prefaces and prologues the adapters give their reasons for altering Shakespeare's plays, often speaking as if they had rendered him and the public some great service in rescuing a few worthwhile parts from an otherwise obsolete and useless work. Some of their ostensible reasons can be listed:

(a) to make a more attractive theatrical vehicle;
(b) to remove metaphors and those instances of 'figurative language' which either seemed too bold for current critical theory or could create difficulties in comprehension;
(c) to remove violations of the unities of place, time and action;
(d) to remove violations of the decorum of action, such as violence or deaths on stage;
(e) to remove violations of the decorum of social position, such as low-life characters being involved in serious plots, or heroes who speak in prose;
(f) to remove violations of the decorum of genre, such as introducing comic characters into tragedy;
(g) to remove violations of poetic justice. □

(Vickers, I, 6)

Underlying this set of practices, as Vickers points out, is the influence of Neo-Classical theory on Restoration critics. The main text which Neo-Classicism drew upon was Aristotle's *Poetics*, which provided ideas about the need for works to conform to the three unities of time, place and action as well as to observe all possible decorum. Such ideas, as Schlegel was to point out in his lectures on Shakespeare in the early nineteenth century, had little basis in Aristotle, coming rather from a reading of French theoreticians who themselves had taken their Aristotle from the Italian critic Castelvetro.[3]

In some senses adaptation might be seen as a passing fashion, but the extent of it and the scale of the changes suggests its importance is more substantial; it is as if, by imposing strict definitions of order and decorum on society and its literature, social order can be preserved. If we look through Vickers's list, it becomes apparent that what is removed from the plays is any sense of social disruption, that the aesthetic is being made to serve moral and political ends. At the same time, there is a certain mechanical air to the implied criteria of good taste and manners as well as a whiff of censorship.

It is tempting at this remove to wonder what the adapters really thought they were doing, but in looking at what other periods have done or said about Shakespeare it is wise to be cautious. Few of us read Shakespeare in editions other than modern ones with modern printing and footnotes; no one has ever seen an original Shakespeare manuscript, so all we ever have is an edited text constructed in accordance with certain ideas. We could, therefore, regard the Restoration adapters as taking to an extreme an impulse that seems inherent in Shakespeare criticism, perhaps in the critical act itself; that is, the reading and making of texts in the light of our own preconceptions. Rather than dismissing the adapters, we should perhaps reflect on their relationship to the larger question of how we constantly reinvent Shakespeare.

Nevertheless, it is the case that there is something bizarre and extreme about the changes wrought on Shakespeare by the adapters. The processes, as suggested above, include adding scenes, characters, stage business, rewriting speeches and altering the whole tone of the play. A sense of this can be gained from the following extracts from Tate's *Richard II*, which needs setting briefly in its own context. The adapted version came out under the title *The Sicilian Usurper* in December 1680, but was banned after two days because of the 'uncomfortable parallels between Shakespeare's play and the contemporary political situation' (Vickers, I, 321), that is the debate surrounding Charles II's position as king. When the theatre revived the play in January 1681 it was under another title, *The Tyrant of Sicily*. This, however, did not prevent the play-house from being closed down for ten days. As with the play's appearance in 1601, it seems to have been regarded as dangerously topical. One of the repeated features of the history of productions of *Richard II* is this kind of intersecting with political contexts where it acts as a focus for sensitive issues of state. And yet the changes which Vickers describes Tate as making to the play give little encouragement for this view:

■ Tate, following the Neo-Classical concept of types and decorum, is particularly concerned to make Richard a good king, and to give him a loving and pathetic wife as proof of his goodness. □

(Vickers, I, 321)

This hardly sounds like a recipe for dangerous theatre. At the same time, it is worth commenting how Tate's strategy bears out modern feminist readings of how ideology uses gender to reinforce the *status quo*: the Queen is made to serve as an example of female domestic love, so excluding her from an active role in history or politics. In turn this suggests that Tate's changes perhaps go further than Vickers implies, and are worth listing briefly.

Tate begins by changing the names and dress of the characters to those of Sicilians (though not in the printed text he brought out in 1681). Second, as Vickers notes, he seeks to heighten respect for Richard and darken Bolingbroke's character by associating the latter with republicanism as well as an implied Catholicism. The parts of both the Queen and the Duchess of York are expanded, with the Queen present at Richard's return from Ireland as well as sending him letters in prison. York becomes a less ambiguous (but possibly more comic) figure who comes to represent bluff loyalty to the crown. All the time the drive is towards a more obvious singularity of meaning, with ambiguities cut from the language and the narrative constructed along clear lines.

Or seemingly so. Shewring argues that the effect of Tate's changes, particularly those affecting the Queen, is 'to guide our sympathy towards Richard even more than Shakespeare has done', adding that the 'tone of personal tragedy is enhanced by the inclusion of songs'.[4] By contrast, Nicholas Brooke suggests that Tate's political sympathies 'were the opposite' of Dryden's who had been revolted by Bolingbroke, and that Tate's dignifying of Richard as a compliment to Charles II is specious 'since the better the King who is shown abdicating, the more obvious the hint that Charles should retire.'[5] There is, of course, no easy way of resolving such differences of interpretation. It is always the case that texts are open to contradictory readings: what appears, from one perspective, to be no more than a piece of sentimental rewriting of Shakespeare, from another perspective has serious political implications. But such differences do suggest that Tate's version is worth a closer look.

II: Tate's adaptation of *Richard II*

The following extracts are intended to give a clearer idea of the way in which Tate changed Shakespeare's play. This first piece is taken from the end of II.i, where Richard seizes Gaunt's land. Norbrook, in his article quoted at the end of Chapter One, suggests that the Essex audience of *Richard II* in 1601 might have been particularly alert to Northumberland's role at this point and to Richard's actions as the play moves towards apparently justified rebellion. Tate's version by contrast, as Vickers suggests, seeks to sanitise Richard:

From *The History of King Richard The Second. Acted . . . Under the Name of the Sicilian Usurper. With a Prefatory Epistle in Vindication of the Author. Occasion'd by the Prohibition of this Play on the Stage* (1681)

■ (Act II scene i)

King. Thanks my good Uncle, bear him to his Bed. [*Exit* Gaunt.]
     Attend him well, and if a Princes Prayers
     Have more than common interest with Heav'n,
     Our Realm shall yet enjoy his honest Councel.
     And now my Souldiers for our Irish Wars,
     We must suppress these rough prevailing Kerns,
     That live like Venom, where no Venom else
     But only they have priviledg to live.
     But first our Uncle *Gaunt* being indispos'd,
     We do create his Brother both in Blood
     And Loyalty our Uncle *York,*

Lord Governour of England, in our absence.
Observe me Lords, and pay him that respect
You give our Royal Presence.

[*Enter* Northumberland]

North. My Liege old *Gaunt* commends him to your Highness.

King. What says our Uncle?

North. Nothing; all is said.
His Tongue is now a stringless instrument,
But call'd on your lov'd name and blest you dying.

King. The ripest fruit falls first and so doe's He;
His course is done, our Pilgrimage to come.
So much for that; return we to our War.
And 'cause our Coffers with too great a Court
And liberal Largess, are grown somewhat Light:
Prest with this exigence, we for a time
Do seize on our dead Uncles large Revenues
In *Herford*'s absence.

York. O my Liege, pardon me if you please;
If not, I please not to be pardon'd. Spare to seize
The Royalties and Rights of banisht *Herford*:
I fear already he's too apt t'engage
Against your Power, and these proceedings will give
Countenance and growth to his Designs.
Forbear to draw such Dangers on your Head.

King. Be Heav'n our judge we mean him nothing fowl
But shortly will with interest restore
The Loan our sudden streights make necessary. —
Weep not my Love nor drown with boding Tears,
Our springing Conquest, bear our absence well,
Nor think that I have joy to part with Thee,
Tho never vacant Swain in silent Bowers,
Cou'd boast a passion so sincere as mine,
Yet where the int'rest of the Subject calls,
We wave the dearest Transports of our Love
Flying from Beauty's Arms to rugged War;
Conscience our first, and Thou our second Care. [*Exeunt*] □

(Vickers, I, 327–8)

The high-flown rhetoric of Tate's Richard might well sound comic to modern ears. What, though, is most noticeable about the changes is Tate's insistence that Richard is only borrowing Bolingbroke's inheritance on a short-loan basis, so altering the political problem of Shakespeare's play. Richard's crime in seizing Bolingbroke's lands is the main reason why the lords support the rebellion and deposition; its removal from the play turns it, therefore, as Shewring notes (p.33), more towards an analysis of factionalism, with Bolingbroke as a manipulator of the rabble, rather than the representative of an aggrieved aristocracy.

The next extract follows a similar pattern. Richard has returned from Ireland and heard the bad news about Bolingbroke's success. Tate begins the scene with lines from Shakespeare, but by the end has inserted a sentimental meeting between Richard and the Queen. It starts with Richard's famous meditation on the death of kings:

■ (From Act III scene iii)

King. ... Some poyson'd by their Wives, some sleeping kill'd;
　　　　All murther'd: for within the hollow Crown
　　　　That rounds the mortal Temples of a King,
　　　　Keeps death his Court, and there the Antique sits,
　　　　Scoffing his State, and grinning at his Pomp! ...
　　　　Cover your heads and mock not flesh and blood,
　　　　With solemn reverence; throw away Respect,
　　　　Obeysance, Form and Ceremonious Duty,
　　　　For you have but mistook me all this while,
　　　　I live with bread like you, feel Wants, tast Grief,
　　　　Therefore am I no King, or a King nothing.
Aum. Give to the Foe my Lord, this cold despair,
　　　　No worse can come of Fight, of Death much better.
　　　　My Fathers Troops are firm let's joyn with them,
　　　　And manage wisely that last stake o'th' War,
　　　　Want's craft can make a body of a limb.
King. You chide me well; proud *Bullingbrook* I come, [*Rises*]
　　　　To change blows with thee for our day of Doom. ...

[Richard then learns that York is not coming with his troops.]

King. Thou hast said enough,
　　　　Beshrew thee Cousin that didst lead me forth
　　　　Of that sweet I was in to despair!
　　　　What say ye now? what comfort have ye now?
　　　　By Heav'n I'll hate him everlastingly,
　　　　That bids me be of comfort any more!

[*Enter* Queen, Dutchess, Ladies *and Attendants*]

　　　　Now by despair my Queen and her fair train!
　　　　Come to congratulate our Victory,
　　　　And claim the triumph we at parting promis'd;
　　　　Go tell 'em Lords, what feats you have perform'd,

> And if ye please tell my adventures too,
> You know I was no Idler in the War.
> Oh! torture, now I feel my miseries sting,
> And this appearance strikes me dead with shame.

Queen. Welcome my Lord,
> This minute is our own, and I'll devote it all
> To extasie; the Realm receives her King,
> And I my Lover, — thou dost turn away!
> Nor are they tears of joy which thou dost shed,
> I give thee welcome, thou replyst with sighs!

King. What language shall my bankrupt fortunes find,
> To greet such Heavenly excellence as thine?
> I promiss'd thee success and bring thee Tears!
> O couldst thou but devorce me from thy Heart!
> But oh! I know thy virtue will undoe thee,
> Thou wilt be still a faithful constant Wife,
> Feel all my Wrongs and suffer in my Fall!
> There is the sting and venom of my Fate,
> When I shall think that I have ruin'd Thee.

Queen. I ask no more my Lord, at Fortunes hands
> Than priviledge to suffer for your sake!
> Who wou'd not share your Grief to share your Love?
> This Kingdom yet, which once you did prefer
> To the worlds sway, this Beauty and this Heart
> Is *Richards* still, millions of Loyal thoughts
> Are always waiting there to pay you homage.
> That glorious Empire yields to you alone,
> No *Bullingbrook* can chase you from that Throne.

King. We'll march no farther, lead to th'Castle here. [*Exeunt*] □

(Vickers, I, 328–30)

It may be that Tate's romantic additions to the play, such as these, and the sketching in of the Queen's character as loyal wife and lover owe something to the fact that the Restoration stage saw the introduction of actresses. Without female parts, plays were less likely to please and so Tate's additions, for all their supposed grounding in decorum and fine sentiment, may have come from more materialistic motives. But the underlying point remains the fact that Tate deflects attention away from political disruption; domestic order within the family, as represented by the picture of the king and his wife, makes the play a kind of middle-class vision of how domestic life can and should echo the order of political life.

If space were limitless it would be illuminating to print further domestic insertions from Tate as well as extended comparisons with Shakespeare's text. That would highlight even further the sort of change at the level of the individual word that Tate makes as well as illustrating the recasting of the play towards a mix of the domestic, bathetic and pompous. A short extract from the prison scene is, however, irresistible. Richard is alone in prison in the final act. He delivers most of the soliloquy Shakespeare gives him, though with lines simplified:

■ (*From* Act V scene iv)

Rich. . . . Thus I and every other Son of Earth
    With nothing shall be pleas'd, till we be eas'd
    With being nothing.
                       [*A Table and Provisions shewn.*]
    What mean my Gaolers by that plenteous Board?
    For three days past I've fed upon my Sighs,
    And drunk my Tears; rest, craving Nature, rest,
    I'll humour thy dire Need and tast this food,
    That only serves to make Misfortune Live.
                 [*Going to sit, the Table sinks down.*]
    Thus *Tantalus* they say is us'd below;
    But *Tantalus* his Guilt is then his Torture.
    I smile at this fantastick Cruelty.
    Ha, Musick too! – Ev'n what my Torturers please.
                      [*Song and soft Musick.*]

[Here a three-stanza song follows.]

           [*After which a Messenger enters, gives him Letters.*]

Mess. Hail Royal Sir, with dang'rous difficulty
    I've enter'd here to bear These to your hand. —
    O killing Spectacle!

Rich. From whom? — my Queen,
    My *Isabel*, my Royal wretched Wife? . . .

[Richard praises his wife for another ten lines before deciding to reply, hiding his feelings.]

    In, hide Thee, and prepare in short to Answer
    To th'infinite Enquiries that my Love
    Shall make of this dear Darling of my Soul.
    Whilst undisturb'd I seize the present Minute
    To answer the Contents of this blest Paper.   [*Ex. Mess.*]
             [*Sits down to write. Enter* Exton *and Servants.*]
    Furies! what means this Pageantry of Death?
    Speak thou the foremost Murderer, thy own hand
    Is arm'd with th'Instrument of thy own Slaughter,

> Go Thou and fill a room in Hell,
> Another Thou
>
> *[Kills 4 of them.]*
> [Exton *here strikes him down.*] □
>
> (Vickers, I, 337–9)

As Vickers points out, the dramatic practices at work in this sort of scene make little sense in terms of the critical and theoretical principles of drama that were articulated in the age, particularly its strict division of plays into comedies or tragedies. Richard, like all kings, is shown as just and humane; his wife is chaste and modest. But what are we to make of the insertions of spectacle and music? The drive here is theatrical entertainment, a deliberate playing to the crowd and an exploitation of the new kind of small indoor theatre with more stage machinery.

Despite attempts to resist, it is hard not to mock Tate's version. We need, however, to consider what Tate perhaps thought he was achieving in order to understand the adaptation. Tate set out his views, like other adapters, in a letter acting as Preface to the play. After explaining how he had not intended the play to be seditious, Tate describes how he had made Richard's character more king-like to draw the audience's pity, but also how he added a few touches of comedy to lighten the whole:

■ To My Esteemed Friend George Raynsford, Esq;
SIR,
I Wou'd not have you surpriz'd with this Address, though I gave you no warning of it. The Buisiness of this Epistle is more Vindication than Complement; and when we are to tell our Grievances 'tis most natural to betake our selves to a Friend. 'Twas thought perhaps that this unfortunate Offspring having been stifled on the *Stage*, shou'd have been buried in Oblivion; and so it might have happened had it drawn its Being from me Alone; but it still retains the immortal Spirit of its first-Father, and will survive in Print, though forbid to tread the *Stage*. They that have not seen it Acted, by its being silenc't, must suspect me to have Compil'd a Disloyal or Reflecting *Play*. But how far distant this was from my Design and Conduct in the Story will appear to him that reads with half an Eye. To form any Resemblance between the Times here written of, and the Present, had been unpardonable Presumption in Me, If the Prohibiters conceive any such Notion I am not accountable for That. I fell upon the new-modelling of this Tragedy, (as I had just before done on the *History of King Lear*) charm'd with the many Beauties I discover'd in it, which I knew wou'd become the *Stage* with as little design of Satyr on present Transactions, as *Shakespeare* himself that wrote this Story before this Age began. I am not ignorant of the posture of Affairs in King *Richard* the Second's

Reign, how dissolute then the Age, and how corrupt the Court; a Season that beheld *Ignorance* and Infamy preferr'd to *Office* and *Pow'r*, exercis'd in Oppressing Learning and Merit; but why a History of those Times shou'd be supprest as a Libel upon Ours, is past my Understanding. 'Tis sure the worst *Complement* that ever was made to a Prince. . . .

Our *Shakespeare* in this Tragedy, bated none of his Characters an Ace of the Chronicle; he took care to shew 'em no worse Men than They were, but represents them never a jot better. . . . His King *Richard* Himself is painted in the worst Colours of History, Dissolute, Unadviseable, devoted to Ease and Luxury . . . without the least palliating of his Miscarriages, which I have done in the new Draft, . . .

I have every where given him the Language of an Active, Prudent Prince, Preferring the Good of his Subjects to his own private Pleasure. . . . Nor cou'd it suffice me to make him speak like a King (who as Mr. *Rymer* says in his *Tragedies of the last Age considered*, are always in Poetry presum'd *Heroes*) but to *Act so too*, viz. with *Resolution* and *Justice*. Resolute enough our *Shakespeare* (copying the History) has made him . . . seizing old *Gaunt's* Revennues. . . . But where was the Justice of this Action? This Passage I confess was so material a Part of the Chronicle (being the very Basis of *Bullingbrook's* Usurpation) that I cou'd not in this new Model so far transgress Truth as to make no mention of it; yet for the honour of my Heroe I suppose the foresaid Revennues to be *Borrow'd* onely for the present Exigence, not *Extorted*. . . .

My Design was to engage the pitty of the Audience for him in his Distresses, which I cou'd never have compass'd had I not before shewn him a Wise, Active and Just Prince. . .

Further, to Vindicate ev'n his *Magnanimity* in Regard of his Resigning the Crown, I have on purpose inserted an intirely new Scene between him and his Queen, wherein his Conduct is sufficiently excus'd by the Malignancy of his Fortune, which argues indeed Extremity of Distress, but Nothing of Weakness.

. . . Yet I took care from the Beginning to adorn my Prince with such heroick Vertues, as afterwards made his distrest Scenes of force to draw Tears from the Spectators; which, how much more touching they would have been had the Scene been laid at Home, let the Reader judge. The additional Comedy I judg'd necessary to help off the heaviness of the Tale, which Design, Sir, you will not only Pardon, but Approve. I have heard you commend this Method in Stage writing, though less agreeable to stricktness of Rule; and I find your Choice confirm'd by our *Laureat's* last Piece, who confesses himself to have broken a Rule for the Pleasure of Variety. . . .

Your obliged Friend and humble Servant,

N. Tate □
(Vickers, I, 321–5)

Tate's Preface is useful because, in a short space, it tells almost the whole story of Neo-Classical criticism. Running through it is the central idea of decorum, of making actions and language appropriate to rank in order to maintain the status quo. But also running through the letter is a concern with moral virtues accompanied by a sense of artifice and restraint. The key critical and moral ideas are contained in words such as 'heroick Vertues', 'stricktness of Rule', 'pitty' and 'Justice'; in brief, the letter offers us a text of the vocabulary of the Neo-Classical view of tragedy.

There are two aspects worth commenting on in Tate's letter in a little more detail as they bear upon Neo-Classical criticism more generally. The first is the point that Tate says he observes beauties in Shakespeare but writes as if these were accidental, or obscured by the rest of the play. In other words, one of the things that eighteenth-century adapters did was try to pick out the best bits of Shakespeare and improve the rest. Such thinking led not merely to structural changes but to literally hundreds of changes of words and phrases, adding up to a rewriting of most speeches. In the bulk of cases the end result is a simplification of the language and a loss of its poetic character.

Second is the idea of the need to make characters behave according to rank or position so that kings, for example, are always kingly: they must behave in a noble fashion, with their motives above suspicion. Unless they did so decorum would be violated. Underlying this, as we have already noted, is the notion of decorum and obedience to a set of rules bringing the aesthetic and the moral into unison. The presuppositions operating here leave little room for anything other than stereotyped figures and stock language, evident in Richard's speeches where motive, behaviour and action are immediately intelligible and always on the surface. There is nothing for the audience to do other than listen and learn.

The case is much the same with Lewis Theobald's adaptation of *Richard II* in 1719, which sought to capitalise on Neo-Classical taste. As with Tate's version, there is an attempt to maintain a unity of action and character, with the play set wholly in the Tower of London. The Queen's part is once again extended, so stretching the play further into sentimentality, while York commits suicide after Richard's death, steering the action into melodrama and empty heroic gestures. For example, Aumerle is executed and his wife Lady Piercy (Northumberland's newly invented daughter) kills herself in grief. The play enjoyed no small success. Its significance seems to lie in what it tells us about the way in which the adapters of Shakespeare tried to overwrite the political action of *Richard II* and turn it into something else. But the crucial point to grasp is that, as much as Tate and Theobald might have turned the play into light entertainment, their adaptations were influenced by conscious or unconscious political motivations of their own. They wished to promote a certain vision of social discipline and political order. This makes it all the more ironic that Tate's adaptation of *Richard II* was banned.

III: Neo-Classical Criticism

We have no contemporary responses to Tate's *Richard II* apart from information about its prohibition. We do, however, have Rymer's essay, to which Tate refers in his Preface, and which is part of the Neo-Classical debate of the period. Shakespeare was at the centre of this critical debate partly because his plays were undoubtedly admired, partly because they did breach the rules of composition apparently set down by Aristotle for tragedy, and partly because, as Tate discovered, Shakespeare could be easily altered by bad writers as well as good. [6]

There is a good reason for looking at extracts from some of the criticism written after 1660 even though it does not bear directly upon *Richard II*; this has to do with the way in which, first, it helped establish tragedy as the norm by which Shakespeare's other plays are judged, and second, how it helped establish tragedy as the main critical area of attention. There is, in fact, very little in the period about the histories either as a genre or as a type of tragedy. Tate refers to *Richard II* as a tragedy even though he knows it is based on chronicle history, and is as much about rule and politics as about the central figure (there is, as Brooke says, something disingenuous about his claim to be unaware of the political relevance of his staging of the play).[7] Neo-Classical criticism, however, had no room for thinking about the implications of such a mix for its theories of genre. What it did have room for was the constant incorporation of Shakespeare into a set of ideas that still remain for some people, even today, the basic framework for understanding tragedy. In other words, more than a residual trace of eighteenth-century thinking about tragedy still persists in modern critical discussions of the tragedies. There is still, for example, in more traditional contemporary criticism a turning to Aristotle and the question of catharsis, of whether we feel pity and terror at the end of tragedy, as if criticism itself is loath to consider other formulations. This may reflect the extent to which eighteenth-century criticism pushed tragedy to the centre of the critical debate.

The extract below comes from Dryden's preface to his adaptation of *Troilus and Cressida*. In the preface Dryden seeks to explain what he has done in changing the play to try and achieve unity of time and place, to reach a proper high tone, and also to insert poetic justice so that the good are rewarded and the evil are properly punished. Poetic justice was a central tenet of Neo-Classical thinking, a necessary condition for works of art, which, in turn, justified such changes as Tate made to *King Lear* by keeping the old king alive and marrying Cordelia to Edgar. We might feel it is precisely Shakespeare's refusal to comply with these rules (or his ignorance of them) that marks his plays out as great rather than formulaic. What is remarkable about Dryden's account, however, is the primacy he gives to the rational ordering of tragedy. Tragedy must make sense at every level so that the audience can perceive it to be working in a clear way:

From John Dryden, *Troilus and Cressida, Or, Truth Found too Late* (1679)

■ The Grounds of Criticism in Tragedy

Tragedy is thus defined by *Aristotle*, (omiting what I thought unnecessary in his Definition). 'Tis an imitation of one intire, great, and probable action; not told but represented, which by moving in us fear and pity, is conducive to the purging of these two passions in our minds. More largly thus, Tragedy describes or paints an Action, which . . . must be one or single, that is, it must not be a History of one Mans life . . . but one single action of theirs. This condemns all *Shakespeare's* Historical Plays, which are rather Chronicles represented, than Tragedies, and all double action of Plays. . . . The natural reason of this Rule is plain, for two different independent actions, distract the attention and concernment of the Audience, and consequently destroy the intention of the Poet: If his business be to move terror and pity, and one of his Actions be Comical, the other Tragical, the former will divert the people, and utterly make void his greater purpose. . . .

As the Action ought to be one, it ought as such, to have Order in it, that is, to have a natural beginning, a middle, and an end: . . .

. . . The last quality of the action is, that it ought to be probable, as well as admirable and great. 'Tis not necessary that there should be Historical truth in it; but always necessary that there should be a likeness of truth, something that is more than barely possible . . . To invent therefore a probability and to make it wonderfull, is the most difficult undertaking in the Art of Poetry: for that which is not wonderfull, is not great, and that which is not probable, will not delight a reasonable Audience. . . .

To instruct delightfully is the general end of all Poetry: . . . To purge the passions by Example, is therefore the particular instruction which belongs to Tragedy. . . . pride and want of commiseration are the most prominent vices in Mankinde; therefore to cure us of these two, the inventors of Tragedy have chosen to work upon two other passions, which are fear and pity. We are wrought to fear, by their seting before our eyes some terrible example of misfortune, which hapned to persons of the highest Quality; for such an action demonstrates to us, that no condition is privileg'd from the turns of Fortune: this must of necessity cause terror in us, and consequently abate our pride. . . . Here 'tis observable, that it is absolutely necessary to make a man virtuous, if we desire he should be pity'd: We lament not, but detest a wicked man, we are glad when we behold his crimes are punish'd, and that Poetical justice is done upon him. . . .

The first Rule . . . is to make the moral of the work; that is, to lay down to yourself what that precept of morality shall be, which you would insinuate into the people: . . . 'Tis the Moral that directs the whole action of the Play to one center; and that action or Fable, is the example built upon the moral, which confirms the truth of it to our experience: . . .

The manners . . . are understood to be those inclinations . . . which move and carry us to actions . . . in a Play; or which incline the person to such, or such actions: . . . To produce a Villain, without other reason than a natural inclination to villainy, is in Poetry to produce an effect without a cause: and to make him more a Villain than he has just reason to be, is to make an effect which is stronger than the cause.

. . . the manners must be suitable or agreeing to the Persons; that is, to the Age, Sex, dignity and the other general heads of Manners: thus when a Poet has given the Dignity of a King to one of his persons, in all his actions and speeches, that person must discover Majesty, Magnanimity, and jealousy of power; because these are suitable to the general manners of a King. □

(Vickers, I, 252–7)

Dryden places considerable emphasis on manners and decorum, but also on fitness and instruction.[8] The underlying thrust of most Neo-Classical criticism is towards didacticism: the purpose of art is not only to entertain but also, through entertainment, to instruct. In the case of tragedy, the instruction was to be about the workings of divine justice. Genres must be kept discrete; otherwise this would undermine and divert attention away from the purpose of instruction in moral virtue. This, of course, makes art no more than a vehicle for trite moral statements, but the real point to grasp about Neo-Classical criticism is how it appropriated Aristotelian ideas such as those of catharsis in the service of its moralistic aesthetic.

Dryden's discussion of the grounds of tragedy helps explain Tate's changes to *Richard II* but also perhaps the neglect of the histories. They are, in an almost literal sense, ruled out of critical attention because the rules have nothing to say about them. The two genres for Neo-Classical criticism are comedy and tragedy, and it is these which dominate the discussion. And yet, later in the preface, discussing Shakespeare's representation of the passions and the nature of his verse, Dryden singles out for special attention the description of Richard's return into London after the deposition:

■ I cannot leave this Subject before I do justice to that Divine Poet, by giving you one of his passionate descriptions: 'tis of *Richard* the Second when he was depos'd, and led in Triumph through the Streets of

London by *Henry of Bullingbrook*: the painting of it is so lively, and the words so moving, that I have scarce read any thing comparable to it, in any other language. Suppose you have seen already the fortunate Usurper passing through the croud, and follow'd by the shouts and acclamations of the people; and now behold King *Richard* entring upon the Scene: consider the wretchedness of his condition, and his carriage in it; and refrain from pitty if you can.

As in a Theatre. the eyes of men
After a well-grac'd Actor leaves the Stage.
Are idly bent on him that enters next.
Thinking his prattle to be tedious:
Even so. or with much more contempt, mens eyes
Did scowl on Richard*: no man cry'd God save him:*
No joyful tongue gave him welcom home.
But dust was thrown upon his Sacred head.
Which with such gentle sorrow he shook off.
His face still combating with tears and smiles
(The badges of his grief and patience)
That had not God (for some strong purpose) steel'd
The hearts of men. they must perforce have melted.
And Barbarism it self have pity'd him. □

(Vickers I, 265)

Dryden's praise of the speech is echoed by other writers later in the period, suggesting something of the influence of Dryden on critical thinking. That thinking is not as rigid as perhaps Tate makes it seem: Dryden recognises in the description of Richard a language and action which appears to be the epitome of tragedy. At the same time, what is interesting about Dryden's account is its direct critical response: though he is reading the text, he asks us to imagine the setting, to see the play in the mind's eye. The rational surface of Neo-Classical criticism slips for a minute as Dryden engages in close analysis of the text and its dramatic effect in a way that Tate's letter never does.

From Dryden's account we can, in fact, begin to construct a sense of the complex exchange between criticism and theatre, and the reception of Shakespeare at the time. Throughout Dryden's criticism there is an emphasis on manners, on decorum, but also on the rules that should shape a play. There is, in addition, a clear emphasis that literature has to instruct, that its serious purpose be maintained, particularly through poetic justice. But at the same time there is also a constant sense of the beauty of Shakespeare's verse and his fineness as a poet. Despite its fondness for the rules, Neo-Classical criticism found itself wrestling with alternative Shakespeares, including one it praised as Nature's child, as a natural genius. Paradoxically, the very uniformity of critical principles the age wished to endorse was implicitly and explicitly challenged in much of the language used to describe Shakespeare.

IV: Alternative Shakespeares

A more extreme version of Neo-Classicism, and one which illustrates the problem of the neglect of the histories, is found in Thomas Rymer's *Tragedies of the Last Age* published in 1677. His purpose, he says, is to discover whether the authors of English tragedy have shown through their designs the working of '*justice* exactly administered', as did the ancients who

■ found that *History*, grosly taken, was neither proper to *instruct*, nor apt to *please* and therefore they would not trust History for their examples, but refin'd upon the History; and thence contriv'd something more *philosophical*, and more *accurate* than History. □

(Vickers, I, 187–8)

In other words, Rymer argues, history cannot please because it cannot instruct; it cannot instruct because it does not offer clear moral lessons. '[I]n History', he writes, 'the same *end* happen[s] to the *righteous* and to the *unjust*, [with] vertue often opprest, and *wickedness* on the throne' (Vickers, I, 187).

History could not be trusted because it did not reward as we might wish; it did not offer universal truths that might instruct. For Rymer, the very key of the work of art must be its vision of justice operating in an unambiguous way. The problem of history was precisely that it had already happened and so was subject to accident that could not be altered or changed. For Rymer, as for Dryden and as for the age in general, art had to be above the contingency of history. On one level it is difficult not to associate this distrust of history with the political situation of the Restoration, an age trying to distance itself from the previous age and the shock of the Civil War. Indeed, it could be argued that just as official Tudor historians sought to use history to their purposes to shape public opinion, so, too, critical writers in the late seventeenth century wished to do a similar thing but by excluding historical examples or by rewriting them.

Rymer's attack on Shakespeare took its most extreme form in his *A Short View of Tragedy* (1693) where, in a long discussion, he ridiculed almost every aspect of *Othello*, especially Desdemona's loss of her handkerchief which leads Othello into believing she has been unfaithful. That ridicule seems to have produced a backlash. Dryden wrote a rebuttal of Rymer as did Charles Gildon who, in 1710, produced an extended commentary on Shakespeare's life and works which was included in Rowe's edition of 1709. This edition and Gildon's essay, we might argue, mark a shift away from mere adaptation towards a new kind of critical interest in what Shakespeare had written. No one, however, would want to pin down a definite change in Shakespeare's critical fortunes to one particular date or publication. Throughout the period that we are looking at there is an intense debate about Shakespeare's virtues and faults, with plenty of evidence of criticism attacking the plays for not conforming to the rules, but also praise of Shakespeare's art.

And not just praise. In 1738, John Rich, the manager at Covent Garden, put on a production of *Richard II* that was 'the first known attempt to perform Shakespeare's unaltered text in over one hundred years'.[9] The production was apparently in 'direct response to a new interest among fashionable society in seeing good English plays on the London stage, an interest largely brought about by the efforts of the "Shakespeare Ladies Club"' (Shewring, p. 40). The production itself appears to have used spectacular pageantry in order to recreate a sense of the Elizabethan stage, and provides evidence of the growing antiquarian interest in Shakespeare after 1700, an interest which is the very antithesis of the disgust expressed by Evelyn in 1661. Instead of a Shakespeare seen as the representative of a barbaric age, Rich's production offered an historic Shakespeare, the representative of an emergent English middle-class culture.

Shewring suggests, however, that Rich may have put *Richard II* on because of 'the current licensing controversy' (p. 44) and that the performance was deliberately intended to be politically risky by suggesting a parallel between Walpole and Richard's flattering advisors. As with Tate's adaptation, the production took place at a sensitive political moment. The difference, though, is important to note: where Tate had altered *Richard II* almost out of recognition, Rich sought to stage an Elizabethan version of the play. Though critics continued to apply Neo-Classical rules to Shakespeare after 1738, they were, in effect, dead from that date on.

The 'Shakespeare Ladies Club' itself appears at a moment that coincides with the increased availability of cheap printed texts of Shakespeare. It is also a time of increased competition between editions, so that at this stage – say, after 1700 – we can begin to talk about Shakespeare being turned into a classic author. Thus Rowe's edition of 1709 was followed by a sequence of others, including Pope (1725), Theobald (1733) and Johnson (1765). And with each edition so the ground moves more and more away from rigid Neo-Classical thinking (which paradoxically had produced the mixed genre adaptations) towards a different kind of thinking about Shakespeare as editors seek to re-establish Shakespeare's texts by, for example, making use of the early Quartos. As with any generalisation, one would not wish to defend it too far, but the shift from adaptation to restoration of Shakespeare's text is of momentous importance to the critical fortunes of Shakespeare's plays.

The different kind of thinking about Shakespeare that began to emerge after 1700 can be illustrated by taking a brief extract from Dr

Johnson's famous preface to his edition of Shakespeare where he defends the dramatist against his detractors but also attacks the application of the unities to the plays:

From Samuel Johnson, Preface to his edition of *The Plays of William Shakespeare* (1765)

■ *Shakespeare* is above all writers, at least above all modern writers, the poet of nature; the poet that holds up to his readers a faithful mirrour of manners and of life. His characters are not modified by the customs of particular places, unpractised by the rest of the world;. . . they are the genuine progeny of common humanity, such as the world will always supply, and observation will always find. . . . In the writings of other poets a character is too often an individual; in those of *Shakespeare* it is commonly a species. . . .

. . . *Shakespeare* has no heroes; his scenes are occupied only by men, who act and speak as the reader thinks that he himself should have spoken or acted on the same occasion. . .

Shakespeare has united the powers of exciting laughter and sorrow not only in one mind but in one composition. . . .

That this is a practice contrary to the rules of criticism will be readily allowed; but there is always an appeal open from criticism to nature. . .

Tragedy was not in those times a poem of more general dignity or elevation than comedy; it required only a calamitous conclusion, with which the common criticism of that age was satisfied, whatever lighter pleasure it afforded in its progress.

History was a series of actions, with no other than chronological succession, independent of each other, and without any tendency to introduce or regulate the conclusion. It is not always very nicely distinguished from tragedy. There is not much nearer approach to unity of action in the tragedy of *Antony and Cleopatra* than in the history of *Richard the Second*. But a history might be continued through many plays; as it had no plan, it had no limits. □

(Vickers, V, 57–62)

As Vickers notes, Johnson was in some ways pulling together ideas and points expressed by previous editors while also still echoing the vocabulary of Neo-Classicism. In that sense he seems to be saying nothing very different from other eighteenth-century writers. Yet the fact remains that, with Johnson's massive preface and those that followed by Stevens and Malone, criticism had become more than notes about this or that play, or a defence of or attack upon Shakespeare. It had become a recognised and recognisable critical discourse and practice. That discourse was, however, to change radically with the arrival of Romanticism.

CHAPTER THREE

Romantic Criticism

Introduction

WITH THE arrival of the Romantic age Shakespeare's history plays begin to receive much more attention; this is especially true of *Richard II*. The third section of this chapter reprints extracts from essays by Schlegel, Coleridge and Hazlitt on the play. These essays were instrumental in bringing *Richard II* out of the shadow of the tragedies, although it remains the case that criticism in the period (approximately, 1789–1824) is still dominated by the four major tragedies, *King Lear, Macbeth, Othello* and *Hamlet*, the last of which became the key text of Shakespeare for the age. Indeed, as Bate says, 'The Romantics' reinvention of Hamlet as a paralysed Romantic was their single most influential critical act.'[1] The Romantics, however, as Bate also notes, 'were not character critics alone'. In effect, they established the foundations of modern Shakespearean criticism:

■ Schlegel was a powerful analyst of structure, Coleridge of language, Hazlitt of theatre and politics. Romantic criticism thus prefigures not only the character analysis of A. C. Bradley's *Shakespearean Tragedy* (1904) and the imagistic approaches of critics, such as G. Wilson Knight and L. C. Knights, who reacted against Bradley but also some of the more recent movements, such as 'Shakespeare in performance' and 'political Shakespeare', which have reacted in turn against the old 'new criticism' of the Knights' generation.[2] □

(Bate, p. 2)

There is, then, good reason to look in some detail at Romantic criticism in terms both of its impact on *Richard II* and its larger significance.

Repeatedly in the eighteenth century we come across the idea that Shakespeare, though at fault and contravening the rules of Neo-Classical taste, is in some ways a natural or primitive force worth reading or seeing, albeit possibly in an adaptation rather than in the original form. Even Voltaire, the French philosopher and dramatist who dominated French Neo-Classical criticism of Shakespeare and who spoke of Shakespeare as a barbarian or inspired idiot, praised him as 'a genius full of force and fecundity' (Bate, p. 4).[3] For the early nineteenth century, however, and in particular for writers and critics such as Schlegel and Coleridge, the eighteenth century represented an age which profoundly misunderstood Shakespeare and his art. It is often the case that criticism works by setting up an earlier generation of critics as figures to be scorned or struggled or argued against, as if in a kind of restless debate with the past. This is certainly so with Romantic criticism as it takes shape and rejects the rules and the unities in favour of its own evolving aesthetic. But the matter goes beyond a mere rejection of Neo-Classicism. There are profound shifts between eighteenth-century culture and Romanticism which are of continuing importance to our own critical understanding.

The shifts are not single or simple. What this chapter does initially, therefore, is consider aspects of the theory underlying Romantic criticism and the new ideas it produces; these concern organic form, character subjectivity and inwardness, and a recognition of the history plays as a separate genre. These ideas, as we will see, are allied with the changing political scene, specifically the constant threat of revolution, an idea embodied in Napoleon. Some of this material may not bear directly on *Richard II*, but it is tied in very closely with the start of modern criticism of the play and also of modern methods of looking at Shakespeare.

There are two key figures who make a difference to criticism in the Romantic period: Samuel Taylor Coleridge and Augustus William Schlegel. The more immediately influential of these is Schlegel, a German scholar chiefly known for his translation of Shakespeare and who, at the start of the nineteenth century, delivered a course of lectures on Shakespearean drama and its significance for German theatre. Shakespeare, quite simply, became the focus for the debate about the need for a national literature in Germany. More particularly, as Bate notes (p. 9), Shakespeare provided an example for German critics of the dramatic principles and practice of a national literature rooted in its own culture, an example that could be imitated without having to follow Neo-Classical rules.

In this kind of thinking about Shakespeare Schlegel had been anticipated to some extent in Germany by the dramatist and critic Gotthold Lessing, and also in France by Madame de Staël. In England, Schlegel's ideas found an echo in those of Coleridge, the Romantic poet and friend of Wordsworth. Like Schlegel, around 1810–13, Coleridge delivered a series of lectures on Shakespeare. This is the time of the rise of Napoleon in France and the threat of war. Coleridge's criticism is influenced by these circumstances in its representation of Shakespeare as a national poet, but also to some extent as a gentrified, conservative thinker, in contrast to the politically subversive dramatist championed by William Hazlitt (Bate, p. 23ff). As Bate says, these three figures – Schlegel, Coleridge and, to a slightly lesser extent, Hazlitt – are responsible for the most significant criticism of the Romantic period, a criticism not just about Shakespeare's texts but about shaping a new critical aesthetic to replace that of the eighteenth century.

I: Romanticism and revolution

Romanticism is not easy to define. In terms of the debate about drama, it is in some ways simply a reaction against the eighteenth century and the attempt to make art fit theories derived from French Neo-Classicism. The reaction, however, is more than merely a case of not liking or not approving. The matter, as Bate shows, is tied up with a broader move-ment across Europe following the French Revolution. At that turning point of history, specifically on 14 July 1789, the Bastille prison was stormed and the royal family moved to Paris. The king was eventually executed in 1793; this was followed by the Reign of Terror during which hundreds of people were guillotined. But then further political changes led to the rise of Napoleon. Bate comments:

■ Under Napoleon, France's aspirations towards pan-European hegemony extended well beyond the cultural. It is of paramount importance to locate the influential lectures of A.W. Schlegel at their particular historical moment. Like several of Coleridge's lectures, they represent Shakespearian criticism written under the shadow of Napoleon. . . . Literary lecturing was a politically charged activity – before they could be delivered, an outline of the proposed lectures had to be submitted to the Vienna police. □

(Bate, p. 10)

What Bate draws out is the extent to which Shakespeare was being used both in England and Europe as a figure to set against the culture of French imperialism, and also how criticism was becoming much more overtly linked to politics. Here we can start to see why the Romantics turn to the histories: Shakespeare is recognised as a national poet, the histories coming into prominence because they foreground national identity and the history of a people.

Also informing this use of Shakespeare was the need to break away from the domination of French cultural ideas and forms, especially the French dramatists of the seventeenth century, Corneille and Racine. There was, too, a desire to get away from the views of Voltaire which had dominated French Neo-Classical criticism. As noted above, Voltaire set the tone of the debate by condemning Shakespeare for his barbarity. Reaction against the eighteenth century was as much as anything a reaction against Voltaire as against Tate or the editors or Dryden or any others. These, too, implicitly and explicitly, came in for criticism, as did Dr Johnson, even though his *Preface to Shakespeare* seemed to do much to undermine the unities. The clearest example of this denigrating of the previous century is found perhaps in Victor Hugo's *William Shakespeare* (1864), the second part of which begins by listing derogatory remarks about Shakespeare from the preceding two hundred years before going on to praise his genius.[4]

It is, of course, difficult to follow all the details and nuances of the debate over Shakespeare as it shifts between French Neo-Classicism, German Romantic criticism, the new critical thinking in England, and French Romanticism. One way of summarising the debate and the changes it brought about, however, is to use the idea of the French Revolution as a metaphor for the way in which the new ideas took hold. Here we can turn to Hugo again. Hugo in 1827 had used the Preface to his play *Cromwell* to promote a case in favour of Shakespeare and Romanticism. But it is in his book on Shakespeare in 1864 that Hugo gives the clearest statement of the connection between the Revolution and Romanticism. Using the metaphor of the French Revolution Hugo gives a vivid sense not only of change but of the different kind of critical language that Romanticism brought into being:

■ . . . the nineteenth century has for its august mother the French Revolution. This redoubtable blood flows in its veins. It honours men of genius, and if need be salutes them when despised, proclaims them when ignored, avenges them when persecuted, re-enthrones them when dethroned: it venerates them, but it does not proceed from them. The nineteenth century has for family itself, and itself alone. It is the characteristic of its revolutionary nature to dispense with ancestors.[5] □

This is the language of a new kind of thinking about human beings and their achievements, a language no longer fixated with judgement about rules and failure. It is a language fired by enthusiasms and ideals, wishing to celebrate and overturn old judgements. Hugo continues:

■ The writers and poets of the nineteenth century have the . . . good fortune of proceeding from a genesis, of arriving late after an end of the world, of accompanying a reappearance of light, of being the organs of a new beginning. This imposes on them . . . the duties of intentional reformers and direct civilizers. They continue nothing; they form everything anew. . . . The function of thinkers in our days is complex; it no longer suffices to think – one must love; it no longer suffices to

think and to love – one must act. To think, to love, and to act, no longer
suffice – one must suffer.[6] □

The different discourse that the term Romantic signals is evident here. Of
course, this language is not invented solely by Hugo; it comes from
Schlegel, Coleridge and the other Romantic writers. It is a language of
emotion, of inwardness, of subjectivity which can transform the world.
Indeed, we can see in miniature here what it is that, on one level, defines
Romantic criticism: it is a commitment to experience against the theory
of Neo-Classicism, of inner being against social form and decorum.

II: Schlegel, Coleridge and Hazlitt

There are, though, other aspects of Romanticism that go with this new
emphasis on the language of feeling. As Bate notes, Johann Herder in
1773 had suggested a new national drama for Germany, with
Shakespeare as the model, developed out of a national culture.[7] This is an
important aspect of Romanticism that is easy to overlook: its connection
with a certain kind of nationalistic thinking. It is important to grasp this
in order to understand why late twentieth-century critics grew suspicious of Romantic criticism and its politics of subjectivity. The stress on
subjectivity, on how characters feel, is not separate from a certain kind of
turning inwards politically. This includes turning inwards geographically,
so giving a new emphasis to the nation state and national identity. In this
context it is easy to see why the Romantics begin to value the history
plays with their stress on England and Englishness.

As Bate argues, Schlegel's lectures were to propose a unity of
Germany that could be forged through art. He does this in part by evok-
ing the middle ages, when the Germans were victorious, and by
suggesting a parallel between artists and soldiers. The effect is to present
Shakespeare as a counter-force, as it were, to Napoleon (Bate, p. 11). This
parallel between Shakespeare and a military force, however, has other
implications. Through art the intention is to forge a new German identity
which Schlegel sees as different from French identity. Where the French
are strict and rule-bound, the Germans can be members of an organic
and evolving culture. Bate summarises Schlegel's argument about
organic form and its political implications this way:

■ French national culture is taken to be characterised by rigorous
adherence to a neo-Aristotelian system of artistic principles, rules far
stricter than those of Aristotle himself, . . . The French are in the thrall
of theoretical mechanisms, of the outward regularity of form. Given
that its context is Schlegel's anti-Gallicism, the attack on mechanical
form is an attack not only on neo-classical aesthetics but also on such

systematic formulations as the Declaration of the Rights of Man, the Civil Constitution of the Clergy, and, preeminently, the Civil Code which Napoleon had promulgated on 21 March 1804. Napoleon was as zealous a propagandist for his Code as Voltaire had been for the Unities; when Schlegel attacks the form that is imposed through external force he has in mind the French Emperor as well as the French Academician. His preference for an organic form that is innate, that unfolds itself from within, that acts according to laws flowing from its essence, is bound up with the idea of an evolving German state which has its own unity despite accidental differences which no external force has a right to interfere with or attempt to reshape. The mechanical French can alter accidentals, such as state boundaries; they cannot touch the germ, the hidden essence of Germany. □

(Bate, p. 12)

This notion of organic form and unity is a key point in Romanticism: what it values is the idea of a form that is natural to, and at one with, its subject matter. Its opposite is the imposed form of the Neo-Classical unities where time, space and action are all limited. Thus Schlegel:

■ most critics . . . interpret [form] merely in a mechanical, and not in an organical sense. Form is mechanical when, through external force, it is imparted to any material merely as an accidental addition without reference to its quality; as, for example, when we give a particular shape to a soft mass that it may retain the same after its induration. Organical form, again, is innate; it unfolds itself from within, and acquires its determination contemporaneously with the perfect development of the germ. We everywhere discover such forms in nature throughout the whole range of living powers, from the crystallisation of salts and minerals to plants and flowers, and from these again to the human body. In the fine arts, as well as in the domain of nature – the supreme artist, all genuine forms are organical, that is, determined by the quality of the work. In a word, the form is nothing but a significant exterior, the speaking physiognomy of each thing, which, as long as it is not disfigured by any destructive accident, gives a true evidence of its hidden essence.[8] □

The idea of organic form is entirely at odds with eighteenth-century thinking because it insists that form and content go together and cannot be regarded separately. Shakespeare's greatness, Schlegel argues,

■ does not consist merely in the bold neglect of the Unities of Place and Time, and in the commixture of comic and tragic elements: . . . [but] far deeper, in the inmost substance of the fictions, and in the essential relations, through which every deviation of form becomes a true requisite, which, together with its validity, has also its significance. □

(Schlegel, p. 342)

In other words, the unity of art is of a different order from that imagined by eighteenth-century theory; it is intrinsic, not imposed. It flows from within the form and content together, combining opposites to move us with its significance.

If Schlegel finds in Shakespeare a new model for organic art, he also offers other ideas that are important corollaries to this. There is, for example, his stress on the need for critics to feel and appreciate the art of different times, to be flexible, to see beyond the merely external. Romanticism, then, is not simply an attack on the previous age but replaces its theory with its own aesthetic of organic form, of unity, of feeling, and also with its own critical position and practice. It offers a body of ideas open to the variety of literary forms instead of a narrow appeal to types and genres. It sees the critic as someone able to sympathise with the text. But not just that. The idea of sympathy also includes a sense of powerful feelings; the shift all the time is towards an interiority, an identity that can suffer and identify with the protagonists and author.

Such ideas appear again and again in the period.[9] It is Schlegel, however, who is the leading voice, because he offers the most methodical attack on Neo-Classical precepts. It is Schlegel who notes that the foundation of Neo-Classicism rests on a misreading of Aristotle. It is Schlegel who ridicules the idea of a unity of time (that the action should take place in a time equal to that which it would in the real world). It is Schlegel who attacks the unity of place as literal-minded folly, denying the very nature of poetry's purpose 'to add all manner of wings to our mind' (p. 250), that is, to enrich and free our imaginations. And it is Schlegel who undermines the unity of action, showing how plot in tragedy involves a much wider set of ideas than mere singleness and completeness.

Schlegel's attack on the unities leaves them in tatters, replacing their threefold strictures with the notion of organic form. He also had a direct influence on English critics, in particular Coleridge. As Bate says, Schlegel's ideas became influential not least because Coleridge borrowed the 'organic/mechanic distinction to express his own conception of inward form' (p. 5) and his own conception of Shakespeare:

■ No work of true genius dare want its appropriate form; neither indeed is there any danger of this. As it must not, neither can it be lawless! For it is even this that constitutes it genius – the power of acting creatively under laws of its own origination. . . . In this statement I have had no reference to the vulgar abuse of Voltaire. . . . The true ground of the mistake, as has been well remarked by a continental critic, lies in the confounding mechanical regularity with organic form. The form is mechanic when on any given material we impress a pre-determined form, not necessarily arising out of the properties of the material, . . . The organic form, on the other hand, is innate; it shapes, as it develops itself from within, and the fullness of its development is one and the same with the perfection of its outward form. Such is the life, such the form. Nature, the prime genial artist, inexhaustible in diverse powers, is equally inexhaustible in forms.[10] □

What we ought to notice in Coleridge's statement is the association of organic form with Nature the great artist; Shakespeare is no longer a primitive force but a rich, mysterious and inexhaustible artist. Nature and art are thus as one, as are Nature and Shakespeare.

Bate claims that along with the notion of organic form Coleridge also took over Schlegel's use of Shakespeare for patriotic purposes, that his lectures were influenced by anti-French and anti-reform sentiment. All the time, informing Coleridge's views is, paradoxically, a conservative picture of Shakespeare – paradoxically because of the extent to which Romanticism identified itself with the rejection of rigid eighteenth-century rules in favour of the natural and the organic. The construction of Shakespeare as a conservative thinker had happened to some extent before Coleridge, but it is important to grasp how those aspects of criticism we associate with Romanticism – the examination of character, the stress on feeling – overlap with a way of reading that has a certain kind of politics attached to it.

The full story of this connection would take a great deal of space to elaborate, but it is worth pointing out that Coleridge was the inventor of the term 'psycho-analytical' as well as the term practical criticism (Bate, pp. 2, 5). As Bate notes, central to Coleridge's method is the idea of seeking the germ of the characters by looking closely at the text (Bate, pp. 5–6). It is when we start to pull these ideas together that we really begin to see the way in which Coleridge is so instrumental in forging modern criticism. Schlegel provides a formal programme replacing Neo-Classicism, but it is Coleridge who demonstrates how Romantic criticism works through the close analysis of language with insights into character. It is this method which the extracts from Coleridge below are primarily chosen to illustrate, showing Coleridge moving carefully through the play and commenting on its effect. In many ways this method is the basis of all modern critical approaches; they may vary in the premises they bring to the text, but their overall method of reading follows Coleridge's practice.

More radical than Coleridge, and often at odds with him, is Hazlitt. An admirer of Schlegel, Hazlitt's criticism is, however, much less theoretical than either Coleridge's or Schlegel's, but also more overtly political. This is evident in the second extract printed below where Hazlitt comments on the power struggle in *Richard II*. While Coleridge's comments focus on the feelings, thoughts and personalities of the characters, Hazlitt notes the class dimensions of the play and its feudal hierarchy. The first of the extracts by Hazlitt in the next section, however, is a review of Kean's performance in the role of Richard II, a performance which Hazlitt found unsatisfactory. What is not clear from Hazlitt's review, but needs pointing out, is that the *Richard II* Hazlitt saw was an adaptation by Richard Wroughton in 1815 which incorporated lines from *2 Henry IV*, *King Lear* and *Titus Andronicus*. The additions were apparently designed to increase the play's pathos and sentiment: Bolingbroke, for example, moved by the Queen's pleas, promises to visit Richard in prison and restore the kingdom to him.[11] The production seems bizarrely at odds with the drive of Romantic criticism outside the theatre to rescue Shakespeare from Tate and the eighteenth century, and it is small wonder that Hazlitt criticised Kean's performance.

There is, however, another point involved here. Both Coleridge and Hazlitt (as well as Charles Lamb) preferred to read Shakespeare as poetry rather than seeing the plays in the theatre. This is because they believed reading the plays gave a better insight into understanding the interior passions of the actions and characters. If this seems to underestimate the importance of the visual meanings of plays and the way in which performance communicates, it is consistent with the aim of Romantic criticism to search out the inner workings of Shakespeare's art through the exercise of sympathy and an imaginative response to the text.

III: Schlegel, Coleridge and Hazlitt on Shakespeare and *Richard II*

A: Schlegel

The preceding section has attempted to provide a context for the extracts that follow so that they can be seen as part of a larger critical project rather than just examples of individual critics writing about a particular play. The extracts are, I feel, relatively straightforward and easy to understand. I have, therefore, included only a few notes or comments about each. It is, however, worth bearing in mind as a general point that each critical statement made is a refutation of eighteenth-century criticism and critical thinking; that every sentence changes and challenges the old by forging a new aesthetic in which the history plays have a new kind of recognised role and importance.

The extracts begin with a passage from Schlegel's *Lectures on Dramatic Art and Literature*, lectures which defend Shakespeare against his detractors and seek to analyse the particular characteristics and genius of his art. The lectures total thirty in all and cover a vast amount of material. Schlegel's praise is for Shakespeare's protean art: that is, his ability to shape new worlds free from the fixity of rigid laws and to match his language to his subject. Like Coleridge, Schlegel speaks constantly of Shakespeare's genius, elevating him above his contemporaries and, by implication, above all other writers. But he also speaks of Shakespeare's correctness, so challenging Neo-Classical definitions of art: correctness is, for the Romantics, the way in which even the smallest detail is integral to the work.

In this extract, from lecture 26 on Shakespeare's history plays, Schlegel explains what he sees as the informing logic of the history play cycle: that the history plays 'form one great whole' and that, taken together, they deal with the politics of kingly rule and the dangers of usurpation. It is an account which is, in essence, repeated, with variations and additions, by later critics. Just as significant as this reading of the history plays as a group, however, is the value that Schlegel places on the history plays as a genre and on their imaginative impact:

From Augustus William Schlegel, *A Course of Lectures on Dramatic Art and Literature* (1808)

■ The dramas derived from the English history, ten in number, form one of the most valuable of Shakespeare's works, and partly the fruit of his maturest age. I say advisedly one of his works, for the poet evidently intended them to form one great whole. It is, as it were, an historical heroic poem in the dramatic form, of which the separate plays constitute the rhapsodies. The principal features of the events are exhibited with such fidelity; their causes, and even their secret springs are placed in such a clear light, that we may attain from them a knowledge of history in all its truth, while the living picture makes an impression on the imagination which can never be effaced. But this series of dramas is intended as the vehicle of a much higher and much more general instruction; it furnishes examples of the political course of the world, applicable to all times. This mirror of kings should be the manual of young princes; from it they may learn the intrinsic dignity of their hereditary vocation, but they will also learn from it the difficulties of their situation, the dangers of usurpation, the inevitable fall of tyranny, which buries itself under its attempts to obtain a firmer foundation; lastly, the ruinous consequences of the weaknesses, errors, and crimes of kings, for whole nations, and many subsequent generations. Eight of these plays, from *Richard the Second* to *Richard the Third*, are linked together in an uninterrupted succession, and embrace a most eventful period of nearly a century of English history. The events portrayed in them not only follow one another, but they are linked together in the closest and most exact connexion; and the cycle of revolts, parties, civil and foreign wars, which began with the deposition of Richard ll., first ends with the accession of Henry VII. to the throne. The careless rule of the first of these monarchs, and his injudicious treatment of his own relations, drew upon him the rebellion of Bolingbroke; his dethronement, however, was, in point of form, altogether unjust, and in no case could Bolingbroke be considered the rightful heir to the crown. This shrewd founder of the House of Lancaster never as Henry IV. enjoyed in peace the fruits of his usurpation: his turbulent Barons, the same who aided him in ascending the throne, allowed him not a moment's repose upon it. On the other hand, he was jealous of the brilliant qualities of his son, and this distrust, more than any really low inclination, induced the Prince, that he might avoid every appearance of ambition, to give himself up to dissolute society.... When this warlike Prince ascended the throne under the name of Henry V., he was determined to assert his ambiguous title; ... and this gave rise to the glorious but more ruinous than profitable war with France which Shakespeare has celebrated in the drama of *Henry the Fifth*. The early death of this king, the legal minority of Henry VI., and his perpetual minority in the art of government, brought the greatest troubles on England. . . . With the accession of Henry VII. to the throne, a new epoch of English history begins: the curse seemed at length to be expiated, and the long series of usurpations, revolts, and civil wars, occasioned by the levity with which the Second Richard sported away his crown, was now brought to a termination. □

(Schlegel, pp. 419–21)

Schlegel here places *Richard II* at the beginning of the larger cycle of history plays and outlines what he sees as the epic design behind the histories. His reading of the plays as a single unit concerned with kingship and the curse that fell on England after Richard's deposition anticipates much of the debate in the twentieth century, in particular, E. M. W. Tillyard's reading of the plays in the 1940s.[12] What is also worth noticing is Schlegel's praise of the history plays as 'one of the most valuable of Shakespeare's works', so giving them a new prominence and worth within the Shakespeare canon.

B: Coleridge

Selecting extracts from Coleridge poses particular problems because most of the material is in notebook form rather than in essays. It is a case of piecing together fragments, such as this report of one of Coleridge's lectures. His subject is the patriotic nature of the history plays, the importance of the opening scenes of *Richard II*, and Shakespeare's creation of Richard's character:

From Samuel Taylor Coleridge, 'The Lectures of 1813–14 at Bristol' on the 'Characteristics of Shakespeare' (1813)

■ One great object of his historic plays, and particularly of that to be examined (*Richard II*), was to make his countrymen more patriotic; to make Englishmen proud of being Englishmen. It was a play not much acted; this was not regretted by the Lecturer, for he never saw any of Shakespeare's plays performed, but with a degree of pain, disgust, and indignation. He had seen Mrs. Siddons as Lady, and Kemble as Macbeth:– these might be the Macbeths of the Kembles, but they were not the Macbeths of Shakespeare; he was therefore not grieved at the enormous size and monopoly of the theatres, which naturally produced many bad and but few good actors; and which drove Shakespeare from the stage, to find his proper place, in the heart and in the closet; where he sits with Milton, enthroned on a double-headed Parnassus; and with whom everything that was admirable, everything praiseworthy, was to be found.

Shakespeare shewed great judgment in his first scenes; they contained the germ of the ruling passion which was to be developed hereafter. Thus Richard's hardiness of mind, arising from kingly power; his weakness and debauchery from continual and unbounded flattery; and the haughty temper of the barons; one and the other alternately forming the moral of the play, are glanced at in the first scenes. An historic play requires more excitement than a tragic, thus Shakespeare never loses an opportunity of awakening a patriotic feeling. For this purpose Old Gaunt accuses Richard of having *'farmed out the island.'* What could be a greater rebuke to a King than to be told that

> This realm, this England,
> . . .
> Is now leased out . . .
> Like to a tenement, or pelting farm.

This speech of Gaunt is most beautiful; the propriety of putting so long a speech into the mouth of an old dying man might easily be shown. It thence partook of the nature of prophecy:–

> Methinks I am a prophet new inspired,
> And thus expiring, do foretell of him.

69

The plays of Shakespeare, as before observed of *Romeo and Juliet*, were characteristic throughout:– whereas that was all youth and spring, this was womanish weakness; the characters were of extreme old age, or partook of the nature of age and imbecility. The length of the speeches was adapted to a delivery between acting and recitation, which produced in the auditors a docility or frame of mind favorable to the poet, and useful to themselves:– how different from modern plays, where the glare of the scenes, with every wished-for object industriously realized, the mind becomes bewildered in surrounding attractions; whereas Shakespeare, in place of ranting, music, and outward action, addresses us in words that enchain the mind, and carry on the attention from scene to scene. . . .

The beautiful *keeping of the character of the play* is conspicuous in the Duke of York. He, like Gaunt, is old, and, full of a religious loyalty struggling with indignation at the king's vices and follies, is an evidence of a man giving up all energy under a feeling of despair. The play throughout is a history of the human mind, when reduced to ease its anguish with words instead of action, and the necessary feeling of weakness which such a state produces. The scene between the Queen, Bushy, and Bagot, is also worthy of notice, from the characters all talking high, but performing nothing; and from Shakespeare's tenderness to those presentiments, which, wise as we will be, will still adhere to our nature.

Shakespeare has contrived to bring the character of Richard, with all his prodigality and hard usage of his friends, still within the compass of our pity; for we find him much beloved by those who knew him best. The Queen is passionately attached to him, and his good Bishop (Carlisle) adheres to the last. He is not one of those whose punishment gives delight; his failings appear to arise from outward objects, and from the poison of flatterers around him; we cannot, therefore, help pitying, and wishing he had been placed in a rank where he would have been less exposed, and where he might have been happy and useful. . . .

The overflowing of Richard's feelings, and which tends to keep him in our esteem, is the scene where he lands –

Dear earth, I do salute thee with my hand,
Tho' rebels wound thee with their horses' hoofs;

so beautifully descriptive of the sensations of a man and a king attached to his country as his inheritance and his birthright. His resolution and determination of action are depicted in glowing words, thus –

So when this thief, this traitor Bolingbroke,
Shall see us rising in our throne,
. . .
For every man that Bolingbroke hath press'd,
God for his Richard hath in heavenly pay
A glorious angel.

Who, after this, would not have supposed great energy of action?
No! all was spent, and upon the first ill-tidings, nothing but despon-
dency takes place, with alternatives of unmanly despair and
unfounded hopes: great activity of mind without any strength of moral
feeling to rouse to action, presenting an awful lesson in the education
of princes. . . .
. . . Richard's parade of resignation is consistent with the other
parts of the play –

. . . Of comfort no man speak;
Let's talk of graves, of worms, of epitaphs. . . .

easing his heart, and consuming all that is manly in words; never anywhere seeking comfort in despair, but mistaking the moment of
exhaustion for quiet. This is finely contrasted in Bolingbroke's
struggle of haughty feeling with temporary dissimulation, in which
the latter says –

Harry Bolingbroke,
On both his knees doth kiss King Richard's hand, . . .

but, with the prudence of his character, after this hypocritical speech,
adds –

March on, – and mark King Richard how he looks. □
(Raysor, II, 278–84)

In contrast to Schlegel, Coleridge turns to the text for his analysis, picking
out characters and speeches in order to demonstrate their effect. In
particular, Coleridge focuses on Richard's alternating moods and contrasts them with Bolingbroke's political acumen.

The second extract from Coleridge complements the first in that it
again presents an analysis of Richard's character, but also of Bolingbroke
and York. We can see in this kind of account of the play how character is
gradually being installed as the centre of interest during the Romantic
period. What we also have in the extract is Coleridge's view of Richard as
unfit for kingship because he is 'womanish' and 'weak'. That view,

however, is only part of Coleridge's analysis, which follows Richard's changes of mood and responses in a complex way.

From 'The Lectures of 1811–12'

■ Having said thus much on the, often falsely supposed, blemishes of our poet – blemishes which are said to prevail in 'Richard II' especially,[13] – I will now advert to the character of the King. He is represented as a man not deficient in immediate courage, which displays itself at his assassination; or in powers of mind, as appears by the foresight he exhibits throughout the play: still, he is weak, variable, and womanish, and possesses feelings, which, amiable in a female, are misplaced in a man, and altogether unfit for a king. In prosperity he is insolent and presumptuous, and in adversity, if we are to believe Dr. Johnson, he is humane and pious. I cannot admit the latter epithet, because I perceive the utmost consistency of character in Richard: what he was at first, he is at last, excepting as far as he yields to circumstances: what he shewed himself at the commencement of the play, he shews himself at the end of it. Dr. Johnson assigns to him rather the virtue of a confessor than that of a king.

True it is, that he may be said to be overwhelmed by the earliest misfortune that befalls him; but, so far from his feelings or disposition being changed or subdued, the very first glimpse of the returning sunshine of hope reanimates his spirits, and exalts him to as strange and unbecoming a degree of elevation, as he was before sunk in mental depression: the mention of those in his misfortunes, who had contributed to his downfall, but who had before been his nearest friends and favourites, calls forth from him expressions of the bitterest hatred and revenge. Thus, where Richard asks:

> Where is the Earl of Wiltshire? Where is Bagot?
> What is become of Bushy? Where is Green?
> That they have let the dangerous enemy
> Measure our confines with such peaceful steps?
> If we prevail, their heads shall pay for it.
> I warrant they have made peace with Bolingbroke.
>
> Act III., Scene 2.

Scroop answers:

> Peace have they made with him, indeed, my lord.

Upon which Richard, without hearing more, breaks out:

O villains! vipers, damn'd without redemption!
Dogs, easily won to fawn on any man!
Snakes, in my heart-blood warm'd, that sting my heart!
Three Judases, each one thrice worse than Judas!
Would they make peace? terrible hell make war
Upon their spotted souls for this offence!

Scroop observes upon this change, and tells the King how they had made their peace:

Sweet love, I see, changing his property
Turns to the sourest and most deadly hate.
Again uncurse their souls: their peace is made
With heads and not with hands: those whom you curse
Have felt the worst of death's destroying wound,
And lie full low, grav'd in the hollow ground.

Richard receiving at first an equivocal answer, – 'Peace have they made with him, indeed, my lord,' – takes it in the worst sense: his prompt-ness to suspect those who had been his friends turns his love to hate, and calls forth the most tremendous execrations.

From the beginning to the end of the play he pours out all the peculiarities and powers of his mind: he catches at new hope, and seeks new friends, is disappointed, despairs, and at length makes a merit of his resignation. He scatters himself into a multitude of images, and in conclusion endeavours to shelter himself from that which is around him by a cloud of his own thoughts. Throughout his whole career may be noticed the most rapid transitions – from the highest insolence to the lowest humility – from hope to despair, from the extravagance of love to the agonies of resentment, and from pretended resignation to the bitterest reproaches. The whole is joined with the utmost richness and copiousness of thought, and were there an actor capable of representing Richard, the part would delight us more than any other of Shakespeare's master-pieces,– with, perhaps, the single exception of King Lear. I know of no character drawn by our great poet with such unequalled skill as that of Richard II.

Next we come to Henry Bolingbroke, the rival of Richard II. He appears as a man of dauntless courage, and of ambition equal to that of Richard III; . . . [I]n Bolingbroke we find a man who in the outset has been sorely injured: then, we see him encouraged by the grievances of his country, and by the strange mismanagement of the government, yet at the same time scarcely daring to look at his own views, or to acknowledge them as designs. He comes home under the pretence of claiming his dukedom, and he professes that to be his object almost to the last: but, at the last, he avows his purpose to its full extent, of which he was himself unconscious in the earlier stages.

This is proved by so many passages, that I will only select one of them; . . . It is where Bolingbroke approaches the castle in which the unfortunate King has taken shelter: York is in Bolingbroke's company – the same York who is still contented with speaking the truth, but doing nothing for the sake of the truth,– drawing back after he has spoken, and becoming merely passive when he ought to display activity. Northumberland says:

> The news is very fair and good, my lord:
> Richard not far from hence hath hid his head.   [III.ii]

York rebukes him thus:

> It would beseem the Lord Northumberland
> To say King Richard:– Alack, the heavy day,
> When such a sacred king should hide his head!

Northumberland replies:

> Your grace mistakes me: only to be brief
> Left I his title out.

To which York rejoins:

> The time hath been,
> Would you have been so brief with him, he would
> Have been so brief with you, to shorten you,
> For taking so the head, your whole head's length.

Bolingbroke observes,

> Mistake not, uncle, farther than you should;

And York answers, with a play upon the words 'take' and 'mistake':

> Take not, good cousin, farther than you should,
> Lest you mistake. The heavens are o'er our heads.

Here, give me leave to remark in passing, that the play upon words is perfectly natural, and quite in character: . . .

At this point Bolingbroke seems to have been checked by the eye of York, and thus proceeds in consequence:

> The which, how far off from the mind of Bolingbroke
> It is, such crimson tempest should bedrench
> The fresh green lap of fair King Richard's land,
> My stooping duty tenderly shall show.

He passes suddenly from insolence to humility, owing to the silent reproof he received from his uncle. This change of tone would not have taken place, had Bolingbroke been allowed to proceed according to the natural bent of his mind, and the flow of the subject. Let me direct attention to the subsequent lines, for the same reason; they are part of the same speech:

> Let's march without the noise of threat'ning drum,
> That from the castle's tatter'd battlements
> Our fair appointments may be well perused.
> Methinks, King Richard and myself should meet
> With no less terror than the elements
> Of fire and water, when their thundering shock
> At meeting tears the cloudy cheeks of heaven.

Having proceeded thus far with the exaggeration of his own importance, York again checks him, and Bolingbroke adds, in a very different strain,

> He be the fire, I'll be the yielding water:
> The rage be his, while on the earth I rain
> My waters; on the earth, and not on him.

I have thus adverted to the three great personages in this drama, Richard, Bolingbroke, and York; and of the whole play it may be asserted, that with the exception of some of the last scenes (though they have exquisite beauty) Shakespeare seems to have risen to the summit of excellence in the delineation and preservation of character. □

(Raysor, II, 186–92)

Coleridge is particularly interested in Richard's inner emotional life, but he is also concerned to convey his sense of the richness of Shakespeare's art. This in part explains the frequent use of quotations: Coleridge sets out the movement of the scenes from speaker to speaker and the intensity of the exchanges. The frequent quotations, however, together with the obvious attention to details of the language, such as the use of puns, also serve to remind us that Coleridge was the inventor of practical criticism.

C: Hazlitt

In some ways Hazlitt offers a different kind of perspective on *Richard II* from Coleridge and Schlegel. In the extract below (from a review) he discusses the play after having watched Kean in the leading role. Coleridge, in the first lecture cited above, said that he had only seen Shakespeare's plays performed with 'a degree of pain, disgust, and indignation', and suggested that the proper place for Shakespeare was the study. Hazlitt seems to agree, but what is also evident is that Hazlitt has an idea, which ties in with both the characters and politics of the text, about how *Richard II* ought to be played.

Hazlitt begins his review of Edmund Kean's performance by arguing that the fine details of the text noticed by the reader are lost in staging and that acting mars the play. It is essentially the same argument that Coleridge put forward, and which Charles Lamb was to echo.[14] But then Hazlitt goes on to suggest how he would wish to see Richard acted:

From William Hazlitt, 'The Examiner' (1815)

■ All that we have said of acting in general applies to his Richard II. It has been supposed that this is his finest part: this is, however, a total misrepresentation. There are only one or two electrical shocks given in it; and in many of his characters he gives a much greater number. – The excellence of his acting is in proportion to the number of hits, for he has not equal truth or purity of style. Richard II was hardly given correctly as to the general outline. Mr Kean made it a character of *passion*, that is, of feeling combined with energy; whereas it is a character of *pathos*, that is to say, of feeling combined with weakness. This, we conceive, is the general fault of Mr Kean's acting, that it is always energetic or nothing. He is always on full stretch – never relaxed. He expresses all the violence, the extravagance, and fierceness of the passions, but not their misgivings, their helplessness, and sinkings into despair. He has too much of that strong nerve and fibre that is always equally elastic. We might instance to the present purpose, his dashing the glass down with all his might, in the scene with Hereford, instead of letting it fall out of his hands, as from an infant's; also, his manner of expostulating with Bolingbroke, 'Why on thy knee, thus low, &c.' which was altogether fierce and heroic, instead of being sad, thoughtful, and melancholy. If Mr Kean would look into some passages in this play, into that in particular, 'Oh that I were a mockery king of snow, to melt away before the sun of Bolingbroke', he would find a clue to this character, and to human nature in general, which he seems to have missed – how far feeling is connected with the sense of weakness as well as of strength, or the power of imbecility, and the force of passiveness.[15] □

Nicholas Brooke comments on this passage that, while Coleridge seems to have sympathised with Richard's 'feminine friendism', Hazlitt is more moralistic. At the same time Brooke notes that Hazlitt's view of Richard's character has become so dominant that 'it requires a strong effort of imagination to recognise the possibility of Kean's interpretation' of Richard as a man of passion rather than pathos.[16]

Hazlitt's view of Richard is developed in a more complex way in this second extract:

From William Hazlitt, *Characters of Shakespeare's Plays* (1817)

■ *Richard II* is a play little known compared with *Richard III* which last is a play that every unfledged candidate for theatrical fame chuses to strut and fret his hour upon the stage in; yet we confess that we prefer the nature and feeling of the one to the noise and bustle of the other; at least, as we are so often forced to see it acted. In *Richard II* the weakness of the king leaves us leisure to take a greater interest in the misfortunes of the man. After the first act, in which the arbitrariness of his behaviour only proves his want of resolution, we see him staggering under the unlooked-for blows of fortune, bewailing his loss of kingly power, not preventing it, sinking under the aspiring genius of Bolingbroke, his authority trampled on, his hopes failing him, and his pride crushed and broken down under insults and injuries, which his own misconduct had provoked, but which he has not courage or manliness to resent. The change of tone and behaviour in the two competitors for the throne according to their change of fortune, from the capricious sentence of banishment passed by Richard upon Bolingbroke, the suppliant offers and modest pretensions of the latter on his return to the high and haughty tone with which he accepts Richard's resignation of the crown after the loss of all his power, the use which he makes of the deposed king to grace his triumphal progress through the streets of London, and the final intimation of his wish for his death, which immediately finds a servile executioner, is marked throughout with complete effect and without the slightest appearance of effort. The steps by which Bolingbroke mounts the throne are those by which Richard sinks into the grave. We feel neither respect nor love for the deposed monarch; for he is as wanting in energy as in principle: but we pity him, for he pities himself. His heart is by no means hardened against himself, but bleeds afresh at every new stroke of mischance, and his sensibility, absorbed in his own person, and unused to misfortune, is not only tenderly alive to its own sufferings, but without the fortitude to bear them. He is, however, human in his distresses; for to feel pain, and sorrow, weakness, disappointment, remorse and anguish, is the lot of humanity, and we sympathize with him accordingly. The sufferings of the man make us forget that he ever was a king.

The right assumed by sovereign power to trifle at its will with the happiness of others as a matter of course, or to remit its exercise as a matter of favour, is strikingly shewn in the sentence of banishment so unjustly pronounced on Bolingbroke and Mowbray, and in what Bolingbroke says when four years of his banishment are taken off, with as little reason.

> How long a time lies in one little word!
> Four lagging winters and four wanton springs
> End in a word : such is the breath of kings.

A more affecting image of the loneliness of a state of exile can hardly be given than by what Bolingbroke afterwards observes of his having 'sighed his English breath in foreign clouds'; or than that conveyed in Mowbray's complaint at being banished for life.

> The language I have learned these forty years,
> My native English, now I must forego;
> And now my tongue's use is to me no more
> Than an unstringed viol or a harp, . . .

How very beautiful is all this, and at the same time how very *English* too!

Richard II may be considered as the first of that series of English historical plays, in which 'is hung armour of the invincible knights of old', in which their hearts seem to strike against their coats of mail, where their blood tingles for the fight, and words are but the harbingers of blows. Of this state of accomplished barbarism the appeal of Bolingbroke and Mowbray is an admirable specimen. Another of these 'keen encounters of their wits', which serve to whet the talkers' swords, is where Aumerle answers in the presence of Bolingbroke to the charge which Bagot brings against him of being an accessory in Gloster's death. . . .

The truth is, that there is neither truth nor honour in all these noble persons: they answer words with words, as they do blows with blows, in mere self defence: nor have they any principle whatever but that of courage in maintaining any wrong they dare commit, or any falsehood which they find it useful to assert. How different were these noble knights and 'barons bold' from their more refined descendants in the present day, who, instead of deciding questions of right by brute force, refer everything to convenience, fashion, and good breeding! In point of any abstract love of truth or justice, they are just the same now that they were then.

The characters of old John of Gaunt and of his brother York, uncles to the King, the one stern and foreboding, the other honest, good-natured, doing all for the best, and therefore doing nothing, are well kept up. The speech of the former, in praise of England, is one of the most eloquent that ever was penned. We should perhaps hardly be disposed to feed the pampered egotism of all countrymen by quoting this description, were it not that the conclusion of it (which looks prophetic) may qualify any improper degree of exultation:

> This royal throne of kings, this sceptred isle,
> This earth of majesty, this seat of Mars,
> This other Eden – demi-paradise . . .
> Hath made a shameful conquest of itself.

The character of Bolingbroke, afterwards Henry IV is drawn with a masterly hand:– patient for occasion, and the steadily availing himself of it, seeing his advantage afar off, but only seizing on it when he has it within his reach, humble, crafty, bold, and aspiring, encroaching by regular but slow degrees, building power on opinion, and cementing opinion by power. His disposition is first unfolded by Richard himself, who however is too self-willed and secure to make a proper use of his knowledge.

> Ourself and Bushy, Bagot here and Green,
> Observed his courtship of the common people
> How he did seem to dive into their hearts,
> With humble and familiar courtesy,
> What reverence he did throw away on slaves;
> Wooing poor craftsmen with the craft of smiles, . . .
> As were our England in reversion his,
> And he our subjects' next degree in hope.

Afterwards, he gives his own character to Percy, in these words:

> I thank thee, gentle Percy, and be sure
> I count myself in nothing else so happy,
> As in a soul rememb'ring my good friends;
> And as my fortune ripens with thy love,
> It shall be still thy true love's recompense.

We know how he afterwards kept his promise. His bold assertion of his own rights, his pretended submission to the king, and the ascendancy which he tacitly assumes over him without openly claiming it, as soon as he has him in his power, are characteristic traits of this ambitious and politic usurper. But the part of Richard himself gives the chief interest to the play. His folly, his vices, his misfortunes, his reluctance to part with the crown, his fear to keep it, his weak and womanish regrets, his starting tears, his fits of hectic passion, his smothered majesty, pass in succession before us, and make a picture as natural as it is affecting. Among the most striking touches of pathos are his wish 'O that I were a mockery king of snow to melt away before the sun of Bolingbroke', and the incident of the poor groom who comes to visit him in prison, and tells him how 'it yearned his heart that Bolingbroke upon his coronation-day rode on roan Barbary'. We shall have occasion to return hereafter to the character of Richard II in speaking of Henry VI. There is only one passage more, the description of his entrance into London with Bolingbroke, which we should like to quote here, if it had not been so used and worn out, so thumbed and got by rote, so praised and painted, but its beauty surmounts all these considerations. . . .[17] □

Hazlitt's criticism is informed by a sharp sense of political value, his analysis anticipating something of the methods of twentieth-century critics in seeing how the history plays work to fashion an English identity. At the same time, he echoes Coleridge's view of Richard as weak while stressing both the pathos of the play and the sympathy it evokes.

Between them Coleridge, Schlegel and Hazlitt set down the main lines for the discussion of *Richard II*: the play's genre, its position in relation to other history plays, the overarching design of the plays, the characters of Richard and Bolingbroke, but above all the play's language and the richness of meaning and feelings surrounding Richard's personal tragedy. In addition, they draw attention to most of the central features of the play, including Richard's great speeches, the garden scene (III.iv), the function of York, Gaunt and the groom, as well as to Bolingbroke's political astuteness and the inevitability of Richard's deposition. Certainly much of what Coleridge wrote, in particular his view of Richard as unfit to be king, was to have a considerable effect on later nineteenth-century criticism, as the next chapter suggests. Essentially, Coleridge constructs a view that focuses upon the individual, the possibilities and potentials, but also the limitations, of the human subject. But, if we stress only this, we do so at the expense of the complex web of ideas that constitute the Romantics' re-reading of Shakespeare.

CHAPTER FOUR

Nineteenth-Century Criticism

Introduction

THIS CHAPTER begins by focusing briefly on the staging of *Richard II* in the 1857 production by Charles Kean. It then looks, again briefly, at Edward Dowden's objections to Shakespeare's play. Dowden's comments were refuted by Walter Pater in a famous essay which has been largely responsible for the creation of the impressions of Richard as poet-king. Pater's essay found support in Frank Benson's performance in 1896, itself the subject of a famous review in 1899 by C. E. Montague. The poet W.B. Yeats also commented on Benson's performance. Like Pater, Yeats sees the play largely in aesthetic terms, and in some ways this might be said to sum up what is happening in late Victorian criticism. Whereas the Romantics had constructed an image of the play in terms of national identity and the poet Shakespeare, the end of the nineteenth century emphasises the poetic quality of the play and its central figure.

While such views might seem less complex than those of Schlegel and Coleridge, they are, none the less, important. A great deal of early twentieth-century criticism took for granted or repeated Pater's image of Richard as a figure of the artist poet, as a man in love with his own words. But what Pater's essay also did was confirm the direction of criticism towards a focus on character and language, something echoed in A. C. Bradley's book *Shakespearean Tragedy*.[1] The end of the nineteenth century, however, also sees the beginnings of English as a university subject, with Shakespeare as a focus of scholarly interest. This is to some extent reflected in Dowden's criticism, but is represented in this chapter by an extract from E. K. Chambers' introduction to his edition of the play.

I: Charles Kean and Edward Dowden

We begin, however, with details of the 1857 production by Charles Kean, son of Edmund Kean whose 1815 performance Hazlitt criticised. The details of both the 1815 and 1857 stagings of *Richard II* are given in Margaret Shewring's excellent book on *Richard II*. The book is not, as the Preface makes plain, theatre history but performance criticism; that is, it is concerned with the cultural significance of productions and the contexts 'which condition audience reception of the play'.[2] What emerges from Shewring's account is how production and performance intersect with and challenge criticism and critical thinking.

The main point about Charles Kean's production was its spectacular nature. A. C. Sprague describes it this way:

■ Kean's spectacular treatment of the interrupted trial by combat, complete even to horses (dummies) for the two contestants, was only eclipsed by his interpolated entry of Bolingbroke into London, a pantomimic episode employing from five hundred to six hundred persons and introducing 'a peal of churchbells', the first, it was thought, 'ever heard within a playhouse walls'.[3] □

Shewring adds to this picture, discussing the 'striking . . . range and detail of the settings', including the Privy Council Chamber at Westminster, the dungeon at Pomfret and the St George's Hall at Windsor (p. 50). There were also painted landscapes and the use of music and costume to create an authentic setting. 'All this', Shewring notes, quoting Kean's biographer J. W. Cole, '"completed a picture which brought back the past to the eyes of the present, and bewildered the spectators with a mingled sensation of astonishment and admiration"' (pp. 52–3). Room for the large amount of spectacle was made by cutting some thirteen hundred lines from the play. Such cuts were also needed in order to focus attention on the significance of the spectacle, which was intended to convey the Victorian idea 'of the medieval world' (p. 54). In other words, Kean was seeking to reconstruct a past for the play through spectacle.

Kean's production of *Richard II* might seem of little critical interest, but Shewring notes that the reason why the production was successful was that it distanced the politics of the play 'into an educational-historical pageant' (p. 57). Far from challenging the audience, it served to reinforce Victorian ideas, while its staging served only to underline the sense of something belonging to the world of romance. The pictorial staging dissipated the play's radical edge and also its resonance. In a way we might compare this both with the early censoring of the text and the various adaptations; what happens in all these instances is that the play's subversive potential is neutralised. As Ralph Berry has pointed out, *Richard II* was once 'the most dangerous, the most politically vibrant play in the canon'.[4] Its subsequent history suggests that other periods have recognised that vibrancy and sought to defuse it.

Not that the play's radical potential was attractive to Edward Dowden, a noted Victorian Shakespearean scholar who had considerable influence on the teaching of Shakespeare in the early twentieth century. Dowden expresses the other side of the Victorian relationship with the work. While Kean staged it in colour and pictures, and so eclipsed its politics, Dowden castigated Richard's lack of moral fibre. It is worth quoting some of his remarks if only because they sometimes reappear in essays by students who criticise Richard's weakness without recognising the bias of such a position:

From Edward Dowden, *Shakespeare – His Mind and Art* (1875)

■ . . . There is a condition of the intellect which we describe by the word 'boyishness'. The mind in the boyish stage of growth 'has no discriminating convictions, and no grasp of consequences'. It has not as yet got hold of realities; it is 'merely dazzled by phenomena instead of perceiving things as they are'. The talk of a person who remains in this sense boyish is often clever, but it is unreal; now he will say brilliant things upon this side of a question, and now upon the opposite side. He has no consistency of view. He is wanting as yet in seriousness of intellect; in the adult mind. Now if we extend this characteristic of boyishness, from the intellect to the entire character, we may understand much of what Shakspere meant to represent in the person of Richard II. Not alone his intellect, but his feelings, live in the world of phenomena, and altogether fail to lay hold of things as they are; they have no consistency and no continuity. His will is entirely unformed; it possesses no authority and no executive power; he is at the mercy of every chance impulse and transitory mood. He has a kind of artistic relation to life, without being an artist. An artist in life seizes upon the stuff of circumstance, and with strenuous will, and strong creative power, shapes some new and noble form of human existence.

Richard, to whom all things are unreal, has a fine feeling for 'situations'. Without true kingly strength or dignity, he has a fine feeling for the royal situation. Without any making real to himself what God or what death is, he can put himself, if need be, in the appropriate attitude towards God and towards death. Instead of comprehending things as they are, and achieving heroic deeds, he satiates his heart with the grace, the tenderness, the beauty, or the pathos of situations. Life is to Richard a show, a succession of images; and to put himself into accord with the aesthetic requirements of his position is Richard's first necessity. He is equal to playing any part gracefully which he is called upon by circumstances to enact. But when he has exhausted the aesthetic satisfaction to be derived from the situations of his life, he is left with nothing further to do. He is an amateur in living; not an artist. . . .

. . . There is in Richard, as Coleridge has finely observed, 'a constant overflow of emotions from a total incapability of controlling them, and thence a waste of that energy, which should have been reserved for actions, in the passion and effort of mere resolves and menaces. The consequence is moral exhaustion and rapid alternations of unmanly despair and ungrounded hope, every feeling being abandoned for its direct opposite upon the pressure of external accident.' A certain unreality infects every motion of Richard; his feelings are but the shadows of true feeling. Now he will be great and a king; now what matters it to lose a kingdom? . . .

Yet Shakspere has thrown over the figure of Richard a certain atmosphere of charm. If only the world were not a real world, to which serious hearts are due, we could find in Richard some wavering, vague attraction. There is a certain wistfulness about him; without any genuine kingly power, he has a feeling for what kingly power must be; without any veritable religion, he has a pale shadow of religiosity. And few of us have ourselves wholly escaped from unreality. . . . Into what glimmering limbo will such a soul as that of Richard pass when the breath leaves the body? The pains of hell and the joys of heaven belong to those who have serious hearts. Richard has been a graceful phantom. Is there some tenuous, unsubstantial world of spirits reserved for the sentimentalist, the dreamer, and the dilettante? Richard is, as it were, fading out of existence. Bolingbroke seems not only to have robbed him of his authority, but to have encroached upon his very personality, and to have usurped his understanding and his will.[5] □

Dowden, in a sense, takes his ideas from the public school system; what he was really interested in was the British Empire and firm government. Here, he treats Richard not as a dramatic figure but as if he were a real person. Given the dominance of the novel in the Victorian era this is perhaps less than surprising, although it does not totally account for the strenuousness of his attack. Dowden writes in a powerful way, and it is not difficult to spot the underlying propositions about the need for manly behaviour that run through the argument. What activates the attack is presumably the fear that accompanies homophobia. Whereas Kean could distance Richard's 'overflow of emotions' into a mythic landscape, or even cut them altogether, Dowden has to confront their implications for Victorian ideas of both manliness and discipline. He does this by castigating Richard as morally bankrupt, and belittling him as 'boyish'. What perhaps is of most interest about Dowden's criticism is the title of his book – *Shakespeare: A Critical Study of His Mind and Art*. Two key terms from Romantic criticism become, in Dowden's hands, vehicles for moralising about character.

II: Walter Pater

Pater is chiefly known for his volume *Studies in the Renaissance* (1873) and for his links with the Pre-Raphaelities – a group of mid-Victorian artists, including Dante Gabriel Rossetti, who wanted to return art to the forms they supposed had existed before the fifteenth-century Italian artist Raphael. They were opposed to the mechanical and technical ethos of Victorian culture, seeing art as necessary to redeem people from the squalor of urban society; above all, they valued beauty and the aesthetic. Taken together these points represent a challenging set of ideas and ideals which have significant political implications.

The extract from Pater below contrasts vividly with Dowden's unsympathetic, bullying analysis. Pater, perhaps following Coleridge, is able to convey much of the play's structure as well as its tone. He also is able to draw out some of the political implications of the ideas about kingship that later criticism was to take up. Indeed, many argue that much of the twentieth-century debate about the play grows out of Pater's essay, which is why it has been given so much room here. The essay is chiefly known, however, for its analysis of Richard as poet-king, as dreamer and artist.

From Walter Pater, *Appreciations* (1889)

■ One gracious prerogative, certainly, Shakespeare's English kings possess: they are a very eloquent company, and Richard is the most sweet-tongued of them all. In no other play perhaps is there such a flush of those gay, fresh, variegated flowers of speech – colour and figure, not lightly attached to, but fused into the very phrase itself – which Shakespeare cannot help dispensing to his characters, as in this 'play of the Deposing of King Richard the Second', an exquisite poet if he is nothing else, from first to last, in light and gloom alike, able to see all things poetically, to give a poetic turn to his conduct of them, and refreshing with his golden language the tritest aspects of that ironic contrast between the pretensions of a king and the actual necessities of his destiny. What a garden of words! With him, blank verse, infinitely graceful, deliberate, musical in inflection, becomes indeed a true 'verse royal', that rhyming lapse, which to the Shakespearean ear, at least in youth, came as the last touch of refinement on it, being here doubly appropriate. His eloquence blends with that fatal beauty, of which he was so frankly aware, so amiable to his friends, to his wife, of the effects of which on the people his enemies were so much afraid, on which Shakespeare himself dwells so attentively as the 'royal blood' comes and goes in the face with his rapid changes of temper. As happens with sensitive natures, it attunes him to a congruous suavity of manners, by which anger itself became flattering; it blends with his merely youthful hopefulness and high spirits, his sympathetic love for gay people, things, apparel – 'his cote of gold and stone, valued at thirty thousand marks', the novel Italian fashions he preferred, as also with those real amiabilities that made people forget the darker touches of his character, but never tire of the pathetic rehearsal of his fall, the meekness of which would have seemed merely abject in a less graceful performer.

Yet it is only fair to say that in the painstaking 'revival' of *King Richard the Second* by the late Charles Kean, those who were very young thirty years ago were afforded much more than Shakespeare's play could ever have been before – the very person of the king based on the stately old portrait in Westminster, 'the earliest extant contemporary likeness of any English sovereign', the grace, the winning pathos, the sympathetic voice of the player, the tasteful archaeology confronting vulgar modern London with a scenic reproduction, for once really agreeable, of the London of Chaucer. In the hands of Kean the play became like an exquisite performance on the violin.

The long agony of one so gaily painted by nature's self, from his 'tragic abdication' till the hour in which he

Sluiced out his innocent soul thro' streams of blood,

was for playwrights a subject ready to hand, and became early the theme of a popular drama, of which some have fancied surviving favourite fragments in the rhymed parts of Shakespeare's work:

The king Richard of Yngland
Was in his flowris then regnand
But his flowris efter sone
Fadyt, and ware all undone:

says the old chronicle. Strangely enough, Shakespeare supposes him an overconfident believer in that divine right of kings, of which people in Shakespeare's time were coming to hear so much; a general right, sealed to him (so Richard is made to think) as an ineradicable gift by the touch – stream rather, over head and breast and shoulders – of the 'holy oil' of his consecration at Westminster; not, however, through some oversight the genuine balm used at the coronation of his successor, given according to legend, by the Blessed Virgin to Saint Thomas of Canterbury. Richard himself found that, it was said, among other forgotten treasures, at the crisis of his changing fortunes and vainly sought reconsecration therewith – understood, wistfully, that it was reserved for his happier rival. And yet his coronation, by the pageantry, the amplitude, the learned care of its order, so lengthy that the king, then only eleven years of age, and fasting, as a communicant at the ceremony, was carried away in a faint, fixed the type under which it has ever since continued. And nowhere is there so emphatic a reiteration as in *Richard the Second* of the sentiment which those singular rites were calculated to produce.

> Not all the water in the rough rude sea
> Can wash the balm from an anointed king,

as supplementing another, almost supernatural, right. 'Edward's seven sons', of whom Richard's father was one,

> Were as seven phials of his sacred blood.

But this, too, in the hands of Shakespeare, becomes for him, like any other of those fantastic, ineffectual, easily discredited, personal graces, as capricious in its operation on men's wills as merely physical beauty, kindling himself to eloquence indeed, but only giving double pathos to insults which 'barbarism itself' might have pitied – the dust in his face, as he returns, through the streets of London, a prisoner in the train of his victorious enemy.

> How soon my sorrow hath destroyed my face!

he cries, in that most poetic invention of the mirror scene which does but reinforce again that physical charm which all confessed. The sense of 'divine right' in kings is found to act not so much as a secret of power over others, as of infatuation to themselves. And of all those personal gifts the one which alone never altogether fails him is just that royal utterance, his appreciation of the poetry of his own hapless lot, an eloquent self-pity, infecting others in spite of themselves, till they too become irresistibly eloquent about him.

In the Roman Pontifical, of which the order of Coronation is really a part, there is no form for the inverse process, no rite of 'degradation', such as that by which an offending priest or bishop may be deprived, if not of the essential quality of 'orders', yet, one by one, of its outward dignities. It is as if Shakespeare had in mind some such inverted rite, like those old ecclesiastical or military ones, by which human hardness, or human justice, adds the last touch of unkindness to the execution of its sentences, in the scene where Richard 'deposes' himself, as in some long, agonizing ceremony, reflectively drawn out, with an extraordinary refinement of intelligence and variety of piteous appeal, but also with a felicity of poetic invention, which puts these pages into a very select class, with the finest 'vermeil and ivory' work of Chatterton or Keats. . . .

No! Shakespeare's kings are not, nor are meant to be, great men: rather, little or quite ordinary humanity, thrust upon greatness, with those pathetic results, the natural self-pity of the weak heightened in them into irresistible appeal to others as the net result of their royal prerogative. One after another, they seem to lie composed in Shakespeare's embalming pages, with just that touch of nature about them, making the whole world akin, which has infused into their tombs at Westminster a rare poetic grace. It is that irony of kingship, the sense that it is in its happiness child's play, in its sorrows, after all, but children's grief, which gives its finer accent to all the changeful feeling of these wonderful speeches: the great meekness of the graceful, wild creature, tamed at last:

Give Richard leave to live till Richard die!

his somewhat abject fear of death, turning to acquiescence at moments of extreme weariness:

My large kingdom for a little grave!
A little little grave, an obscure grave!

his religious appeal in the last reserve, with its bold reference to the judgment of Pilate, as he thinks once more of his 'anointing'.

And as it happens with children he attains contentment finally in the merely passive recognition of superior strength, in the naturalness of the result of the great battle as a matter of course, and experiences something of the royal prerogative of poetry to obscure, or at least to attune and soften men's griefs. As in some sweet anthem of Handel, the sufferer, who put finger to the organ under the utmost pressure of mental conflict, extracts a kind of peace at last from the mere skill with which he sets his distress to music.

Beshrew thee, Cousin, that didst lead me forth
Of that sweet way I was in to despair!

'With Cain go wander through the shades of night!'– cries the new king to the gaoler Exton, dissimulating his share in the murder he is thought to have suggested; and in truth there is something of the mur-dered Abel about Shakespeare's Richard. The fact seems to be that he died of 'waste and a broken heart': it was by way of proof that his end had been a natural one that, stifling a real fear of the face, the face of Richard, on men's minds, with the added pleading now of all dead faces, Henry exposed the corpse to general view; and Shakespeare, in bringing it on the stage, in the last scene of his play, does but follow out the motive with which he has emphasized Richard's physical beauty all through it – that 'most beauteous inn', as the Queen says quaintly, meeting him on the way to death-residence, then soon to be deserted, of that wayward, frenzied, but withal so affectionate soul. Though the body did not go to Westminster immediately, his tomb,

> That small model of the barren earth
> Which serves as paste and cover to our bones

the effigy clasping the hand of his youthful consort, was already prepared there, with 'rich gilding and ornaments', monument of poetic regret, for Queen Anne of Bohemia, not of course the 'Queen' of Shakespeare, who however seems to have transferred to this second wife something of Richard's wildly proclaimed affection for the first. In this way, through the connecting link of that sacred spot, our thoughts once more associate Richard's two fallacious prerogatives, his personal beauty and his 'anointing'.

. . . Like some melodiously contending anthem of Handel's, I said, of Richard's meek 'undoing' of himself in the mirror-scene; and, in fact, the play of *Richard the Second* does, like a musical composition, possess a certain concentration of all its parts, a simple continuity, an evenness in execution, which are rare in the great dramatist. With *Romeo and Juliet*, that perfect symphony . . . it belongs to a small group of plays, where, by happy birth and consistent evolution, dramatic form approaches to something like the unity of a lyrical ballad, a lyric, a song, a single strain of music. Which sort of poetry we are to account the highest, is perhaps a barren question. Yet if, in art generally, unity of impression is a note of what is perfect, then lyric poetry, which in spite of complex structure often preserves the unity of a single passionate ejaculation, would rank higher than dramatic poetry, where, especially to the reader, as distinguished from the spectator assisting at a theatrical performance, there must always be a sense of the effort necessary to keep the various parts from flying asunder, a sense of imperfect continuity, such as the older criticism vainly sought to obviate by the rule of the dramatic 'unities'. It follows that a play attains artistic perfection just in proportion as it approaches that unity of lyrical effect, as if a song or ballad were still lying at the root of it, all the various expression of the conflict of character and circumstance falling at last into the compass of a single melody, or musical theme. As, historically, the earliest classic drama arose out of the chorus, from which this or that person, this or that episode, detached itself, so, into the unity of a choric song the perfect drama ever tends to return, its intellectual scope deepened, complicated, enlarged, but still with an unmistakable singleness, or identity, in its impression on the mind. Just there, in that vivid single impression left on the mind when all is over, not in any mechanical limitation of time and place, is the secret of the 'unities' – the imaginative unity – of the drama.[6] □

Several phrases and ideas from Pater are repeated in later criticism, in particular the notion of Richard as 'sweet-tongued'; the analysis of Richard's self-deposition as 'some long agonizing ceremony', the undoing of a king in an 'inverted rite'; the dramatic form of the play as approaching the unity of lyric. These are perceptive counters to Dowden's crude moralistic reading and by contrast emphasise the play's poetic qualities and rhetorical effects as well as its complex structure.

Underlying Pater's comments is a sense of the play as tragedy, as a ritual in which Richard suffers as a weak human being. This is accompanied by Pater's insights into Richard's eloquence and power 'over others in spite of themselves'. But Pater also draws attention to the gap between Richard's language and the harsh political realities of the play, including the failure of the myth of the divine right of kings to protect him. While Pater, then, foregrounds character and poetry in his analysis, he also sees how the personal and the tragic are interwoven with the political in the play.

III: Benson's *Richard II* and W. B. Yeats

The significance of Frank Benson's performance of *Richard II* lies in the way it brought a seriousness to the production in terms of both language and characterisation, so replacing the extravagance of Kean's spectacular show. Indeed, what emerged in Benson's performance was a figure very much in line with Pater's analysis of a sensitive Richard; later critics have turned this idea into one of Richard simply as poet, missing the complex figure created in late nineteenth-century interpretations. We get a sense of that complexity from C. E. Montague's review printed in 1899. The review, it will be noticed, mentions Dowden, who seemed to dominate criticism at the time.

From C. E. Montague, 'F. R. Benson's *Richard II*' (1899)

■ The chief interest of the day, however, attached to Mr. Benson's Richard II, a piece of acting which is much less known here, and to whose chief interest we do not think that critical justice has ever been done. An actor faulty in some other ways, but always picturesque, romantic, and inventive, with a fine sensibility to beauty in words and situations and a voice that gives this sensibility its due, Mr. Benson brings out admirably that half of the character which criticism seems almost always to have taken pains to obscure – the capable and faithful artist in the same skin as the incapable and unfaithful King. With a quite choice and pointed infelicity, Professor Dowden has called Shakespeare's Richard II, 'an amateur in living, not an artist'; Mr. Boas, generally one of the most suggestive of recent writers on Shakespeare, has called his grace of fancy 'puerile' and its products 'pseudo-poetic'. The general judgment on the play reads as if the critics felt they would be 'only encouraging' kings like the Richard of this play if they did not assure him throughout the ages that his poetry was sad stuff at the best. 'It's no excuse', one seems to hear them say, and 'Serve you right, you and your poetry'. It is our critical way to fall thus upon the wicked or weak in books and leave him half-dead, after taking from him even the good side that he hath. Still it is well to see what Shakespeare meant us to, and we wonder whether any one who hears Mr. Benson in this part with an open mind can doubt that Shakespeare meant to draw in Richard not only a rake and muff on a throne and falling off it but, in the same person, an exquisite poet; to show with one hand how kingdoms are lost and with the other how the creative imagination goes about its work; to fill the same man with the attributes of a feckless wastrel in high place and with the quite distinct but not incompatible attributes of a typical, a consummate artist. . . .

[At this point Montague gives a long description of what characterises the artist, including the 'heightened and delighted personal sense of fact' and 'a veritable passion for arresting and defining in words'.]

We have drawn out this tedious description of the typical artist because the further it goes the more close a description does it become of the Richard whom Mr. Benson shows us in the last three acts. In him every other feeling is mastered, except at a few passing moments, by a passion of interest in the exercise of his gift of exquisite responsiveness to the appeal made to his artistic sensibility by whatever life throws for the moment in his way. Lamb said it was worthwhile to have been cheated of the legacy so as not to miss 'the idea of' the rogue who did it. That, on a little scale, is the kind of aesthetic disinterestedness which in Shakespeare's Richard, rightly presented by Mr. Benson, passes all bounds. The 'idea of' a King's fall, the 'idea of' a wife and husband torn apart, the 'idea of' a very crucifixion of indignities – as each new idea comes he revels in his own warmed and lighted apprehension of it as freely as in his apprehension of the majesty and mystery of the idea of a kingship by divine right. He runs out to meet the thought of a lower fall or a new shame as a man might go to his door to see a sunset or a storm. It has been called the aim of artistic culture to witness things with appropriate emotions. That is this Richard's aim. Good news or bad news, the first thing with him is to put himself in the right vein for getting the fullest and most poignant sense of its contents. Is ruin the word – his mind runs to steep itself in relevant pathos with which in turn to saturate the object put before it; he will 'talk of graves and epitaphs', 'talk of wills', 'tell sad stories of the death of kings'. Once in the vein, he rejoices like a good artist who has caught the spirit of his subject. The very sense of the loss of hope becomes 'that sweet way I was in to despair'. To his wife at their last meeting he bequeaths, as one imaginative writer might bequeath to another some treasure of possibilities of tragic effect, 'the lamentable tale of me'. And to this intoxicating sense of the beauty or poignancy of what is next him he joins the true passion of concern for its perfect expression. At the height of that preoccupation enmities, fears, mortifications, the very presence of onlookers are as if they were not. At the climax of the agony of the abdication scene Shakespeare, with a magnificent boldness of truth, makes the artist's mind, in travail with the lovely poetical figure of the mirror, snatch at the possibility of help at the birth of the beautiful thing, even from the bitterest enemy, –

> say that again;
> The shadows of my sorrow; ha, let's see.

And nothing in Mr. Benson's performance was finer than the King's air, during the mirror soliloquy, as of a man going about his mind's engrossing business in a solitude of its own making. . . .

. . . But indeed the whole performance . . . was brilliant in its equal grasp of the two sides of the character, the one which everybody sees well enough and the one which nearly everybody seems to shun seeing, and in the value it which rendered to the almost continuous flow of genuine and magnificent poetry from Richard to the descant on mortality in kings for instance, and the exquisite greeting to English soil and the gorgeous rhetoric of the speeches on divine right in kings. Of Mr. Benson's achievements as an actor his Richard II strikes us as decidedly the most memorable.[7] □

Montague's review confirms the shift from mid-Victorian spectacle in productions of the play to a focus on its language and pathos. With that shift a new emphasis is placed on Richard's speeches in acts three and four, with their meditations on mortality, and especially on the mirror scene with its fragmenting of Richard's character between man and king. The review thus highlights the extent to which the play depends for its tragic effect on Richard's speeches as he deposes himself, and his self-conscious awareness of the paradoxes of that action.

Benson's sensitive performance of Richard is one of many turning points in the history of *Richard II*. For Yeats, who, like Montague, also responded to the production, it provided, in Shewring's words, 'confirmation that such poetic sensitivity could be significant in its own right and, indeed, equal to the practical, harsh, more pragmatic approach of a worldly, successful Bolingbroke' (p. 68). Yeats's analysis of the play is thus invested with a kind of belief about the place and value of poetry in a culture which more and more had come to despise everything apart from grinding material success. Yeats had gone to Stratford in 1901 to see Benson in a series of plays – the second tetralogy plus *King John*. His account of his visit includes a discussion of the town's theatre and contemporary stage conventions as well as an attack on Dowden and his 'commonplace' values. In this extract, however, Yeats focuses on what he sees as the significance of *Richard II*. In particular, Yeats argues that 'Shakespeare cared little for the state', that he did not value human beings in political terms, but rather saw the emptiness of political systems:

From W. B. Yeats, *Ideas of Good and Evil* (1903)

■ . . . I have seen this week *King John*, *Richard II*, the second part of *Henry IV*, *Henry V*, the second part of *Henry VI*, and *Richard III* played in their right order, with all the links that bind play to play unbroken; and partly because of a spirit in the place, and partly because of the way play supports play, the theatre has moved me as it has never done before. That strange procession of kings and queens, of warring nobles, of insurgent crowds, of courtiers, and of people of the gutter has been to me almost too visible, too audible, too full of an unearthly energy. I have felt as I have sometimes felt on grey days on the Galway shore, when a faint mist has hung over the grey sea and the grey stones, as if the world might suddenly vanish and leave nothing behind, not even a little dust under one's feet. The people my mind's eye has seen have too much of the extravagance of dreams, like all the inventions of art before our crowded life had brought moderation and compromise, to seem more than a dream, and yet all else has grown dim before them. . . .

[In the sections that follow Yeats discusses Stratford and various aspects of staging and acting.]

I cannot believe that Shakespeare looked on his Richard II with any but sympathetic eyes, understanding indeed how ill-fitted he was to be King, at a certain moment of history, but understanding that he was lovable and full of capricious fancy, 'a wild creature' as Pater has called him. The man on whom Shakespeare modelled him had been full of French elegancies, as he knew from Hollingshead, and had given life a new luxury, a new splendour, and been 'too friendly' to his friends, 'too favourable' to his enemies. And certainly Shakespeare had these things in his head when he made his King fail, a little because he lacked some qualities that were doubtless common among his scullions, but more because he had certain qualities that are uncommon in all ages. To suppose that Shakespeare preferred the men who deposed his King is to suppose that Shakespeare judged men with the eyes of a Municipal Councillor weighing the merits of a Town Clerk; and that had he been by when Verlaine cried out from his bed, 'Sir, you have been made by the stroke of a pen, but I have been made by the breath of God', he would have thought the Hospital Superintendent the better man. He saw indeed, as I think, in Richard II the defeat that awaits all, whether they be Artist or Saint, who find themselves where men ask of them a rough energy and have nothing to give but some contemplative virtue, whether lyrical phantasy, or sweetness of temper, or dreamy dignity, or love of God, or love of His creatures. He saw that such a man through sheer bewilderment and impatience can become as unjust or as violent as any common man, any Bolingbroke or Prince John, and yet remain 'that sweet lovely rose'. The courtly and saintly ideals of the Middle Ages were fading, and the practical ideals of the modern age had begun to threaten the unuseful dome of the sky; Merry England was fading, and yet it was not so faded that the Poets could not watch the procession of the world with that untroubled sympathy for men as they are, as apart from all they do and seem, which is the substance of tragic irony.

Shakespeare cared little for the State, the source of all our judgments, apart from its shows and splendours, its turmoils and battles, its flamings out of the uncivilized heart. He did indeed think it wrong to overturn a King, and thereby to swamp peace in civil war, and the historical plays from *Henry IV* to *Richard III*, that monstrous birth and last sign of the wrath of Heaven, are a fulfilment of the prophecy of the Bishop of Carlisle, who was 'raised up by God' to make it; but he had no nice sense of utilities, no ready balance to measure deeds, like that fine instrument, with all the latest improvements, Gervinus and Professor Dowden handle so skilfully. He meditated as Solomon, not as Bentham meditated, upon blind ambitions, untoward accidents, and capricious passions, and the world was almost as empty in his eyes as it must be in the eyes of God. . . .

———

The Greeks, a certain scholar has told me, considered that myths are the activities of the Daemons, and that the Daemons shape our characters and our lives. I have often had the fancy that there is some one Myth for every man, which, if we but knew it, would make us understand all he did and thought. Shakespeare's Myth, it may be, describes a wise man who was blind from very wisdom, and an empty man who thrust him from his place, and saw all that could be seen from very emptiness. It is in the story of Hamlet, who saw too great issues everywhere to play the trivial game of life, and of Fortinbras, who came from fighting battles about 'a little patch of ground' so poor that one of his Captains would not give 'six ducats' to 'farm it', and who was yet acclaimed by Hamlet and by all as the only befitting King. And it is in the story of Richard II, that unripened Hamlet, and of Henry V, that ripened Fortinbras. To poise character against character was an element in Shakespeare's art, and scarcely a play is lacking in characters that are the complement of one another, and so, having made the vessel of porcelain Richard II, he had to make the vessel of clay Henry V. He makes him the reverse of all that Richard was. He has the gross vices, the coarse nerves, of one who is to rule among violent people, and he is so little 'too friendly' to his friends that he bundles them out of doors when their time is over. He is as remorseless and undistinguished as some natural force, and the finest thing in his play is the way his old companions fall out of it broken-hearted or on their way to the gallows; and instead of that lyricism which rose out of Richard's mind like the jet of a fountain to fall again where it had risen, instead of that phantasy too enfolded in its own sincerity to make any thought the hour had need of, Shakespeare has given him a resounding rhetoric that moves men, as a leading article does to-day. His purposes are so intelligible to everybody that everybody talks of him as if he succeeded, although he fails in the end, as all men great and little fail in Shakespeare, and yet his conquests abroad are made nothing by a woman turned warrior, and that boy he and Katherine were to 'compound', 'half French, half English', 'that' was to 'go to Constantinople and take the Turk by the beard', turns out a Saint, and loses all his father had built up at home and his own life.

Shakespeare watched Henry V not indeed as he watched the greater souls in the visionary procession, but cheerfully, as one watches some handsome spirited horse, and he spoke his tale, as he spoke all tales, with tragic irony.[8] □

Like Pater, Yeats sees Richard's failings but also what he calls his 'uncommon' qualities, that is, his 'contemplative virtues', his sense of beauty. Yeats's analysis, however, goes beyond character discussion to suggest that informing the history plays is a larger vision of things. Shakespeare, he argues, deliberately sets character against character, Richard against Bolingbroke and, later, Henry V. This contrast is not simply between weak and strong kings but between figures who can see 'great issues' in events and those who see nothing. In essence, it is a contrast between tragic heroes such as Richard and military leaders such as Bolingbroke. It is this contrast which lends the history plays their tragic irony: that whatever Bolingbroke wins has little value when set against the kind of insight Richard possesses.

Like Pater, then, Yeats sees Shakespeare rejecting political success as the measure of human worth. Like Pater, too, Yeats responds to Richard's rhetoric and attacks Dowden's small-minded imperialism. In many ways Yeats looks back to Coleridge and Romantic criticism. The difference is that, whereas Coleridge had been interested in Richard's inner moods and feelings, Yeats and Pater see in Richard a character to set against Victorian aggression. What they both seek to defend are the ideas of beauty and poetry in a culture interested only in political success.

IV: E.K. Chambers

E.K. Chambers brought out his edition of *Richard II* some ten years before Yeats's essay appeared. Chambers is one of the great Shakespearean scholars. His massive volumes on the *Shakespearean Stage* collect much of the primary information about the Elizabethan theatres, the players and the dramatists. The tone of the essay below is, as one might expect, in marked contrast to that of Yeats and Pater, and is a sign of the movement of Shakespeare's texts into the academic world of university English:

From E.K. Chambers (ed.), *The Tragedy of King Richard the Second* (1891)

■ The histories of Shakespeare have a threefold burden. They are largely epical in character, a bead-roll, as it were, of English kings. . . . It is easy to find the motive for such a drama-cycle in the 'new spring' of patriotic enthusiasm born in England of the Spanish Wars. . . . In the sixteenth century, History was just beginning to fill the place of mere contemporary Chronicle; Englishmen were just awakening to a wider outlook over the world, and with it to a sense that they had, as a people, a past in which they were bound to take an interest and pride. . . .

Secondly, there is the element of purely human, of tragic interest in the spectacle of so many men called one after another, not from any grace or gift of their own, but by the accident of being kings, to grapple with dangerous moral and social forces, and, most often, failing in their task. . . .

Though this is much, there is 'more in it'. At bottom Shakespeare is always a student, and these plays are the outcome of a student's reflection on grave questions concerning the well-being of a nation. For Shakespeare, as for Thucydides, History becomes at once a judgment of the past and a forecast of the future; no longer merely a tale of 'forgotten, far off things', it is an 'eternal possession', and a potent factor in determining the conduct of life. Thus *Richard II* and the rest are studies in kingship, wherein, to those who can read, the poet has laid bare his mind upon the problems of government in the form which they appeared in to our ancestors. His answer to them is one which Plato might have applauded. He finds the true foundation of regal authority neither in an imaginary divine right nor in the will of a parliamentary assembly: the genuine king and leader of men is he who best understands and sympathizes with the needs and aspirations of his people, and is best fitted to guide them in the working out of their proper destiny. John forgot this, and left his country in the hands of a foreign invader; Richard II and Henry IV failed to regard it, and overwhelmed her with all the horrors of the Wars of the Roses.

In the days in which this message was delivered, it was sorely needed. The Tudors wrought a great work for England, but their task was already achieved when Shakespeare wrote. The country was at last free, united, prosperous, a pleasant and a merry land to dwell in. And now the evils inherent in the Tudor conception of monarchy began to outweigh its influence for good; the gradual extension of the royal prerogative threatened to swamp the liberties of the people. As yet the danger was hardly felt; it was reserved for the next century to preach once more the doctrines, dangerous to princes as princes themselves to those who put their trust in them, of the 'divine right of kings', but Shakespeare saw more clearly than People, Parliament, or Queen: his wider vision stretched back to Runnymede and to Pontefract, and on, with vague poetic foresight, to the scaffold outside Whitehall. The English histories are his word of warning to a regardless nation, and the fatality which has always hung around revivals of *Richard II* forms a curious commentary on the text.

There are thus threads of unity running through all these plays; in all we find a common dramatic treatment of history; but the smaller group, almost an English trilogy, which deals with Richard II and his two immediate successors, is woven even more closely into one web. It exhibits to us three types of king, one of them perfect, Shakespeare's ideal ruler, the other two imperfect, because lacking in the essential elements of that ideal. Henry V has all the notes of a true king. He has gone through no degrading intrigues to win his crown; neither is he weak and vain, but rather full of resource and overflowing with energy. This superabundant vitality made him wanton in his youth, but once he is on the throne it is soon converted into more fitting channels. Above all, he is neither unjust nor self-seeking; fully in harmony with the life of his people, he is ready to put himself at their head and lead them on to the accomplishment of their high fortunes. It is true that Shakespeare regards these fortunes as inextricably bound up with foreign conquest; there he is the child of his age; but, however much his spirit may resound to the 'pomp and circumstance of glorious war', yet we feel that the horrors and the 'pity of it' are never far from his thoughts.

The other two kings, in different ways, fall short of the ideal. Both are purely selfish in their aims, and unscrupulous of the rights of the nation in their pursuit of uncontrolled power. Moreover, Richard is unstable and frivolous; Henry has the blot of treachery and murder upon his soul. Thus both their lives are failures; it is good to be a lawful king, and it is good to be strong and self-reliant, but it is only devotion to a people's cause that can save from ruin. Yet Shakespeare does not choose to paint in crude colours; both these men have the outward aspect, the speech and bearing of a king.

Richard II forms part of a trilogy, and its meaning is amplified and enriched by comparison with the plays that follow it; yet, as it stands, it has a self-centred, independent unity of its own. It seems to have been written some years before *Henry IV* and *Henry V*, and perhaps slightly modified at a subsequent period in order to take its place in the series. The first essential of every work of art is a principle of unity, and the English romantic drama – having rejected the so-called classical or formal unities of place, time, and action – gradually evolved for itself an inner spiritual unity of thought. In Shakespeare this takes the form of an underlying central idea whose truth is illustrated by the development of the action. These ideas are generally human in their bearing; they deal with Character and Love and Kingship, or, in many of the later plays, with the deepest problems of the origin and destinies of man and the government of the world. The central idea of *Richard II* is a tragical one; it is a tragedy of failure, the necessary failure of a king, however rightfully he may reign, however 'fair a show' he may present, if he is weak and self-seeking and lawless. The action of the play presents the working-out of this tragedy; it traces the downfall of Richard from the scenes where he appears as a powerful monarch, disposing with a word of the lives of his subjects, to that where his unkinged, murdered corpse is borne on to the stage. The instrument of his ruin is his cousin Henry, and therefore Bolingbroke's rise becomes a natural parallel to Richard's fall. The king's own image of the two buckets holds good: in the first act Richard is supreme, Henry at the lowest depth; gradually one sinks, the other ascends, until they are on a level, when they meet at Flint Castle. As is often the case, the turning-point of the action is put precisely in the middle of the play. Still the same process continues, and when the final catastrophe of the last act occurs, the original positions of the two are exactly reversed; it is now Henry's word that is potent to doom Richard. Whether the play has been revised or not, it is at least a marvel of careful workmanship; situations and phrases constantly occur in the second half of the play which are pointed inversions of others at the beginning. The moving forces of the play are thus to be found in the characters of the chief personages, in the clash of two spirits, one capable, the other incapable, of making circumstances the stepping-stones to his own end. This is carefully brought out in the first scene; the opposition between the kings, hidden as yet from others, is here clearly revealed to themselves, and the key-note of the whole play is touched. A comparison of the two natures is ample to explain the outcome of the struggle between them.

On the delineation of Richard all the resources of Shakespeare's genius have been poured: it is a work of art and of love. We have presented to us the portrait of a finely tempered man, gifted and graced in mind and body. He 'looks like a king' for beauty and majesty, with his fair face in which the blood comes and goes. His marvellous wealth of eloquent imaginative speech irradiates the play. His power of personal fascination, no less than his intense selfishness and pitiful fate, remind us of Charles Stuart, the melancholy-eyed man, who lured Strafford to his doom; it enthrals the queen, it enthrals Aumerle, it enthrals even the 'poor groom of his stable'. He meets them with answering affection that twines itself around not men and women only, but the horse he rides upon and the earth he treads. The very root of his nature is an exquisite sensitiveness, intellectual and emotional; he reads his cousin's thoughts in his face; he is a lover of music and of pageantry, of regal hospitality and refined luxurious splendour. And withal there are lacking in him the elements which go to make up the backbone of a character. This beautiful, cultured king, for all his delicate half-tones of feeling and thought, is a being devoid of moral sense, treacherous, unscrupulous, selfish; he murders his uncle, robs his cousin, and oppresses his people; he trails the fair name of England in the dust; even in the days of his captivity he regrets his follies, but scarcely regards his crimes. It is not in moral sense only that he is deficient, but in moral and intellectual fibre; like Plato's 'musical man' he has 'piped away his soul with sweet and plaintive melodies'; he can divine Bolingbroke's wishes, but he cannot judge his character aright, nor can he forecast the results of his own lawless acts. In prosperity he yields himself to flatterers; in adversity he puts an idle confidence in a supposed God-given commission to reign. Contrary events are for him not a spur to action, but an incentive to imagination; he plays around them with lambent words; he is always 'studying how to compare'. The best side of him appears when he is fallen; he becomes the part of victim better than that of tyrant; the softer qualities in him move our pity, the sterner ones that he has not are less needed. True, he strikes no blow, and finds a ready comfort in despair, but he keeps his plaining and poetic laments for his friends, and meets the rebel lords with subtle scorn and all the dignity of outraged royalty. Yet even here he betrays, like another of Shakespeare's characters – Orsino in *Twelfth Night* – what we are accustomed to think of as essentially modern faults; he is a shade too self-conscious, a touch too theatrical in his attitude.

To the checkered lights and shadows of such a disposition Bolingbroke presents the most complete contrast. He leaves the impression of little grace and intense power. A man of iron will and subtle pertinacious intellect, a true 'crown-grasper', he clearly envisages his end and remorselessly pursues it, playing with a masterly hand upon the hates and loves and ambitions of other men. Rarely does he betray any emotion; very rarely does he speak an uncalculated word. He can 'steal courtesy from heaven' to win the hearts of the citizens or the favours of the Percies, but his genuine temper is shown in the undertone of studied sarcasm which runs through his bearing towards Richard in the first act, and makes itself heard at intervals throughout the play. His life is a web of intrigue; the disillusioned Hotspur in *Henry IV* calls him 'subtle king' and 'vile politician', while upon his unhappy death-bed he whispers to the watching prince 'by what bypaths and indirect crooked ways he met his crown'. His schemes are for the time successful, but before long they recoil upon him in the alienation of the nobles he has tricked and the wild life of his son.[9] □

Chambers' introduction takes up many of the threads of earlier criticism of the play. For example, he mentions the epic quality of the histories, their concern with kingship, the sharp contrast between Richard and Bolingbroke and the tragic action of the play. To this extent his essay marks a kind of synthesis as *Richard II* comes to take on a certain critical identity with certain features being emphasised. What, however, is interesting about Chambers' introduction is that it links the play in a much fuller way than previously with Tudor politics and the dangers of absolutism. 'The gradual extension of the royal prerogative', Chambers writes, 'threatened to swamp the liberties of the people', and he goes on to suggest that the play itself 'with vague poetic foresight' anticipates the 'scaffold outside Whitehall'. In other words, the deposition of Richard II prefigures the execution of Charles I, while the struggle in the play embodies the struggle throughout the period between the rights of the crown and the rights of ordinary men and women set out in Magna Carta at Runnymede.

Chambers' introduction, in its analysis, anticipates the debate about Tudor politics and the history plays in the criticism of the 1940s, epitomised in the work of E. M. W. Tillyard. But it also anticipates more recent debates about the play's concern with authority and power. In this sense it serves as an introduction to twentieth-century criticism of *Richard II* as well as representing a kind of summary of previous critical thinking; it is a pivotal piece of work, taking stock of the past in a scholarly way, but also beginning to establish a critical course for the future.

CHAPTER FIVE

E. M. W. Tillyard and Historical Criticism

Introduction

IN THE words of David M. Bergeron:

■ All criticism of the histories emanates from E.M.W. Tillyard's pioneering work, *Shakespeare's History Plays* (1944). Whether one agrees or disagrees with it, Tillyard's has become the traditional interpretation of the history plays.[1] □

As this quotation suggests, Tillyard's work has established itself as the standard interpretation of Shakespeare's history plays. This standard reading is that the plays, in line with orthodox political Tudor doctrine, condemn rebellion as sinful and support the divine right of kings. Tillyard's views have been challenged by recent radical critics and also by traditional literary and historical critics. Nevertheless, Tillyard still occupies a central place in the discussion of the histories.

The reasons for Tillyard's critical prominence are not hard to find. In part Tillyard came to prominence because the arguments he advanced, though doctrinaire, were so simple: that Shakespeare's plays reflected the political and moral thinking of the Elizabethan state. What could be more natural or commonsensical? In part, too, Tillyard seemed to sum up the reaction against the Victorian and early twentieth-century emphasis on character by considering the plays in their historical context. There were critics before Tillyard who had looked at Shakespeare in terms of Elizabethan political writings, but no one had managed to stir the critical debate in the way that Tillyard was to do. At the heart of that debate lies the question of how to read the histories.

Before turning to Tillyard and some of the objections to his arguments, however, it may be helpful to fill out the wider context. As we saw in the last chapter, both Pater and Yeats responded to the lyrical qualities of *Richard II*: the play is written entirely in verse with much use of rhyme, and Richard's major speeches are packed with images and conceits. The lyrical quality of the play, as Richard Dutton notes, has often been brought out in the theatre, particularly in the 1929 and 1937 John Gielgud performances.[2] Margaret Shewring points out that, although Gielgud was influenced by the Benson performance of 1896, other changes in the attitude towards Shakespeare also had an impact. There was, for example, the establishment of the new Shakespeare Society, the research work of William Poel into staging, and the influence of Granville Barker the director and actor. All led to a rejection of the Victorian emphasis on spectacle 'in favour of the everyday'.[3] Other changes in theatre practice led to Shakespeare's plays being staged with the scenes in the order they were originally written rather than rearranged by the producer, and changed speech styles meant no more long drawn-out performances.

Such changes in theatrical practice were matched in critical writing. As we saw in the previous chapter, E.K. Chambers had already sounded a different kind of historical critical approach in 1891, and that was to some extent taken up by Dover Wilson in his 1939 edition of the play (an extract from this appears below). In addition, ground-breaking work by Caroline Spurgeon on imagery had traced out patterns of ideas and images that later scholars were to add to.[4] These circumstances are of note: Tillyard was not writing in a vacuum but was part of a developing Shakespeare industry, reshaping the inherited views of Shakespeare on every front as well as reshaping English as an academic subject. At Cambridge, for example, I.A. Richards had introduced the idea of practical criticism and with it the idea of criticism as an act of interpretation rather than evaluation. But there is another dimension to Tillyard's thinking that we must take account of.

I: E.M.W. Tillyard's *Elizabethan World Picture*

Behind Tillyard's criticism is the experience of the 1939–45 war. This is reflected in the direction of his central arguments. Reduced to the simplest terms, Tillyard argues that Shakespeare was on the side of order: that his plays value and espouse the notion of civil order put forward by the Elizabethans as state policy; that disobedience was wrong; that the crown ruled by right of divine power.

At a more complex level, Tillyard's thesis argues that Shakespeare's history plays, in common with the work of the sixteenth-century chronicle writer Edward Hall, embrace the notion of the Tudor Myth as put forward by Elizabethan officialdom. This presented the Wars of the Roses as God's punishment for the deposition of Richard II. England was, according to the myth, subject to a divine curse which was only finally expiated when Richard III was killed at Bosworth and Henry Tudor came to the throne, joining the houses of York and Lancaster through his marriage to Elizabeth of York.

The myth has three important implications. First, it presents history as under the control of a divine providence rather than as the result of human actions or political policy. Second, this is essentially a medieval, Christian view of history in which the state (or 'body politic') is seen as part of a universal order created by God. The state itself should reflect that order, with the monarch at the head, and with any disruption of the hierarchy seen as leading to chaos. Third, in Tillyard's reading, the whole of Shakespeare's history plays, from *Richard II* through the *Henry VI* plays and to *Richard III*, become a grand narrative illustrating this order of things.

Tillyard, then, sees the history plays as endorsing political stability and celebrating the Tudor monarchy. Dutton suggests that Tillyard, in his interpretation of the histories, was not just responding to the war but also 'the decades of mass-destruction and totalitarianism before it', so that the elaborate schema he sees at work in Elizabethan literature is a sort of nostalgic longing for a time when the world order was settled, stable and hierarchical. Above all, Dutton continues, the order Tillyard conceives has at its roots an idea of the correspondence between the political state and the 'God-given harmony of the cosmos'.[5] This point needs expanding a little.

Tillyard's views were first propounded in his book *The Elizabethan World Picture* (1943), an attempt to describe those ideas which all Elizabethans, Tillyard suggested, believed in; it was to be a picture of Elizabethan thought, its commonly held world-view. Most critics today would accept that the ideas Tillyard puts forward were powerful in the culture of the time, but insert the reservation that these were only part of a vigorous debate about political order, government, rebellion and history itself. What follows is a brief extract from Chapter 2 of *The Elizabethan World Picture*. The chapter is entitled 'Order', and in it Tillyard explains his thesis, in particular, his argument that Elizabethans had an abhorrence of disorder.

■ Those . . . who take their notion of the Elizabethan age principally from the drama will find it difficult to agree that its world picture was ruled by a general conception of order, for at first sight that drama is anything but orderly. . . . Actually . . . the conception of order is so taken for granted, so much part of the collective mind of the people, that it is hardly mentioned except in explicitly didactic passages. It is not absent from non-didactic writing, for it appears in Spenser's *Hymn of Love* and in Ulysses' speech on 'degree' in Shakespeare's *Troilus and Cressida*. It occurs frequently in didactic prose: in Elyot's *Governor*, the Church Homily Of *Obedience*, the first book of Hooker's *Laws of Ecclesiastical Polity*, and the preface to Raleigh's *History of the World*.

Shakespeare's version is the best known. For this reason, and because its full scope is not always perceived, I begin with it.

> The heavens themselves, the planets, and this centre
> Observe degree priority and place
> Insisture course proportion season form
> Office and custom, in all line of order;
> And therefore is the glorious planet Sol
> In noble eminence enthron'd and spher'd
> Amidst the other, whose med'cinable eye
> Corrects the ill aspects of planets evil
> And posts like the commandment of a king,
> Sans check, to good and bad. But when the planets
> In evil mixture to disorder wander,
> What plagues and what portents, what mutiny,
> What raging of the sea, shaking of earth,
> Commotion in the winds, frights changes horrors,
> Divert and crack, rend and deracinate
> The unity and married calm of states
> Quite from their fixure. Oh, when degree is shak'd,
> Which is the ladder to all high designs,
> The enterprise is sick. How could communities,
> Degrees in schools and brotherhoods in cities,
> Peaceful commerce from dividable shores,
> The primogenitive and due of birth,
> Prerogative of age, crowns sceptres laurels,
> But by degree stand in authentic place?
> Take but degree away, untune that string,
> And hark, what discord follows. Each thing meets
> In mere oppugnancy. The bounded waters
> Should lift their bosoms higher than the shores
> And make a sop of all this solid globe.
> Strength should be lord to imbecility,
> And the rude son should strike his father dead.
> This chaos, when degree is suffocate,
> Follows the choking.

Much of what I have to expound is contained in this passage, and I shall revert to its details later. The point here is that so many things are included simultaneously within this 'degree' or order, and so strong a sense is given of their interconnexions. The passage is at once cosmic and domestic. The sun, the king, primogeniture hang together; the war of the planets is echoed by the war of the elements and by civil war on earth; the homely brotherhoods or guilds in cities are found along with an oblique reference to creation out of the confusion of chaos. Here is a picture of immense and varied activity, constantly threatened with dissolution, and yet preserved from it by a superior unifying power. The picture, however, though so rich, is not complete. There is nothing about God and the angels, nothing about animals vegetables and minerals. For Shakespeare's dramatic purposes he brought in quite enough, but it would be wrong to think that he did not mean to imply the two extremes of creation also. . . .

The conception of order described above must have been common to all Elizabethans of even modest intelligence. . . .

. . . Above all cosmic or earthly orders or laws there is Law in general, 'that Law which giveth life unto all the rest which are commendable just and good, namely the Law whereby the Eternal himself doth work'. . . .

Though little enlarged on by the poets, cosmic order was yet one of the master-themes of Elizabethan poetry. It has its positive and its negative expressions. First there is an occasional full statement, as in Spenser's *Hymns*. Then there are the partial statements or the hints. Ulysses' 'degree' speech is a partial statement. The long scene between Malcolm and Macduff at the English court and the reference to the healing power of the English king draw their strength from the idea. There is a short passage in the first part of *Henry VI* whose pivotal meaning any other than a contemporary reader might easily miss. It shows Talbot during a truce with the French doing homage to Henry VI, who has arrived at Paris to be crowned, and Henry rewarding him with the earldom of Shrewsbury. The scene is an example of the sort of thing that ought to happen in an orderly kingdom and it serves as a norm by which the many disorders in the same play are judged. Talbot's speech in its references to the places of God, the king, and himself in their due degrees carries with it the whole context of Hooker and the great Homily of obedience:

> My gracious prince and honorable peers,
> Hearing of your arrival in this realm,
> I have awhile given truce unto my wars,
> To do my duty to my sovereign.
> In sign whereof this arm, that hath reclaim'd
> To your obedience fifty fortresses
> Twelve cities and seven walled towns of strength,
> Beside five hundred prisoners of esteem,
> Lets fall his sword before your highness' feet
> And with submissive loyalty of heart
> Ascribes the glory of his conquest got
> First to my God and next unto your grace. . . .

The notion of cosmic order pervades the entire *Fairy Queen* and prompts such a detail as Spenser's iteration of the phrase 'in comely rew [row]' or 'on a row'. The arrangement is comely not just because it is pretty and seemly but because it harmonizes with a universal order.

But the negative implication was even more frequent and emphatic. If the Elizabethans believed in an ideal order animating earthly order, they were terrified lest it should be upset, and appalled by the visible tokens of disorder that suggested its upsetting. They were obsessed by the fear of chaos and the fact of mutability; and the obsession was powerful in proportion as their faith in the cosmic order was strong. To us *chaos* means hardly more than confusion on a large scale; to an Elizabethan it meant the cosmic anarchy before creation and the wholesale dissolution that would result if the pressure of Providence relaxed and allowed the law of nature to cease functioning. Othello's 'chaos is come again', or Ulysses' 'this chaos, when degree is suffocate', cannot be fully felt apart from orthodox theology. . . . If Shakespeare in *Henry VI*, *Troilus and Cressida*, and *Macbeth* gives us his version of order, it bulks small compared with the different kinds of chaos that reign or threaten in all these plays. Yet Shakespeare's chaos is without meaning apart from the proper background of cosmic order by which to judge it.[6] □

In essence, Tillyard's analysis echoes that of Ulysses' speech in Shakespeare's *Troilus and Cressida* on the need for order or 'degree'; like Ulysses, Tillyard argues that all orders of life in Elizabethan thinking are arranged in a fixed hierarchy that duplicates the divine law. For example, all the planets have a proper place in the universe; the seasons flow in order; cities and families have a set structure. As against this, Tillyard suggests that any disruption of order appalled the Elizabethans who would have read it as a sign of a return to the chaos before the creation.

Modern critics have raised various objections to this monolithic picture. For one thing, within forty years the Elizabethan state which Tillyard says abhorred chaos was set to be plunged into civil war, and there is evidence before 1642 of political discontent. But there are other objections, too, to the way Tillyard constructs a world picture that ignores the rapid changes of Elizabethan culture, such as its contradictions, tensions, inconsistencies, gaps, diversity and, indeed, its dramatic nature. Such issues will become apparent as we move on to Tillyard's detailed view of the history plays.

II: E. M. W. Tillyard's *Shakespeare's History Plays*

I have already provided a general outline of Tillyard's reading of the history plays, in particular how he sees them as reflecting orthodox Tudor doctrine and presenting a providential view of history: that the Tudor dynasty was the logical end of God's ordering of history following the sinful deposition of Richard II. Irving Ribner argues that in constructing this reading Tillyard compresses a wide range of contemporary views on history into one, and sets the plays in too narrow a framework:

■ . . . There were other schools of historiography in Elizabethan England. The providential history of Hall, in fact, represents a tradition which . . . was already in decline. To dismiss, for instance, as Tillyard does, Machiavelli as lying 'outside the main sixteenth-century interest' is clearly short-sighted. In historiography, as in other intellectual areas, the Elizabethan age was one of flux and uncertainty, with new and heretical notions competing in men's minds against old established ideas which could no longer be accepted without doubt and questioning.[7] □

Machiavelli was the author of *The Prince* (1513), a handbook of pragmatic, often sceptical advice to princes on how to gain and keep power. In effect, *The Prince* turns history into a political science as well as a matter of ruthless ambition. There is little doubt that Tillyard's thesis, as Ribner and others have noted, by dismissing the sort of new humanist thinking about history and power that Machiavelli represents, is seriously flawed. Bolingbroke, for example, in his actions can be seen as a kind of Machiavellian figure ready to exploit opportunities as well as people such as Northumberland.

Ribner, then, sees Tillyard as short-sighted and limited in his approach. This criticism could equally be applied to Tillyard's analysis of order: in some ways it is a naive reflectionist view, that we can construct and verify critical interpretations by an appeal to history. But it was probably this approach that made Tillyard's work so attractive when it appeared. Instead of a critical method based on character, here was a way of locating the plays in their historical context which gave them a much more serious intellectual dimension than had previously been suggested.

The extract from *Shakespeare's History Plays* which follows comes from the second part of Tillyard's book. The first part examines various backgrounds to the plays – cosmic, historical, literary and dramatic – and incorporates some of the ideas from *The Elizabethan World Picture*. This extract deals specifically with *Richard II* and the significance of its formal, ceremonial qualities which Tillyard sees as the essence of the play. They serve, Tillyard suggests, to dramatise the medieval world to which Richard belongs, a world overtaken by the modern world of Bolingbroke:

From E. M. W. Tillyard, *Shakespeare's History Plays* (1944)

■ Of all Shakespeare's plays *Richard II* is the most formal and ceremonial. It is not only that Richard himself is a true king in appearance, in his command of the trappings of royalty, while being deficient in the solid virtues of the ruler; that is a commonplace: the ceremonial character of the play extends much wider than Richard's own nature or the exquisite patterns of his poetic speech.

First, the very actions tend to be symbolic rather than real. There is all the pomp of a tournament without the physical meeting of the two armed knights. There is a great army of Welshmen assembled to support Richard, but they never fight. Bolingbroke before Flint Castle speaks of the terrible clash there should be when he and Richard meet: . . . But instead of a clash there is a highly ceremonious encounter leading to the effortless submission of Richard. There are violent challenges before Henry in Westminster Hall, but the issue is postponed. The climax of the play is the ceremony of Richard's deposition. And finally Richard, imprisoned at Pomfret, erects his own lonely state and his own griefs into a gigantic ceremony. He arranges his own thoughts into classes corresponding with men's estates in real life; king and beggar, divine, soldier, and middle man. His own sighs keep a ceremonial order like a clock: . . .

Second, in places where emotion rises, where there is strong mental action, Shakespeare evades direct or naturalistic presentation and resorts to convention and conceit. . . . Emotionally Richard's parting from his queen could have been a great thing in the play: actually it is an exchange of frigidly ingenious couplets.

> *Rich.* Go, count thy ways with sighs; I mine with groans.
> *Qu.* So longest way shall have the longest moans.
> *Rich.* Twice for one step I'll groan, the way being short,
>   And piece the way out with a heavy heart.

This is indeed the language of ceremony not of passion. . . .

The case of Gaunt is different but more complicated. When he has the state of England in mind and reproves Richard, though he can be rhetorical and play on words, he speaks the language of passion:

> Now He that made me knows I see thee ill.
> Thy death-bed is no lesser than thy land
> Wherein thou liest in reputation sick.
> And thou, too careless patient as thou art,
> Commit'st thy anointed body to the cure
> Of those physicians that first wounded thee.

A thousand flatterers sit within thy crown,
Whose compass is no bigger than thy head.

But in the scene of private feeling, when he parts from his banished son, both speakers, ceasing to be specifically themselves, exchange the most exquisitely formal commonplaces traditionally deemed appropriate to such a situation.

Go, say I sent thee for to purchase honour
And not the king exil'd thee; or suppose
Devouring pestilence hangs in our air
And thou art flying to a fresher clime. . . .

Superficially this may be maturer verse than the couplets quoted, but it is just as formal, just as mindful of propriety and as unmindful of nature as Richard and his queen taking leave. Richard's sudden start into action when attacked by his murderers is exceptional, serving to set off by contrast the lack of action that has prevailed and to link the play with the next of the series. His groom, who appears in the same scene, is a realistic character alien to the rest of the play and serves the same function as Richard in action.

Thirdly, there is an elaboration and a formality in the cosmic references, scarcely to be matched in Shakespeare. These are usually brief and incidental, showing indeed how intimate a part they were of the things accepted and familiar in Shakespeare's mind. But in *Richard II* they are positively paraded. The great speech of Richard in Pomfret Castle is a tissue of them: first the peopling of his prison room with his thoughts, making its microcosm correspond with the orders of the body politic; then the doctrine of the universe as a musical harmony; then the fantasy of his own griefs arranged in a pattern like the working of a clock, symbol of regularity opposed to discord; and finally madness as the counterpart in man's mental kingdom of discord or chaos. Throughout the play the great commonplace of the king on earth duplicating the sun in heaven is exploited with a persistence unmatched anywhere else in Shakespeare. Finally . . . there is the scene (III.iv) of the gardeners, with the elaborate comparison of the state to the botanical microcosm of the garden. But this is a scene so typical of the whole trend of the play that I will speak of it generally and not merely as another illustration of the traditional correspondences.

The scene begins with a few exquisitely musical lines of dialogue between the queen and two ladies. She refines her grief in a vein of high ceremony and sophistication. She begins by asking what sport they can devise in this garden to drive away care. But to every sport proposed there is a witty objection. . . . Shakespeare uses language here like a very accomplished musician doing exercises over the whole compass of the violin. Then there enter a gardener and two servants: clearly to balance the queen and her ladies and through that balance to suggest that the gardener within the walls of his little plot of land is a king. Nothing could illustrate better the different expectations of a modern and of an Elizabethan audience than the way they would take the gardener's opening words:

> Go, bind thou up yon dangling apricocks,
> Which, like unruly children, make their sire
> Stoop with oppression of their prodigal weight.

The first thought of a modern audience is: what a ridiculous way for a gardener to talk. The first thought of an Elizabethan would have been: what is the symbolic meaning of those words, spoken by this king of the garden, and how does it bear on the play? And it would very quickly conclude that the apricots have grown inflated and overweening in the sun of the royal favour; that oppression was used with a political as well as a physical meaning; and that the apricots threatened, unless restrained, to upset the proper relation between parent and offspring, to offend against the great principle of order. And the rest of the gardener's speech would bear out this interpretation.

> Go thou, and like an executioner
> Cut off the heads of too fast growing sprays,
> That look too lofty in our commonwealth.
> All must be even in our government.
> You thus employ'd, I will go root away
> The noisome weeds, which without profit suck
> The soil's fertility from wholesome flowers.

In fact the scene turns out to be an elaborate political allegory, with the Earl of Wiltshire, Bushy, and Green standing for the noxious weeds which Richard, the bad gardener, allowed to flourish and which Henry, the new gardener, has rooted up. It ends with the queen coming forward and joining in the talk. She confirms the gardener's regal and moral function by calling him 'old Adam's likeness', but curses him for his ill news about Richard and Bolingbroke. The intensively symbolic character of the scene is confirmed when the gardener at the end proposes to plant a bank with rue where the queen let fall her tears, as a memorial:

> Rue, even for ruth, here shortly shall be seen
> In the remembrance of a weeping queen.

111

In passing, for it is not my immediate concern, let me add that the gardener gives both the pattern and the moral of the play. The pattern is the weighing of the fortunes of Richard and Bolingbroke:

> Their fortunes both are weigh'd.
> In your lord's scale is nothing but himself
> And some few vanities that make him light;
> But in the balance of great Bolingbroke
> Besides himself are all the English peers,
> And with that odds he weighs King Richard down.

For the moral, though he deplores Richard's inefficiency, the gardener calls the news of his fall 'black tidings' and he sympathizes with the queen's sorrow. And he is himself, in his microcosmic garden, what neither Richard nor Bolingbroke separately is, the authentic gardener-king, no usurper, and the just represser of vices, the man who makes 'all even in our government'.

. . . Why was it that in *Richard II*, when he was so much more mature, when his brilliant realism in *King John* showed him capable of making his gardeners as human and as amusing as the gravediggers in *Hamlet*, Shakespeare chose to present them with a degree of formality unequalled in any play he wrote? It is, in a different form, the same question as that which was implied by my discussion of the other formal or ceremonial features of the play: namely, why did Shakespeare in *Richard II* make the ceremonial or ritual form of writing, . . . not merely one of the principal means of expression but the very essence of the play?

These are the first questions we must answer if we are to understand the true nature of *Richard II*. And here let me repeat that though Richard himself is a very important part of the play's ceremonial content, that content is larger and more important than Richard. . . . [I]n *Richard II* . . . we are invited, again and again, to dwell on the sheer ceremony of the various situations. The main point of the tournament between Bolingbroke and Mowbray is the way it is conducted; the point of Gaunt's parting with Bolingbroke is the sheer propriety of the sentiments they utter; the portents, put so fittingly into the mouth of a Welshman, are more exciting because they are appropriate than because they precipitate an event; Richard is ever more concerned with how he behaves, with the fitness of his conduct to the occasion, than with what he actually does; the gardener may foretell the deposition of Richard yet he is far more interesting as representing a static principle of order; when Richard is deposed, it is the precise manner that comes before all –

With mine own tears I wash away my balm,
With mine own hands I give away my crown,
With mine own tongue deny my sacred state,
With mine own breath release all duty's rites.

We are in fact in a world where means matter more than ends, where it is more important to keep strictly the rules of an elaborate game than either to win or to lose it.

Now though compared with ourselves the Elizabethans put a high value on means as against ends they did not go to the extreme. It was in the Middle Ages that means were so elaborated, that the rules of the game of life were so lavishly and so minutely set forth. *Richard II* is Shakespeare's picture of that life.

Of course it would be absurd to suggest that Shakespeare pictured the age of Richard II after the fashion of a modern historian. But there are signs elsewhere in Shakespeare of at least a feeling for historical verity; and there are special reasons why the age of Richard II should have struck the imaginations of the Elizabethans.

[Here Tillyard argues Shakespeare was influenced by the fifteenth-century chronicle writer Froissart's emphasis on ceremony and heraldry. '*Richard II*', he writes, 'may be his intuitive rendering of Froissart's medievalism'.]

But there were other reasons why the reign of Richard II should be notable. A.B. Steel, his most recent historian, begins his study by noting that Richard was the last king of the old medieval order:

the last king ruling by hereditary right, directed and undisputed, from the Conqueror. The kings of the next hundred and ten years . . . were essentially kings *de facto* not *de jure*, successful usurpers recognised after the event, upon conditions, by their fellow-magnates or by parliament.

Shakespeare, deeply interested in titles as he had showed himself to be in his early History Plays, must have known this very well; and Gaunt's famous speech on England cannot be fully understood without this knowledge. He calls England

This nurse, this teeming womb of royal kings,
Fear'd by their breed and famous by their birth,
Renowned for their deeds as far from home,
For Christian service and true chivalry,
As is the sepulchre in stubborn Jewry
Of the world's ransom, blessed Mary's son.

113

Richard was no crusader, but he was authentic heir of the crusading Plantagenets.... Richard ... had the full sanctity of medieval kingship and the strong pathos of being the last king to possess it. Shakespeare probably realized that however powerful the Tudors were and however undisputed their hold over their country's church, they had not the same sanctity as the medieval kings. He was therefore ready to draw from certain French treatises, anti-Lancastrian in tone, that made Richard a martyr and compared him to Christ and his accusers to so many Pilates giving him over to the wishes of the London mob. Shakespeare's Richard says at his deposition:

> Though some of you with Pilate wash your hands,
> Showing an outward pity; yet you Pilates
> Have here deliver'd me to my sour cross,
> And water cannot wash away your sin.

Holy and virtuous as the Earl of Richmond is in *Richard III*, he does not pretend to the same kingly sanctity as Richard II. Such sanctity belongs to a more antique, more exotically ritual world; and Shakespeare composed his play accordingly. . . .

[Here Tillyard suggests the play has a style in common with medieval art and illumination.]

The case for the essential medievalism of *Richard II* is even stronger when it is seen that the conspirators, working as such, do not share the ceremonial style used to represent Richard and his court. Once again the usual explanation of such a contrast is too narrow. It has been the habit to contrast the 'poetry' of Richard with the practical common sense of Bolingbroke. But the 'poetry' of Richard is all part of a world of gorgeous tournaments, conventionally mournful queens, and impossibly sententious gardeners, while Bolingbroke's common sense extends to his backers, in particular to that most important character, Northumberland. We have in fact the contrast not only of two characters but of two ways of life.

One example of the two different ways of life has occurred already: in the contrast noted between the mannered pleading of the Duchess of York for Aumerle's life and Henry's vigorous resolve immediately after to punish the conspirators. The Duchess and her family belong to the old order where the means, the style, the embroidery matter more than what they further or express. Henry belongs to a new order, where action is quick and leads somewhere. But other examples are needed to back up what to many readers will doubtless seem a dangerous and forced theory of the play's significance. First, a new kind of vigour, the vigour of strong and swift action, enters the verse of the play at II.i.224, when, after Richard has seized Gaunt's property and announced his coming journey to Ireland, Northumberland, Ross, and Willoughby remain behind and hatch their conspiracy. . . . It is not for nothing that the next scene shows the Queen exchanging elegant conceits about her sorrow for Richard's absence with Bushy and Green. But the largest contrast comes at the beginning of the third act. It begins with a very fine speech of Bolingbroke recounting to Bushy and Green all their crimes, before they are executed. It has the full accent of the world of action, where people want to get things and are roused to passion in their attempts: . . . The scene is followed by Richard's landing in Wales, his pitiful inability to act, and his wonderful self-dramatization. As a play of externals, as an exaltation of means over ends (here carried to a frivolous excess), it is wonderful; yet it contains lines that for the weight of unaffected passion come near Bolingbroke's single fine line,

Eating the bitter bread of banishment.

The world for which Bolingbroke stands, though it is a usurping world, displays a greater sincerity of personal emotion.

Thus *Richard II*, although reputed so simple and homogeneous a play, is built on a contrast. The world of medieval refinement is indeed the main object of presentation but it is threatened and in the end superseded by the more familiar world of the present. . . .

It must not be thought, because Shakespeare treated history, as described above, in a way new to him that he has lost interest in his old themes. On the contrary he is interested as much as ever in the theme of civil war, in the kingly type, and in the general fortunes of England. And I will say a little on each of these before trying to sum up the play's meaning in the tetralogy to which it belongs.

Richard II does its work in proclaiming the great theme of the whole cycle of Shakespeare's History Plays: the beginning in prosperity, the distortion of prosperity by a crime, civil war, and ultimate renewal of prosperity. The last stage falls outside the play's scope, but the second scene with the Duchess of Gloucester's enumeration of Edward III's seven sons, her account of Gloucester's death, and her call for vengeance is a worthy exordium of the whole cycle. The speeches of the Bishop of Carlisle and of Richard to Northumberland [in IV.i] . . . are worthy statements of the disorder that follows the deposition of the rightful king. In doctrine the play is entirely orthodox. Shakespeare knows that Richard's crimes never amounted to tyranny and hence that outright rebellion against him was a crime. He leaves uncertain the question of who murdered Woodstock and never says that Richard was personally responsible. The king's uncles hold perfectly correct opinions. Gaunt refuses the Duchess of Gloucester's request for vengeance, the matter being for God's decision alone. Even on his deathbed, when lamenting the state of the realm and calling Richard the landlord and not the king of England, he never preaches rebellion. And he mentions deposition only in the sense that Richard by his own conduct is deposing himself. York utters the most correct sentiments . . . supporting the existing government. And though he changes allegiance he is never for rebellion. As stated above, the gardener was against the deposition of Richard.

As well as being a study of medievalism, Richard takes his place among Shakespeare's many studies of the kingly nature. He is a king by unquestioned title and by his external graces alone. But others have written so well on Richard's character that I need say no more.

Lastly, for political motives, there is the old Morality theme of Respublica. One of Shakespeare's debts in *Richard II* is to *Woodstock* and this play is constructed very plainly on the Morality pattern, with the king's three uncles led by Woodstock inducing him to virtue, and Tressilian Bushy and Green to vice. There are traces of this motive in Shakespeare's play, but with Woodstock dead before the action begins and Gaunt dying early in it the balance of good and evil influences is destroyed. Bushy, Green, and Bagot, however, remain very plainly Morality figures and were probably marked in some way by their dress as abstract vices. Once again, as in the earlier tetralogy, England herself, and not the protagonist, is the main concern. Gaunt speaks her praises, the gardener in describing his own symbolic garden has her in mind. As part of the great cycle of English history covered by Hall's chronicle the events of the reign of Richard II take their proper place. But here something fresh has happened. The early tetralogy had as its concern the fortunes of England in that exciting and instructive stretch of her history. *Richard II* has this concern too, but it also deals with England herself, the nature and not merely the fortunes of England. In *Richard II* it is the old brilliant medieval England of the last Plantagenet in the authentic succession; in *Henry IV* it will be the England not of the Middle Ages but of Shakespeare himself. We can now see how the epic comes in and how *Richard II* contributes to an epic effect. Those works which we honour by the epic title always, among other things, express the feelings or the habits of a large group of men, often of a nation.

Of this great new epic attempt *Richard II* is only the prelude. What of England it pictures is not only antique but partial: the confined world of a medieval courtly class. In his next play Shakespeare was to picture (with much else) the whole land, as he knew it, in his own day, with its multifarious layers of society and manners of living.[8] ☐

Tillyard's discussion of *Richard II* centres on the play's formality as a sign of the medieval world Shakespeare was creating. Richard was 'the last king of the old medieval order'; his 'poetry' is part of this world and its ceremony. Such ceremony is set against 'the more familiar world of the present', represented by Bolingbroke and his followers. In addition, Tillyard argues, *Richard II* proclaims 'the great theme' of the histories – the curse that overtook England following Richard's illegal deposition leading to the Wars of the Roses. To this extent it is also a study of kingship.

Tillyard sees *Richard II* in terms of a portrait of the medieval world, an illuminated manuscript, but also as a piece of orthodox doctrine. Graham Holderness, the most thorough of the modern writers on the history plays, suggests that Tillyard's study seeks to establish a kind of link back to the Elizabethans almost without reference to any intervening cultural events. It is, Holderness contends, a piece of deeply conservative scholarship but also sentimental in its idea of the Elizabethan well-ordered state. For Holderness, Tillyard sets out to establish, and deliver us back into, an organic, immutable society like Shakespeare's.[9] This is seen at the end of the extract above where Tillyard talks about the theme of England, as if to bring that theme once again to prominence in the 1940s.

III: John Dover Wilson and Lily B. Campbell

Holderness's critique of Tillyard is too long to quote, but it is in itself evidence of Tillyard's centrality to the critical argument about the history plays. Tillyard, however, was not an isolated voice, and his name is often used as a kind of shorthand, as Holderness says, for a whole school of historicist criticism which sees literature as a reflection of historical events or even as historical documents.[10] That, in turn, becomes a kind of shorthand that obliterates differences between critics. Tillyard had, in fact, been anticipated to some extent by Dover Wilson in his Cambridge edition of the play in 1939, though with a different emphasis. Dover Wilson takes up various issues that Tillyard was to ignore – the Essex rebellion, Coleridge's criticism, Richard's tragedy – and produces a different reading of the text. It is a reading that is much more centrally engaged than Tillyard's with the previous debate about the play, and in some ways is more acute and informative:

From John Dover Wilson, 'Introduction' to *Richard II* (1939)

■ To the contemporaries of Shakespeare Richard was no ordinary man; and it is by failing to realize this that modern criticism, despite all its penetrating, and for the most part just, analysis of his human qualities, leaves every thoughtful reader and spectator of the drama baffled and dissatisfied. Richard was a king, and a good deal more. First of all he stood in the eyes of the later middle ages as the type and exemplar of royal martyrdom; of a king not slain in battle, not defeated and killed by a foreign adversary, not even deposed owing to weakness or tyranny in favour of his heir, but thrust from the throne in his May of youth by a mere usurper, under colour of a process at law, utterly illegal, and then foully murdered. . . .

. . . [T]he fall of Richard fascinated the late medieval and Elizabethan world as much by its magnitude and its unaccountableness as by its pathos and the sacrilege that brought it to pass.

> Down, down I come, like glist'ring Phaethon:
> Wanting the manage of unruly jades,

are words which Shakespeare places in his mouth, and some critics have taken them as the keynote of the play. But though in their sun-imagery they express the splendour of the catastrophe . . . they do not touch its mystery, of which all at that period who studied the young king's career were conscious, and which is one of the main impressions that Shakespeare's play still leaves upon our minds. This mystery was closely associated with the supposed workings of Fortune, a Roman deity which continued to exercise under Providence a potent influence over men's thought during the middle ages, and was conceived of by Elizabethan England far more concretely than by the England of our own day, despite its daily race-meetings, its football pools and its almost universal habit of gambling. The symbol and attribute of Fortune was, of course, her wheel, which is hardly ever absent from any of the countless pictures and references to her in medieval art and literature. Shakespeare makes no mention of the wheel in *Richard II*, though he employs the less familiar figure of Fortune's buckets in the deposition scene.

His reticence, however, is part of his subtlety. For the wheel is constantly in his mind throughout the play. Indeed, it determines the play's shape and structure, which gives us a complete inversion. The first act begins immediately after the death of the Duke of Gloucester, when, as Froissart notes, Richard was 'hygh upon the whele' and exhibiting all the hubris and tyranny expected of persons in that position, while, at the same time, his opponent, Bolingbroke, is down at the lowest point of his fortune, at the bottom. But from the beginning of Act II the wheel begins to turn mysteriously of itself, or rather by the action of Fortune. The will of the King seems paralysed; he becomes an almost passive agent, Bolingbroke acts, and acts forcibly; yet he too appears to be borne upward by a power beyond his volition.

This last is an important point, since it rules out those indications of deep design which some subtle critics, following Coleridge, think they discover in the character of the usurper from the very beginning, but which I feel sure were not intended by Shakespeare. Circumstance drives Bolingbroke on from point to point: he takes what Fortune and Richard throw in his path. The attitude of the nobles toward him in II.iii shows that they regard him as a claimant to the throne, and by that time the larger horizon has begun to open out before him. But this is quite a different thing from entertaining deep designs. Bolingbroke is an opportunist, not a schemer. . . .

The second great attraction, then, of the story of Richard of Bordeaux and Henry, Duke of Lancaster, for the men of the fifteenth and sixteenth centuries was that it afforded, in its spectacle of the 'dejecting of the one and advancing of the other', a perfect example of the mysterious action of Fortune, working of course under the inscrutable 'providence of God', according to the quasi-mechanical symbolism under which they conceived that action. And this in turn constituted one of the main appeals of *Richard II* for the spectators who first witnessed it. For, though the operations of Fortune were most evident and potent in the lives of the great, everything human was subject to them. It is a point which did not escape Pater, who has seen so much in this play. 'His grief', he writes of Richard, 'becomes nothing less than a central expression of all that in the revolutions of Fortune's wheel goes *down* in the world.' Shakespeare's play was a mirror, not only for magistrates, but for every son of woman; and when on Shakespeare's stage the 'dejected' king gazed into the glass – incomparable symbol for that age! – what he saw there was the brittleness both of his own glory and of all earthly happiness.

In the third place, the reign of Richard II possessed a peculiar significance in the history of England, as the Elizabethans understood that history. In itself, and for the two protagonists who brought it to an end, a striking example of a turn of Fortune's wheel, it marked the beginning of a much greater revolution in the story of the nation's fortunes. Shakespeare and his contemporaries, rejoicing in the Tudor peace and looking back with horror to the period of civil strife, known as the Wars of the Roses, which preceded the accession of Henry VII, were haunted by fears of a return of such anarchy, and found its origin in the events of the last few years of Richard II's reign. And rightly so; for the deposition and murder of Richard not only shocked the conscience of Christendom, they struck at the legal basis of the monarchical, that is to say the whole constitutional system of England. . . .

———

But while Elizabeth lived, the older anxieties governed men's thoughts and in their fears that her reign might be the prelude to yet another period of anarchy, they naturally bent eagerly enquiring eyes upon the events of the reign of Richard II which had led up to the earlier period of trouble and particularly upon the actions of the usurper Henry IV, . . .

The most remarkable of all occurrences, however, connecting the fortunes of Elizabeth and Essex with those of Richard and his rival was the performance at the Globe theatre, by the express wish of the Earl's supporters, who added an honorarium to their other persuasions, of a play, *Richard II*, generally assumed to be Shakespeare's, on the eve of the attempted rebellion, which took place on 8 February 1601, and came . . . utterly to grief. The transaction at the Globe was discussed at length in the trial that followed; but Shakespeare was not among the Globe players brought to book, and there is no evidence that he and his company suffered in any way for their part therein. On the contrary, they are found playing at Court before the Queen on the day preceding Essex's execution. . . .

———

Whatever, then, Shakespeare's personal attitude toward Essex may have been, the association of his *Richard II* with the Earl's schemes was an accidental one, and has no relevance either to the purpose of the dramatist or to our understanding of the play. The play is, nevertheless, steeped in Elizabethan political notions, and unless we grasp them we are likely to miss much that the author intended us to perceive. Not that he was attempting anything in the nature of a political argument. On the contrary, the political situation he dealt with was merely the material for drama. He takes sides neither with Richard nor with Bolingbroke; he exhibits without concealment the weakness of the King's character, but he spares no pains to evoke our wholehearted pity for him in his fall. Indeed, it is partly because it succeeds in holding the balance so even that *Richard II* is a favourite play with historians. It develops the political issue in all its complexity, and leaves judgment upon it to the spectator. Shakespeare's only prejudices are a patriotic assertion of the paramount interests of England above those of king or subject, an assertion which, following a hint in Froissart, he places upon the lips of the dying John of Gaunt, and a quasi-religious belief in the sanctity of an anointed monarch; and it is part of his dramatic setting that these two prejudices or ideals are irreconcilable under the historical circumstances with which the play deals. . . .

And yet, if we follow Coleridge and most modern critics in isolating the figure of Richard from the dramatic composition of which it is only a part, and ignoring the political prepossessions of the audience for whom the play was written, we miss much, perhaps most, that Shakespeare intended. For his Richard, as often happens with his characters for one reason or another, is to be viewed on a double plane of vision: at once realistically as a man, and symbolically as the royal martyr whose blood, spilt by the usurper, cries out for the vengeance which tears England asunder for two generations. Looked at merely from within the framework of the play of which he is the central figure, he seems the rather contemptible person that Coleridge has depicted; seen in the secular perspective of the whole cycle, his personal failings . . . [and] tragedy become the occasion of something much larger than himself, the deposition and death of the Lord's anointed. For that break in the lineal succession of God's deputies elect meant the beginning of political chaos.

> Take but degree away, untune that string,
> And hark what discord follows!

is the moral of Shakespeare's series of English chronicles as of everything else he wrote that touches political issues.

And what is true of Richard is true also of the lesser characters in the play. The prophetic voice of Gaunt, for example, pronounces judgment not only upon the spendthrift King, whose deposition it foretells, but also by implication upon Bolingbroke, the son who lifts

> An angry arm against God's minister,

and becomes the sacrilegious instrument of his deposition. As I have said above, Bolingbroke is not rightly understood until he is regarded as in part at least the puppet of Fortune. And, successful as he is in *Richard II*, we feel even here that he has been caught up into the tragic net by usurpation, so that it is with no surprise we find him at the beginning of the sequel not only renewing his vow to go on a crusade in expiation of his guilt, but pronouncing himself 'shaken' and 'wan with care'. Indeed, the whole play is as full of foreboding as it is of patriotic sentiment. Civil war is already implicit in the strife between Bolingbroke and Mowbray, with which it opens, and in the wrangling of the nobles before Richard's deposition, while it is explicit in the prophecy of the Bishop of Carlisle (IV.i.129–49) and in the scarcely less significant words of Richard to Northumberland at V.i.55–68. Thus when Richard's tragedy is ended, we are left with the feeling that England's has only just begun.[11] □

Dover Wilson picks up on the tensions of *Richard II*, specifically its powerful use of the ideas of Fortune's wheel and prophecy as governing events. He also develops the idea of Richard as at once man and martyr in the play, so suggesting a double perspective on the action as both a personal and political tragedy. That tragedy includes Bolingbroke whom Dover Wilson sees as a puppet of Fortune, 'borne upward by a power beyond his volition'. In other words, unlike the majority of critics Dover Wilson argues that Bolingbroke does not have 'deep designs' on the crown but rather, like Richard, is 'caught up' in events that will lead to yet greater disaster for England.

Two years after Tillyard's book another influential study appeared, *Shakespeare's Histories* (1947) by Lily B. Campbell. The book confirmed the post-war direction of the study of the histories towards their contemporary significance. Campbell is more concerned with the *Henry VI* plays than the second tetralogy, and in the extract that follows I have highlighted just the outline of her argument – that *Richard II* explores the problem of deposition in a context of concern about Elizabeth and the succession.

From Lily B. Campbell, *Shakespeare's Histories* (1947)

■ Shakespeare's intentions can only be discussed after consideration of his play, which, as I have said earlier, opens exactly where Halle began his introduction into the troubles of the houses of Lancaster and York, with the quarrel between Bolingbroke and Mowbray. It is a proper scene to introduce a play of kingship, for, to the sixteenth century, above all else a king was an administrator of justice, acting as God's deputy. And it is as God's justicer that Richard first appears. Shakespeare has given us the measuring rod of Richard's own conception of his office by which to judge how far short he fails of his ideals. The charges and counter-charges which are hurled between the two dukes are very like those heard more than once at Elizabeth's court, but they derived from Holinshed. . . .

In the minds of many Elizabethans the blood of Mary Stuart cried from the ground against Elizabeth as did that of Thomas of Woodstock against Richard II, . . . But to any who would avenge the royal blood spilled by the king, Shakespeare has Gaunt give the answer that every loyal subject of Elizabeth gave to those who would avenge the death of Mary, 'God's is the quarrel'.

After this scene [Act I scene ii], which does not further the action, and which can have been introduced only to restate the Tudor theory of kingship, we return to Richard as the agent of justice in the quarrel between Bolingbroke and Mowbray. . . .

[Here Campbell analyses the play's action.]

. . . From the beginning of her reign the charge most often brought against Elizabeth . . . was that she was swayed by favourites. But like Gaunt and York and Gloucester, . . . who thought themselves true advisers and branded any whom the king preferred as favourites, all those to whom Elizabeth would not listen denounced those to whom they thought she was listening too much. Leicester, the accused of all accusers, thought himself in danger from the false reports that were whispered in the queen's ear by those whom she unjustly favoured. Essex, the most spoiled young man at court, directed his rebellion, he said, only to rescuing the queen from such men as Raleigh and Cobham whom she was favouring.

As to the second charge, Elizabeth too was censured for spilling the royal blood in permitting Mary Stuart to die, and there were many who thought she pointed the way to her own destruction thereby, . . .

The third charge as well was made against Elizabeth, that she leased out her kingdom. Such favourites as Leicester and Essex became rich through her grants of lands and special privileges, the farm of sweet wines to Essex, for instance. . . .

These are the three sins which represent the antecedent action of the play of *Richard II*; they are the sins which posed the question repeatedly asked, whether Richard II were justly deposed – or no. But they are also the sins which were brought up time after time when the fate of Richard II was pointed out to Elizabeth as a warning. The question as to whether Richard II deserved to be deposed might have remained an academic question, however, had he not in his folly committed a new sin, which brought about his destruction [the taking of Gaunt's lands]. . . .

In his play of *Richard II* Shakespeare thus offered the follies of Richard II only as a background for the presentation of the problem that was so often discussed during Elizabeth's reign, the problem of the deposition of a king. That problem received its most disturbing treatment in Parsons' *Conference about the Next Succession to the Crowne of Ingland*, published in 1594, and Parsons was concerned to justify the deposition of Richard II and the accession of Henry IV. It seemed dangerous to Elizabeth's friends and the supporters of her government because it was sent forth in a time of discontent, when charges were being bandied about that were reminiscent of those presented as charges against Richard II. About this time Shakespeare wrote a play of Richard II which showed the deposition and murder of the king. It seems to me most natural that he should do so, for the question was uppermost in men's minds. In the play Shakespeare reiterated the charges against Richard that had been so often laid at Queen Elizabeth's door. He adjudged Richard guilty of sinful folly, but Gaunt and Richard himself and Carlisle, all the sympathetic characters, insist that 'God's is the quarrel', that a subject may not give sentence on his king. Furthermore, the picture of Henry IV at the end of the play as a king whose soul is full of woe is scarcely conducive to the encouragement of would-be usurpers.

Yet the fact remains that a play on the same subject, probably Shakespeare's, was played on the eve of Essex's rebellion at the request of the conspirators. Perhaps the young Percies and their friends only recognized that there was a deposition in it, proving that such things could be. But it is also true that a book of Hayward's which told the same story was under suspicion at the same time, though the author later said he wrote it always with the interest of the true heir, King James, in mind. I do not know the answer to the riddle, though it is quite clear that Elizabeth's enemies compared her to Richard II, and that Essex's enemies compared him to Henry IV.

What seems to me more important than personalities that may or may not be involved is that Shakespeare here set forth a political problem that was engaging the interest of the nation, and that he set it forth fairly. He did not ask whether a good king might be deposed, but whether a king might be deposed for any cause. He used Richard II as the accepted pattern of a deposed king, but he used his pattern to set forth the political ethics of the Tudors in regard to the rights and duties of a king. It might equally well have served as a warning to Elizabeth and to any who desired to usurp her throne. The way of the transgressing king was shown to be hard, but no happiness was promised to the one who tried to execute God's vengeance or to depose the deputy elected by the Lord.[12] □

Like Dover Wilson, Campbell sees the ambivalence of the play but also its possible links with Elizabeth's situation and the question of Mary Stuart's death. What Campbell adds to this is a discussion of the significance of kingship in the play and in the Renaissance. The king, she notes, is or should be a figure of justice, God's deputy on earth. Out of this arises the central political crisis of the play: how to depose lawfully a king who has broken the law but who, in theory at least, embodies that law. Campbell's reading thus takes the historical and political analysis of the play on a stage further, connecting it with both contemporary events and contemporary arguments about the law and the monarch.

Campbell's book, together with those of Tillyard and Wilson, represents the standard approach to Shakespeare's history plays and to *Richard II*. It is an approach that most readers have probably come across in some form or other. Most readers, that is, will have come across the assumption that Shakespeare's plays value order and kingship; that the histories endorse the official Tudor view of history in which the deposition of Richard led to England being cursed and punished by violent civil strife; and that the curse was only expiated with the coming of Henry Tudor, Elizabeth I's grandfather. It is also possible that most readers might share these assumptions simply because they have been presented as the standard approach in, for example, introductions to the play, and as the informing thesis in, for example, amateur productions. This standard approach, however, is not the only approach. Indeed, in many ways it is now outdated. The rest of this book sets out the challenges to Tillyard, both by New Criticism and by more recent criticism, and discusses some of the new readings of *Richard II* that inform the current debate about the play.

CHAPTER SIX

New Criticism

Introduction

THIS CHAPTER considers the New Critics, although the label is not a very exact one. It is used to refer to critics writing after 1950 through to 1970, practising a form of close reading that pays little attention to history or politics. The quest of New Criticism is the text itself, the words on the page. New Criticism starts with the idea that the meaning of a text is not to be found in the author's intention but in analysis of its language.[1] The previous chapter looked at the criticism of E.M.W. Tillyard, Dover Wilson and Lily B. Campbell. In critical terms, these can all be classified as historicist critics: that is to say, their approach is to contextualise the play in its contemporary history and read it as a reflection of history. Although they reach different conclusions about the play's meaning, what they share is a set of values and ideas about criticism. Underlying their approach is the idea that the author's intention can be located by considering the history of the period. They are, in this sense, intentionalist critics. New Criticism, which developed around the same time as Tillyard was writing, rejects much of this framework, especially the notion that what concerns us is the author's intention. What New Criticism favours is an approach that seeks to unravel the text, especially its systems of opposites (such as appearance and reality) while affirming its innate unity.

New Criticism, by and large, claims to be non-political, but in fact it does represent a political stance. Its values are those of liberal humanism: that is, it believes human nature remains the same and that the key political values are freedom and autonomy.[2] But this is not immediately obvious, as the approach of New Critics is formalist: that is, they concern themselves with how the unity of the text is achieved. Generally the New Critics focus on formal features of works, especially imagery. Particular attention is then paid to the complexity of the text, to the ambiguities, tensions and paradoxes achieved in its language and structure. Almost inevitably, however, as we will see with the extracts on *Richard II* below, this kind of close attention to the complexities of the language leads to a reconsideration of the text's content and, indeed, its history and politics.

In terms of *Richard II*, New Criticism produced articles dealing with nearly every aspect of the play: the themes of kingship, time, rebellion, acting; the genre of the play as history and tragedy; Bolingbroke's motives and behaviour; the garden imagery of the play; the play as a tragedy in which Richard is unsuited for the role of king by his nature or by being a player-king; the question of Richard's claim to divine kingship, and the play's Christian symbolism. In addition, New Criticism could not avoid being pulled back to a discussion of the political significance of *Richard II*. The impetus was to focus on form, but time and time again this led to questions that extended beyond considerations of form. One reason for this is that this new generation of critics had to work out how they stood in relation to the massively influential views of E. M. W. Tillyard.

I: Challenges to Tillyard

There were several different kinds of challenge to Tillyard's reading of the histories by New Criticism. The quirkiest is that of A. P. Rossiter, whose book *Angel with Horns* (1961) was much admired for its attack on accepted ways of thinking. His analysis of *Richard II* is concerned with what he sees as the larger process of 'retributive reaction' in the pattern of events: 'Richard is *wrong*, but Bolingbroke's coronation is *not right*'. This leads Rossiter to argue that history in the history plays is apprehended as an 'obscure tragedy in which men are compelled, constrained, baffled and bent by circumstances'.[3] Where Tillyard, then, had seen a clear moral and historical pattern in the text, Rossiter proposes an altogether more ambiguous set of meanings for the play.

A more direct challenge to Tillyard came from Robert Ornstein's book *A Kingdom for a Stage* (1972). Its central thesis is that the histories are not, as Tillyard suggested, about the Tudor myth but about rebellion. *Richard II* does not, Ornstein contends, present an ideal medieval world under Richard; nor does the play 'declare the universality of cosmic harmony; it speaks instead of the universality of contention and change'. More importantly, Richard is guilty of 'the lawlessness which medieval and Renaissance theorists defined as tyranny' and which justified rebellion.[4] Tillyard had simply denied Richard's crimes amounted to tyranny, but Ornstein suggests the question of Richard's actions cannot be dismissed so easily.

Both Rossiter and Ornstein suggest that *Richard II* is a more ambiguous, and more politically ambivalent, play than Tillyard had allowed for. A similar point is made by Norman Rabkin, another critic who took issue with Tillyard. Rabkin's argument, an extract from which appears below, is that *Richard II* sets out an irresolvable problem of rule and that this is evident in the play's structure.

From Norman Rabkin, *Shakespeare and the Common Understanding* (1967)

■ It is a truism in certain schools that Shakespeare's plays are the defining embodiment of Elizabethan ideals of order and degree, the Tudor myth of the polity as beehive and history as the working out of a providence that sanctions kings as divine agents and condemns regicide or anything that might lead in its direction as sacrilege. For this view, promulgated with eloquence, learning, and insight by E. M. W. Tillyard and others, there is much to be said, and innumerable passages and incidents from the plays leap to mind in support of it. There can be no doubt that with the possible exception of Dante no great western writer has so dearly loved the ideal of hierarchical social order as Shakespeare, whose vision of it helped England through its severest trials in the twentieth century and has given to English-speaking peoples a local habitation and a name for much that we hope for in the state. On the other hand, many readers have realized for a long time that this reading of Shakespeare's politics is too simple. One need not go so far as Jan Kott, who sees the history plays as embodying 'the image of the Grand Mechanism', an image in which the precepts of Machiavelli and the blind movement of the wheel of fortune are fused to reflect a cruel and meaningless process in which only power counts, to recognize that against ideal and wishful dramatic images of Tudor political ideals Shakespeare poses a powerful sense of *Realpolitik*. In politics as in everything else Shakespeare incites contradictory readings. . . .

As always, the problem shapes the structure of the play. The question that *Richard II* poses is the question of what to do about a king whose continuance on the throne is essential to the continued order of a state governed by hereditary monarchy, but who is manifestly unfit personally for what is required of him. Shakespeare plunges us immediately into the problem by setting it up in the opening scene in a debate – its circumstances and issues veiled both because they are too dangerous even to be discussed in public in the play's fictional world and because they are familiar to an audience which knows the history and has recently seen it performed on the stage. Richard has secretly employed Thomas Mowbray, Duke of Norfolk, to murder the Duke of Gloucester, uncle to the King and possibly dangerous to his control of England; and Richard's cousin Henry Bolingbroke, obviously unable to suggest the King's complicity even if he is aware of it, has challenged Richard's position by attempting to expose Mowbray. . . .

The problem is explicitly stated, and one traditional answer to it given, by John of Gaunt, Duke of Lancaster and father to Bolingbroke, as he responds to the plea of his widowed sister-in-law that he avenge the crime:

> God's is the quarrel; for God's substitute,
> His deputy anointed in His sight,
> Hath caused his death: the which if wrongfully,
> Let heaven revenge; for I may never lift
> An angry arm against His minister.   (I.ii.37–41)

In a sense Gaunt shares the view of Mowbray, who is not presented as a blackguard, yet has served the wishes of a monarch who felt the murder necessary to uphold his own position as king. If the unthreatened rule of the King is the principle of the state's survival, there may be some justification for what he has caused to be done. At any rate, to take arms against God's minister is to Gaunt an even more egregious crime than Richard's. And if history is providentially governed, then to oppose its course is sacrilegious. What happens in history is what heaven wants.

An obvious answer to Gaunt's position underlies all the action; ironically Shakespeare puts it into advice delivered to Richard himself as in the deposition scene the King helplessly falls back on the idea that God controls history and will protect his minister: 'Fear not,' the Bishop of Carlisle instructs the King, now mournfully yielding to passive anticipation of impending disaster;

> Fear not, my Lord: that Power that made you king
> Hath power to keep you king in spite of all.
> The means that heaven yields must be embraced,
> And not neglected; else if heaven would,
> And we will not, heaven's offer we refuse. (III.ii.27–32)

And Aumerle, son of the Duke of York and loyal to Richard, immediately translates Carlisle's meditative statement into practical power politics: Bolingbroke is growing strong while we hold ourselves back. Richard's advisors, then, share Gaunt's belief in providence's stake in history, but they oppose to his and Richard's passive fatalism, the notion that providence depends on the actions it makes available to individuals who know how to use power.

To their advice Richard responds with a deeply felt statement of his belief that heaven will take care of him:

Not all the water in the rough rude sea
Can wash the balm off from an anointed king;
The breath of worldly men cannot depose
The deputy elected by the Lord.   (54–57)

The statement is clearly presumptuous and ultimately wrong in terms of the plot, yet difficult to refute, since Bolingbroke and England will have to pay dearly for what happens to prove it wrong. No matter how much Shakespeare makes us understand that Richard is here whistling in the dark, playing at being kingly instead of defending his threatened crown, he will not allow us to think of the problem entirely in terms of power politics. Again, simply on the level of plot, the play's world reacts precisely as Richard believes it will to the deposition of a king whose legitimacy is a matter as much of religion as of politics. At the moment that Richard officially yields all to Bolingbroke, the same Bishop of Carlisle pronounces a curse against those who strike out against 'the figure of God's majesty, / His captain, steward, deputy-elect, / Anointed, crowned, planted many years' (IV.i.125–127) and predicts, as Richard will do shortly again (V.i.55–68) in language which his successor will ruefully remember later (*II Henry IV*, III.i.67–79), the bloody civil wars that all the audience is fully aware of. If Richard argues in surrendering his throne that 'With mine own tears I wash away my balm' (IV.i.207), we know that he cannot. Divinity does seem to hedge the seat of royal power and to punish those who oppose it with power no matter for how good a reason. Yet it allows Richard himself to be destroyed; and to make the paradox even more unsettling, providence will, in the fullness of time, place on the throne a son of the usurping Bolingbroke who will save England from its enemies, within and without, as the sacrilegiously deposed Richard could not.

Thus Gaunt's 'God's is the quarrel' states the question of the play and the tetralogy but does not answer it. The question is inevitable in a state whose political stability is defined in the light of a benevolent providence that places absolute sanctions on the power of fallible rulers. It is no wonder that, given such postulates, historiography and political theory should find themselves caught in almost insuperable contradictions and conflicts in the age that most explicitly defines the royal prerogatives and puts them to the test; the problem is built into the European idea of kingship . . . men are simply incapable of creating the kind of political stability that the Tudor myth envisions. . . . [L]ike Israel, England discovers that the new and benign order brought about by the creation of monarchical stability has legitimized in the process of its creation a kind of permanent challenge to the crown that will ultimately destroy kingship itself.

This is the insoluble problem of history as the chronicle plays make us see it. Shakespeare poses it brilliantly in little in the scene (III.iv) in which the gardeners, employing a familiar analogy, discuss the state as garden and Richard II as incompetent caretaker. The well-tended garden, in which natural process properly controlled brings forth flower and fruit in their appointed season and the community of the whole lives in wholesome balance, is the ideal to which we must contrast the disorder and disease rampant in the England of *Richard II*, and with its appeal to nature the analogy conveys the Elizabethan sense that the well-ordered polity is both a reflection of cosmic order and the product of a benevolent providence. But the ideal is only an ideal; the terms of the analogy do not provide adequate guidelines for translating it into statecraft. Reproaching Richard for not having acted as a king should, the gardeners suggest only that he should have been more autocratic. Through the myth of the garden Shakespeare suggests the King's providential function, his sacred place in the natural order, and the inevitable ruin of those who attack it, but he does not allow us to share Gaunt's momentary and Richard's perennial sense that with the aid of providence the garden will somehow take care of itself as long as the King retains his power. The problem of *Richard II* is the problem of England; it is not accidental that the most moving hymn to England ever composed occurs here in the passionate words of the dying Gaunt. Shakespeare does not solve the problem – only history and a new set of assumptions unimaginable in the sixteenth century were to do that; rather, he understands it as few of his contemporaries did, and he makes us fully and painfully aware of it. . . .

I have indicated that the ambivalence of *Richard II* is built into its structure. But that structure, even as I have thus far described it, depends entirely on character, for our response to the politics of the play is a response not to theory but to the men whose lives and actions make theory necessary in the world. Bolingbroke's situation as Shakespeare dramatizes it almost necessitates an ambivalent response, but it is his character that makes it difficult for us to reach conclusions about him easily. At once patriotic and ambitious, manly and ruthless, he is above always mysterious. . . .

The presentation of Richard is similarly ambiguous, but as the play's tragic centre he is a far more complex character, and the extremes of our response to him are farther apart. Where Bolingbroke is adequately competent and strong, Richard is appallingly incompetent. Where Bolingbroke earns our rational admiration and at times our moral approval, Richard commands our deepest emotions. It is a notorious fact that productions of *Richard II* which stress the King's faults while playing down his virtues make the play fail; for the real power of this historical tragedy lies in its ability to elicit our increasing sympathies for the King whose fall we recognize as inevitable and even desirable.[5] □

In many ways Rabkin sums up the objections of New Criticism to Tillyard's thesis: that his reading of Shakespeare was too political and took little account of the play's complexities. But New Criticism also objected to Tillyard's historical method, which suggested that *Richard II* means what Elizabethans thought it might mean rather than what the text tells us. Rabkin illustrates the way in which New Criticism, rather than looking behind the play, explores the text itself in terms of its ambiguity and its effect on the reader.

II: New readings – M. M. Mahood

New Criticism, however, was not solely concerned with rebutting Tillyard's argument. One of the marks of New Criticism was, indeed, that it offered a new method of reading which led to some new ways of considering *Richard II*. One particular feature of New Criticism, as noted above, was a focus on imagery. An early post-war study of imagery in *Richard II* was Richard Altick's essay 'Symphonic Imagery in *Richard II*'.[6] This examined what Altick called iterative – repeated – images to show how they grow ever more complex and powerful as the action unfolds. The essay is an exhaustive account of the images of earth, blood, tears, speech and gardens. The only objection to the essay is that it works like a catalogue rather than as a dramatic analysis. This shortcoming is remedied in M. M. Mahood's widely praised essay 'Wordplay in *Richard II*', which examines the imagery in the context of an argument about how the play is about words and the power of language. In cutting the essay some of its fine points are lost, but its stylishness remains apparent (the italicisation of the text is Mahood's and serves to indicate the individual words she discusses in the essay):

From M.M. Mahood, *Shakespeare's Wordplay* (1957)

■ *Richard II* is a play about the efficacy of a king's words. Shakespeare here sets 'the word against the word': the words of a poet against the words of a politician. Richard is a poet, but not, of course, for the reason that as a character in a poetic drama he speaks verse which is magnificent in its imagery and cadence. If the whole play were in prose, he would still be a poet by virtue of his faith in words; his loss of this faith and his consequent self-discovery that for all the wordy flattery of others he is not agueproof, constitute Richard's tragedy. Bolingbroke, on the other hand, knows words have no inherent potency of meaning, but by strength of character and force of arms he is able to make them mean what he wants them to mean. The historical, as distinct from the tragic, action of the play lies in Bolingbroke's perilous contravention of the divine decree which made Richard king; and this historical action is not self-contained but belongs to the whole sequence of the mature Histories.

These two themes are supported and often impelled by the play's verbal ambiguities which nearly all have to do with language. The words most often played upon include *breath* in the meaning of 'respiration', 'life', 'time for breathing', 'utterance' and 'will expressed in words'; *title* in meanings ranging from 'legal right', through 'appellation of honour' to 'a label'; *name* either as a superficial labelling or as inherent reputation; *honour* in a range of meanings to be further developed when Falstaff answers his own question: 'What is honour? a word!'; *tongue* as the mere organ that makes sounds or as the whole complex organisation of a language; *sentence* meaning 'a unit of speech', 'judgment', 'an apophthegm' or 'significance'; and the word *word* itself, signifying on the one hand 'an element of speech' and on the other, 'contention', 'command', 'promise', 'apophthegm' or 'divine utterance'. The almost polar extremes of meaning in many of these words contribute to the rigid symmetry of the play's action, the descent of Richard and rise of Bolingbroke like buckets in a well. At the same time, the most delicate nuances of meaning between these extremes are used to give a poetic subtlety which can only be suggested here in a brief survey of the play's development.

Shakespeare uses his favourite device of a play-within-a-play at the very beginning of *Richard II*. As soon as the playhouse trumpet has sounded and the actors are entered Richard, with his own triple blast of resonant language, stages a miniature drama between Bolingbroke and Mowbray, which he promises himself shall be a good show:

> Then call them to our presence face to face,
> And frowning brow to brow our selves will heare,
> The accuser and the accused freely speake. (I.i.15–17)

The poet is never more a maker than when he enacts the very semblance of life in a play; and the poet Richard combines the work of producer and chief actor when he attempts to stage, by royal command, a drama of quarrel and reconciliation in which he himself will play the controlling part of *deus ex machina*. But Bolingbroke and Mowbray, for all the splendour of their rhetoric, are not content with words. . . .

The king has no wish to see Mowbray's guilt exposed by a trial of arms, and he attempts to end this scene of quarrel by his own trite epilogue on the theme of 'Forget, forgive'. But neither contestant will swallow his words. Mowbray's 'fair *name*' is more to him than an appellation: it is his reputation, the dearest part of him – 'Mine honour is my life, both grow in one.' Bolingbroke will not be *crestfallen*: unless he can prove his words in battle, he has no right to the armorial bearings which signify his nobility. The words of both are pitted against the king's words, and by force of character they carry the day. The king who was 'not borne to sue, but to commaund' must wait until the meeting at Coventry for his decree in Council to carry the authority which his own words lack. . . .

. . . But the King asserts the authority of his word in Council, the fight is called off and the champions banished the kingdom. At this point Mowbray, not an important character in the plot, is given a significant speech full of puns upon breath, sentence and tongue – words which shuttle back and forth to weave the elaborate verbal fabric of the play. In contrast to the 'golden uncontrould enfranchisment' promised by the contest, he now faces an enforced inactivity among people whose language he cannot speak. . . .

At Coventry, Gaunt protested that the King's words which should, in the nature of things, give life to their country, could deal only death; and at the beginning of Act II Gaunt himself dies, uttering with his last breath words which would be life to both King and kingdom if only Richard would heed them. We are made aware of the depth and weight of the language in this scene by the way Shakespeare has framed it between two pieces of dialogue in which words are identified with life: the opening quibbles on *breath* and *breathe*:

GAUNT Wil the King come that I may *breathe* my last?
In holsome counsell to his unstaied youth.
YORKE Vex not your selfe, nor striue not with your breath,
For all in vaine comes counsell to his eare.
GAUNT Oh but they say, the tongues of dying men,
Inforce attention like deepe harmony:
Where words are scarce they are seldome spent in vaine,
For they breathe truth that breathe their wordes in paine,

(II.i.1–8)

and the announcement of Gaunt's death:

NORTHUMBERLAND My liege, old Gaunt commends him to your Maiestie.
KING What saies he?
NORTHUMBERLAND Nay nothing, all is said :
His tongue is now a stringlesse instrument,
Words, life, and al, old Lancaster hath spent. (147–51)

The Sceptred Isle speech has a much richer meaning within this sharply-defined context than when it is extracted for a patriotic set piece, and it is worth seeing what are the elements that go to its composition. 'This earth of maiestie, this seate of Mars' fits in with the garden theme which is a *motif* of the play from its first hints in the opening scenes . . . to its full statement in Act III scene iv. Here garden is that of Eden symbolic of security ('this fortresse built by Nature') and of fertility ('this happy breede . . . this teeming wombe of royall Kings'). But we do not expect to find Mars in Eden; and this same line – 'This earth of maiestie, this seate of Mars' operates in another way by introducing a string of paradoxes and oxymora. *Earth* can be mere soil or the great globe itself, *seat* is any stool till Mars makes it a throne, *stone* would be any pebble if the restrictive adjective did not make it a jewel. The effect is of something which might appear without value but is in fact of untold value, and 'this *dear dear* land' sharpens the paradox: what is dear in the sense that it is loved cannot be dear in the sense that it is priced for sale. By this time a third element has been introduced: England's rulers are

> Renowned for theyr deeds as far from home,
> For christian seruice, and true chiualry,
> As is the sepulchre in stubburn Jewry,
> Of the worlds ransome blessed Maries sonne.   (53–6)

Gaunt may mean that some of England's kings have won fame fighting to regain Jerusalem, the kind of fame which his son will crave throughout his reign. But the grammatical ambiguity of the passage also yields the meaning that their virtues have made the English kings as famous as the sepulchre of Christ. Then, after the point at which most quotations end (short of a main verb), this King-Christ parallel, the garden-of-Paradise image and the paradoxes upon the theme of value are all brought together in a powerful climax :

> This land of such deare soules, this deere deere land,
> Deare for her reputation through the world,
> Is now leasde out; I dye pronouncing it,
> Like to a tenement or pelting Farme.   (57–60)

What is beyond all value has been valued and leased. The king, whose relation to his kingdom should be that of God to Paradise, who ought to 'regain the happy seat' has, instead of redeeming it (and here I suspect some Herbertish wordplay on the legal sense of *redemption*), jeopardised its security and fertility by farming it out. The God-King analogy is a real one to Gaunt who has already been shown, in the second scene of the play, to have such belief in the divine right of kings that he 'may neuer lift An angry arme against his minister'. Yet he knows how little there is of the godlike in Richard's nature, and his bitter awareness of this gap between the ideal and the actual passes to the audience and later conditions our response to Richard's 'dear earth' speech over the land he has farmed out, or to his identification of himself with the betrayed and condemned Christ at a further stage of the drama.

From the profound wordplay of this speech to Gaunt's quibbles on his own name may seem a sharp descent; but the 'Gaunt as a grave' puns have a force which the king acknowledges when he asks 'Can sicke men play so *nicely* with their names?' *Nicely* means 'subtly' as well as 'trivially'. Gaunt's pun is not only true to the trivial preoccupations of the dying; it also reminds us of the play's dominant theme, the relationship between names and their bearers. Gaunt is saying in effect: 'I am true to my name, Gaunt, but you are not true to the name you bear of King'. Besides this, *gaunt* in the sense of 'wasted' prepares us for his long speech of remonstrance, in which wordplay underlines that relationship between the spiritual health of the king and the well-being of his kingdom which was a living concept for the Elizabethans, . . .

This by no means exhausts the puns with which Gaunt endeavours to pack the most meaning into the few words left for him to utter. But his efforts are in vain. Richard seizes Bolingbroke's estates and leaves for Ireland. . . .[7] □

In the eighteenth century Shakespeare had been condemned for his use of puns and quibbles. Mahood's analysis, however, shows how through such features the text is packed with meaning and is rich in ambiguities and paradoxes. The analysis, however, is not just concerned with surface wordplay but rather with a reading of the play in which language becomes a central theme foregrounded by the text. In many ways Mahood anticipates later developments in poststructuralist criticism in this kind of exploration of the role of language as the location of plural meanings in the text.

III: New readings – Ernst H. Kantorowicz and Jan Kott

Language was one area of significant new readings of Shakespeare produced by New Criticism. A second area might be called history of ideas. Here, the most important study is Ernst H. Kantorowicz's book called *The King's Two Bodies*, which argues that medieval and Renaissance political theory recognised the king as having two bodies – one was his body natural subject to human infirmity; the other was the king as figure of the body politic and so not subject to human error. The idea, initially strange, starts to make sense if we think of the phrase 'The King is dead; long live the King'. What Kantorowicz did was to show how the idea can be applied to a reading of *Richard II*, and how the play shows Richard disintegrating.

From Ernst H. Kantorowicz, *The King's Two Bodies* (1957)

■   Twin-born with greatness, subject to the breath
    Of every fool, whose sense no more can feel
    But his own wringing. What infinite heart's ease
    Must kings neglect that private men enjoy! . . .
    What kind of god art thou, that suffer'st more
    Of mortal griefs than do thy worshippers?

Such are, in Shakespeare's play, the meditations of King Henry V on the godhead and manhood of a king. The king is 'twin-born' not only with greatness but also with human nature, hence 'subject to the breath of every fool'.

It was the humanly tragic aspect of royal 'gemination' which Shakespeare outlined and not the legal capacities which English lawyers assembled in the fiction of the King's Two Bodies. However, the legal jargon of the 'two Bodies' scarcely belonged to the arcana of the legal guild alone. That the king 'is a Corporation in himself that liveth ever' was a commonplace found in a simple dictionary of legal terms. . . .

The legal concept of the King's Two Bodies [found in Plowden's *Reports*] cannot, for other reasons, be separated from Shakespeare. For if that curious image, which from modern constitutional thought has vanished all but completely, still has a very real and human meaning today, this is largely due to Shakespeare. It is he who has eternalized that metaphor. He has made it not only the symbol, but indeed the very substance and essence of one of his greatest plays: *The Tragedy of King Richard II* is the tragedy of the King's Two Bodies. . . .

Gradually, and only step by step, does the tragedy proper of the King's Two Bodies develop in the scene on the Welsh coast. There is as yet no split in Richard when, on his return from Ireland, he kisses the soil of his kingdom and renders that famous, almost too often quoted, account of the loftiness of his royal estate. What he expounds is, in fact, the indelible character of the king's body politic, god-like or angel-like. The balm of consecration resists the power of the elements, the 'rough rude sea', since

The breath of worldly man cannot depose
The deputy elected by the Lord.   (III.ii.54f.)

Man's breath appears to Richard as something inconsistent with king-ship. Carlisle, in the Westminster scene, will emphasize once more that God's Anointed cannot be judged 'by inferior breath' (IV.i.128). It will be Richard himself who 'with his own breath' releases at once kingship and subjects (IV.i.210), so that finally King Henry V, after the destruction of Richard's divine kingship, could rightly complain that the king is 'subject to the breath of every fool'.

When the scene (III.ii) begins, Richard is, in the most exalted fash-ion, the 'deputy elected by the Lord' and 'God's substitute . . . anointed in his sight' (I.ii.37f.). . . . He still is sure of himself, of his dignity, and even of the help of the celestial hosts, which are at his disposal.

> For every man that Bolingbroke hath press'd . . .
> God for his Richard hath in heavenly pay
> A glorious angel.   (III.ii.60ff.)

This glorious image of kingship 'By the Grace of God' does not last. It slowly fades, as the bad tidings trickle in. A curious change in Richard's attitude – as it were, a metamorphosis from 'Realism' to 'Nominalism' – now takes place. The Universal called 'Kingship' begins to disintegrate; its transcendent 'Reality', its objective truth and god-like existence, so brilliant shortly before, pales into a nothing, a *nomen*. And the remaining half-reality resembles a state of amnesia or of sleep.

> I had forgot myself, am I not king?
> Awake thou coward majesty! thou sleepest
> Is not the king's name twenty thousand names
> *Arm, arm, my name!* a puny subject strikes
> At thy great glory.   (III.ii.83)

This state of half-reality, of royal oblivion and slumber, adumbrates the royal 'Fool' of Flint Castle. And similarly the divine prototype of gemination, the God-man, begins to announce its presence, as Richard alludes to Judas' treason:

> Snakes, in my heart-blood warm'd, that sting my heart!
> Three Judases, each one thrice worse than Judas!   (III.ii.131f.)

It is as though it has dawned upon Richard that his vicariate of the God Christ might imply also a vicariate of the man Jesus, and that he, the royal 'deputy elected by the Lord', might have to follow his divine Master also in his human humiliation and take the cross. . . .

The structure of the second great scene (III.iii) resembles the first.

Richard's kingship, his body politic, has been hopelessly shaken, it is true; but still there remains, though hollowed out, the semblance of kingship. At least this might be saved. 'Yet looks he like a king,' states York at Flint Castle (III.iii.68); and in Richard's temper there dominates, at first, the consciousness of his royal dignity. . . . The 'cascades' then begin to fall as they did in the first scene. The celestial hosts are called upon once more, this time avenging angels and 'armies of pestilence', which God is said to muster in his clouds – 'on our behalf' (III.iii.85f.). Again the 'Name' of kingship plays its part:

> O, that I were as great
> As is my grief, or lesser than my *name*!   (III.iii.136f.)

> Must (the king) lose
> The *name* of king? a God's *name*, let it go.   (III.iii.145f.)

From the shadowy name of kingship there leads, once more, the path to new disintegration. No longer does Richard impersonate the mystic body of his subjects and the nation. It is a lonely man's miserable and mortal nature that replaces the king as King:

> I'll give my jewels for a set of beads:
> My gorgeous palace for a hermitage:
> My gay apparel for an almsman's gown:
> My figured goblets for a dish of wood:
> My sceptre for a palmer's walking-staff:
> My subjects for a pair of carved saints,
> And my large kingdom for a little grave,
> A little little grave, an obscure grave.   (III.iii.147ff.)

The shiver of those anaphoric clauses is followed by a profusion of gruesome images of High-Gothic *macabresse*. However, the second scene – different from the first – does not end in those outbursts of self-pity which recall, not a Dance of Death, but a dance around one's own grave. There follows a state of even greater abjectness. . . .

As the third scene (IV.i) opens, there prevails again – now for the third time – the image of sacramental kingship. On the Beach of Wales, Richard himself had been the herald of the loftiness of kingship by right divine; at Flint Castle, he had made it his 'program' to save at least the face of a king and to justify the 'Name', although the title no longer fitted his condition; at Westminster, he is incapable of expounding his kingship himself. Another person will speak for him and interpret the image of God-established royalty; and very fittingly, a bishop. The Bishop of Carlisle. . . .

The scene in which Richard 'undoes his kingship' and releases his body politic into thin air leaves the spectator breathless. It is a scene of sacramental solemnity, since the ecclesiastical ritual of undoing the effects of consecration is no less solemn or of less weight than the ritual which has built up the sacramental dignity. . . . Since none is entitled to lay finger on the Anointed of God . . . King Richard, when defrocking himself, appears as his own celebrant: . . . Bit by bit he deprives his body politic of the symbols of its dignity and exposes his poor body natural to the eyes of the spectators:

> Now mark me how I will undo myself:
> I give this heavy weight from off my head,
> And this unwieldy sceptre from my hand,
> The pride of kingly sway from out my heart;
> With mine own tears I wash away my balm,
> With mine own hands I give away my crown,
> With mine own tongue deny my sacred state,
> With mine own breath release all duteous oaths:
> All pomp and majesty do I foreswear. . . .   (IV.i.203ff.)

Self-deprived of all his former glories, Richard seems to fly back to his old trick of Flint Castle, to the role of Fool, as he renders to his 'successor' some double-edged acclamations. This time, however, the fool's cap is of no avail. . . . Invisible his kingship, and relegated to within: visible his flesh, and exposed to contempt and derision or to pity and mockery – there remains but one parallel to his miserable self: the derided Son of man. . . . The parallel of Bolingbroke–Richard and Pilate–Christ . . . was revived to some extent in Tudor times. But this is not important here; for Shakespeare, when using the biblical comparison, integrates it into the entire development of Richard's misery, of which the nadir has yet not been reached. . . . For of a sudden Richard realizes that he, when facing his Lancastrian Pilate, is not at all like Christ, but that he himself, Richard, has his place among the Pilates and Judases, because he is no less a traitor than the others, or is even worse than they are: he is a traitor to his own immortal body politic and to kingship such as it had been to his day:

> Mine eyes are full of tears, I cannot see. . . .
> But they can see a sort of traitors here.
> Nay, if I turn mine eyes upon myself,
> I find myself a traitor with the rest:
> For I have given here my soul's consent
> T'undeck the pompous body of a king . . .   (IV.i.244ff.)

That is, the king body natural becomes a traitor to the king body politic, to the 'pompous body of a king'. It is as though Richard's self-indictment of treason anticipated the charge of 1649, the charge of high treason committed by the king against the King. . . .

The mirror scene is the climax of that tragedy of dual personality. The looking-glass has the effects of a magic mirror, and Richard himself is the wizard who, comparable to the trapped and cornered wizard in the fairy tales, is forced to set his magic art to work against himself. The physical face which the mirror reflects no longer is one with Richard's inner experience, his outer appearance, no longer identical with inner man. . . . When finally, at the 'brittle glory' of his face, Richard dashes the mirror to the ground, there shatters not only Richard's past and present, but every aspect of a super-world. His catoptromancy had ended. The features as reflected by the looking-glass betray that he is stripped of every possibility of a second or super-body – of the pompous body politic of king, of the God-likeness of the Lord's deputy elect, of the follies of the fool, and even of the most human griefs residing in inner man. The splintering mirror means, or is, the breaking apart of any possible duality. All those facets are reduced to one: to the banal face and insignificant *physis* of a miserable man, a *physis* now void of any metaphysis whatsoever. It is both less and more than Death. It is the *demise* of Richard, and the rise of a new body natural.[8] □

Kantorowicz's argument combines a discussion of Renaissance political theory with a close reading of Richard's tragedy as he strips himself of 'the pompous body politic of king'. It thus brings together the historical and tragic aspects of the play but sets them in a new light, offering a new interpretation of the significance of the play's central action, and in particular the mirror scene in Act IV scene i. Like Mahood's essay, Kantorowicz's argument, with its stress on the notion of the body, was to have considerable impact on later criticism of Shakespeare.

Whereas Kantorowicz explored a set of Renaissance ideas, Jan Kott in his book *Shakespeare Our Contemporary* sought to show how Shakespeare could be read as part of the modern world. Not everyone agreed with Kott's radical stand, but his perception of the unrelenting process of history was a timely jolt to tired ways of thinking about the plays.

From Jan Kott, *Shakespeare Our Contemporary* (1964)

■ . . . Shakespeare's Histories deal with the struggle for the English crown that went on from the close of the fourteenth to the end of the fifteenth century. They constitute an historical epic covering over a hundred years and divided into long chapters corresponding to reigns.

But when we read these chapters chronologically, following the sequence of reigns, we are struck by the thought that for Shakespeare history stands still. Every chapter opens and closes at the same point. In every one of these plays history turns full circle, returning to the point of departure. These recurring and unchanging circles described by history are the successive kings' reigns.

Each of these great historical tragedies begins with a struggle for the throne, or for its consolidation. Each ends with the monarch's death and a new coronation. In each of the Histories the legitimate ruler drags behind him a long chain of crimes. He has rejected the feudal lords who helped him to reach for the crown; he murders, first, his enemies, then his former allies; he executes possible successors and pretenders to the crown. But he has not been able to execute them all. From banishment a young prince returns – the son, grandson, or brother of those murdered – to defend the violated law. The rejected lords gather round him, he personifies the hope for a new order and justice. But every step to power continues to be marked by murder, violence, treachery. And so, when the new prince finds himself near the throne, he drags behind him a chain of crimes as long as that of the until now legitimate ruler. When he assumes the crown, he will be just as hated as his predecessor. He has killed enemies, now he will kill former allies. And a new Pretender appears in the name of violated justice. The wheel has turned full circle. A new chapter opens. A new historical tragedy: . . .

Emanating from the features of individual kings and usurpers in Shakespeare's History plays, there gradually emerges the image of history itself. The image of the Grand Mechanism. Every successive chapter, every great Shakespearian act is merely a repetition:

> The flattering index of a direful pageant;
> One heav'd a-high, to be hurl'd down below
>
> (*Richard III*, IV.4)

It is this image of history, repeated many times by Shakespeare, that forces itself on us in a most powerful manner. Feudal history is like a great staircase on which there treads a constant procession of kings. Every step upwards is marked by murder, perfidy, treachery. Every step brings the throne nearer. Another step and the crown will fall. One will soon be able to snatch it.

———

Let us begin by tracing the working of the Grand Mechanism as Shakespeare shows it in his theatre. . . .

Let us begin with the great abdication scene in *Richard II*, the scene omitted in all editions published in Queen Elizabeth's lifetime. It revealed the working of the Grand Mechanism too brutally: the very moment when power was changing hands. Authority comes either from God, or from the people. A flash of the sword, the tramping of the guards; applause of intimidated noblemen; a shout from the forcibly gathered crowd; behold: the new authority, too, comes from God, or from the will of the people. . . .

. . . The act of dethronement has to be completed quickly and absolutely. The King's royal majesty must be extinguished. The new King is waiting. If the former King is not a traitor, then the new one is a usurper. One can well understand Queen Elizabeth's censors:

Northumberland	My lord, dispatch; read o'er these articles.
Richard	Mine eyes are full of tears, I cannot see:
	And yet salt water blinds them not so much
	But they can see a sort of traitors here.
	Nay, if I turn mine eyes upon myself,
	I find myself a traitor with the rest;
	For I have given here my soul's consent
	T'undeck the pompous body of a king . . .

. . . It is nearly the end. There is just one more act to come. The last one. But this act will at the same time be the first act of a new tragedy. It will have a new title, of course: *Henry IV*. In *Richard II* Bolingbroke was a 'positive hero'; an avenger. He defended violated law and justice. But in his own tragedy he can only play the part of Richard II. The cycle has been completed. The cycle is beginning again. Bolingbroke has mounted half-way up the grand staircase of history.[9] □

As Rabkin (in the first extract in this chapter) notes, Kott offers a picture of history as a 'cruel and meaningless process in which only power counts'. Kott links this view of history to his experience of living in the police states of eastern Europe. Shakespeare, he argues, is our contemporary because he offers us a view of history which we recognise as both modern and painfully accurate. It is a view that looks through the ceremonies and rhetoric of kingship to the repeated events of 'murder, violence, treachery'.

IV: Synthesis

Kott's view is the very antithesis of Tillyard's ideal of order and hierarchy. For many critics, however, both views were too extreme, and often in new critical readings of the histories there is a combination of the two positions: a recognition of the ideas Tillyard put forward as important, but also a more rigorous examination of the effects of the plays and their presentation of power politics. The final extract rounding off this chapter, by Alvin Kernan, represents a kind of synthesis of twentieth-century critical thinking up to 1970. In the essay Kernan coins the term 'Henriad' to describe the second tetralogy. Although a number of critics object to it, the term is now common in modern American criticism. Its purpose is to suggest that *Richard II* together with the two parts of *Henry IV* and *Henry V* constitute a group of plays dealing with and dramatising a specific political problem.

From Alvin Kernan, '*The Henriad*: Shakespeare's Major History Plays' (1969)

■ Taken together, Shakespeare's four major history plays, *Richard II, 1 Henry IV, 2 Henry IV*, and *Henry V* constitute an epic, *The Henriad*. Obviously these four plays are not an epic in the usual sense – there is no evidence that Shakespeare even planned them as a unit – but they do have remarkable coherence and they possess that quality which in our time we take to be the chief characteristic of epic: a large-scale, heroic action involving many men and many activities, tracing the movement of a nation or people through violent change from one condition to another. In the *Iliad* that action involves the wrath of Achilles and the misfortunes which it brought to the Achaeans before Troy. In the *Aeneid* the action is the transferal of the Empire of Troy to Latium. And in *Paradise Lost* the action is man's first disobedience and the fruit of that forbidden tree.

In *The Henriad*, the action is the passage from the England of Richard II to the England of Henry V. This dynastic shift serves as the framework for a great many cultural and psychological transitions which run parallel to the main action, giving it body and meaning. In historical terms the movement from the world of Richard II to that of Henry V is the passage from the Middle Ages to the Renaissance and the modern world. In political and social terms it is a movement from feudalism and hierarchy to the national state and individualism. In psychological terms it is a passage from a situation in which man knows with certainty who he is to an existential condition in which any identity is only a temporary role. In spatial and temporal terms it is a movement from a closed world to an infinite universe. In mythical terms the passage is from a garden world to a fallen world. In the most summary terms it is a movement from ceremony and ritual to history and drama.

It is by means of ceremony and ritual that the old kingdom is presented in the beginning of *The Henriad*. *Richard II* opens on a scene in which two furious peers, Mowbray and Hereford, confront and accuse one another of treason before their king. The place of judgment is the court itself, where in a traditional setting with its ancient emblems and established procedures, the pattern of innumerable former assemblies will be repeated in an attempt to absorb and reorder once again the disorderly elements in man and society.

When this ritual fails, an even more solemn ritual is ordered, trial by combat. The combatant knights enter in the proper manner and take their assigned places in the lists. The king makes his traditional speech, the marshal of the lists asks the ceremonial questions, and the knights answer in the assigned way: . . . Here, and throughout the early acts of the play, the individual is submerged within the role imposed upon him by prescribed ways of thinking, acting, and speaking.

Even as it expresses itself, this old world is breaking up. The patriarchs of England – the seven sons of Edward II – are, like the sons of Jacob, passing from the land, and with them their old world passes. The sense of an ancient, more perfect world, fading from existence into memory, is focused in John of Gaunt's comparison of England, as it was only yesterday, to another Eden:

> This royal throne of kings, this scept'red isle,
> This earth of majesty, this seat of Mars,
> This other Eden, demi-paradise,
> This fortress built by Nature for herself
> Against infection and the hand of war,
> This happy breed of men, this little world,
> This precious stone set in the silver sea,
> Which serves it in the office of a wall,
> Or as a moat defensive to a house,
> Against the envy of less happier lands;
> This blessed plot, this earth, this realm, this England.
>
> (II.i.40–50)

By III.iv when the 'sea-walled garden' appears again, presided over by a gardener in 'old Adam's likeness', it is full of weeds, the flowers choked, the trees unpruned, the hedges in ruin, the herbs eaten by caterpillars, and the great tree in its centre dead and lifeless.

What is passing in the course of *Richard II* is innocence, a sense of living in a golden world and no one is more innocent than Richard himself. When Bolingbroke begins his rebellion, Richard confidently expects that God himself will send down soldiers to defend him and blast the usurper. The order of nature and the laws of men, he believes, guarantee his kingship:

> Not all the water in the rough rude sea
> Can wash the balm off from an anointed king;

145

> The breath of worldly men cannot depose
> The deputy elected by the Lord.
> For every man that Bolingbroke hath press'd
> To lift shrewd steel against our golden crown,
> God for his Richard hath in heavenly pay
> A glorious angel. Then, if angels fight,
> Weak men must fall; for heaven still guards the right.
>
> (III.ii.54–62)

Richard, here and elsewhere, expresses the conservative world view which has been variously called 'The Great Chain of Being', 'The Elizabethan World Picture' and 'The Tudor Political Myth', those ritual views of the cosmos and the state. Richard takes this great imaginative projection of human values for absolute fact, mistakes metaphor for science, fails to distinguish human desire from actuality, and therefore fails to understand that he cannot trust to 'Nature' to maintain him as a king, simply because he *is* king. From the outset of the play powerful political and personal forces are at work undermining the social system, making a mockery of ritual and ceremony. Mowbray has been involved in graft and assassination. Henry Hereford has been courting popularity with the common people, and he accuses Mowbray of treason knowing that he is innocent. His motive may be to embarrass Richard, who is himself deeply implicated in the murder of his uncle, the crime of which Mowbray is accused. Richard is violently jealous and suspicious of his cousin Hereford and uses the trial as an occasion for banishing him under the pretence of being merciful. Pressed by the perpetual need for money, Richard sells his right to gather taxes to profiteers. He neglects affairs of state to spend his time revelling with male favourites. Each of these acts indirectly undermines the order which Richard thinks immutable, and when upon John of Gaunt's death he seizes the banished Hereford's lands, he strikes a direct blow, as the Duke of York points out, against the great law of orderly succession on which his kingship rests:

> Take Hereford's rights away, and take from Time
> His charters and his customary rights;
> Let not to-morrow then ensue to-day;
> Be not thyself – for how art thou a king
> But by fair sequence and succession? (II.i.195–99)

His responsibility for his own destruction is dramatically realized in a later scene in which he agrees to uncrown himself and resign his throne to Bolingbroke.

In *Paradise Lost* the results of the fall, Adam and Eve's disobedience to God, are immediate and spectacular: the earth tilts and the seasons become intemperate, the animals become vicious and prey on one another and on man, and man himself knows fear, anger, lust, and shame. What Milton presents on the scale of the universe, Shakespeare presents on the scale of the kingdom and the individual. Most immediately, Richard's disorders release a variety of other disorders on all levels of life. Richard having rebelled against the order which made and kept him king, Henry Bolingbroke immediately rebels against Richard. By the end of the play there is already another group of plotters planning to overthrow Henry. Throughout the three succeeding plays political scheming, plotting, raids on the commonwealth, and civil wars never cease.

As the old order breaks up, a profound psychological confusion parallels the political confusion. In that Edenic world which Gaunt describes and Richard destroys, every man knew who he was. His religion, his family, his position in society, his assigned place in processions large and small, his coat of arms, and his traditional duties told him who he was, what he should do, and even gave him the formal language in which to express this socially-assigned self. But once, under the pressures of political necessity and personal desires, the old system is destroyed, the old identities go with it. Man then finds himself in the situation which Richard acts out in IV.i, the deposition scene. Richard is speaking, and when Northumberland attempts to break in with the exclamation 'My lord', he responds with words which reveal how thoroughly shattered is his sense of his identity as Richard Plantagenet, King of England:

> No lord of thine, thou haught insulting man,
> Nor no man's lord; I have no name, no title –
> No, not that name was given me at the font –
> But 'tis usurp'd. Alack the heavy day,
> That I have worn so many winters out,
> And know not now what name to call myself!   (IV.i.254–59)

Richard is not the first man in this play to discover that he no longer knows who he is. He has already forced the question of identity on Bolingbroke by banishing him from England and robbing him of his succession as Duke of Lancaster. Bolingbroke – whose names change rapidly: Hereford, Bolingbroke, Lancaster, and Henry IV – has understood the lesson well. Speaking to Bushy and Green, two of Richard's favourites, the man who had once confidently answered the question 'What is thy name?' with the proud words 'Harry of Hereford, Lancaster, and Derby am I', now tells the bitterness of banishment and the pain that comes from loss of those possessions and symbols which had heretofore guaranteed identity:

> Myself – a prince by fortune of my birth,
> Near to the King in blood, and near in love
> Till you did make him misinterpret me –
> Have stoop'd my neck under your injuries
> And sigh'd my English breath in foreign clouds,
> Eating the bitter bread of banishment,
> Whilst you have fed upon my signories,
> Dispark'd my parks and fell'd my forest woods,
> From my own windows torn my household coat,
> Raz'd out my imprese, leaving me no sign
> Save men's opinions and my living blood
> To show the world I am a gentleman. (III.i.16–27)

Man has broken into a strange, new existence where he is free to slide back and forth along the vast scale of being, coming to rest momentarily at various points, but never knowing for certain just who and what he is. John of Gaunt's awkward punning on his name as he lies dying suggests the pervasiveness of the feeling that names and the identities they carry are no longer real and permanent but only the roles of the moment. This fluctuation in identity is the basic rhythm of the play, and we feel it everywhere: in Richard's ever-changing moods, in Bolingbroke's rising fortunes and changing names, in Richard's decline from King of England to his last appearance on stage, a body borne in by his murderer. The pattern of up-down, of restless change in the self, appears in its most complete and concentrated form in Richard's great speech, when he sits in the dungeon of Pomfret Castle, about to die, and tries desperately to understand himself and this strange world into which he has fallen. Richard began as a great and secure king, seated on a throne, surrounded by pomp, confirmed by ceremony, looking out over a world of light where everything in the universe was open and ordered. At the end of the play he is the isolated individual, solitary, sitting in a small circle of light, surrounded by darkness and by a flinty prison wall, uncertain of any reality or truth. Isolated, like some hero of Kafka, in a mysterious and a containing world, Richard takes the confusing and conflicting evidence which his mind offers him and attempts, by means of reason and the poetic power to construct analogies, to 'Hammer it out', to give it shape and form, to achieve some new coherence. The results are not comforting. As hard as he hammers, he can discover only endless mutability in the life of man and endless restlessness in his soul. All evidence is now ambiguous: where the Bible promises an easy salvation in one passage, 'come little ones', only turn the page and it speaks of the passage to the Kingdom of Heaven being as difficult as a camel threading the eye of a needle. Man's powers at one moment seem infinite and he feels that he can 'tear a passage through the flinty ribs/Of this hard world', but at the next moment he is the most helpless of creatures and can only comfort himself that many others have endured like misery. Reality has now become theatrical, a playing of many roles in a constantly changing play:

> Thus play I in one person many people,
> And none contented. Sometimes am I king;
> Then treasons make me wish myself a beggar.
> And so I am. Then crushing penury
> Persuades me I was better when a king;
> Then am I king'd again; and by and by
> Think that I am unking'd by Bolingbroke,
> And straight am nothing. But whate'er I be,
> Nor I, nor any man that but man is,
> With nothing shall be pleas'd till he be eas'd
> With being nothing.   (V.v.31–41)

To accommodate the newly perceived, paradoxical, shifting reality Richard abandons the formal, conventional style of the beginning of the play and changes to a metaphysical style capable of handling irony and a reality in which the parts no longer mesh, capable of carrying deep, intense agitation and the passionate effort of thought.

The world continues to speak ambiguously to Richard in the form of two visitors. The first is a poor groom from his stables who, having seen the King before only from a distance, now risks his life to come to speak of sympathy and duty which alters not when it alteration finds. The second visitor is the murderer Exton, come to kill Richard in hopes of reward from Henry. Richard, having tried to define himself by means of poetry and failed, now takes the way of drama, and acts. He seizes a sword from one of Exton's thugs and strikes two of them down before being killed himself. And so he defines himself in a dramatic or historic, not a philosophic way. He, like the rest of men, has no stable identity certified by the order of things immutable. He is instead tragic man, whose identity fluctuates between hero and victim, king and corpse; whose values are not guaranteed by anything but his own willingness to die for them; whose life is a painful and continuing process of change. Richard traces the way that the other major characters must each follow in their turn.[10] □

Kernan's analysis draws together many of the ideas of Tillyard and New Criticism: that the histories mark a shift from a medieval to modern world, from a 'garden world' of an ideal England to a 'fallen world' of Machiavellian politics, from ritual to history, from feudalism to the beginnings of a 'modern state and individualism'. *Richard II* is the beginning of this process, but also, in its action, traces out the pattern of all the plays. Kernan's is a reading of the plays which seeks to do justice to their richness and to the problems they present.

This seems an appropriate point at which to take stock and sum up the implications of the present chapter. Tillyard had looked at the history plays in their political and historical contexts. New Criticism looks at the words on the page; this might seem an innocent move, but its force is to make us more aware of the complexity of all contexts. This includes the political and historical contexts of the text, and also the whole context of interpretation. New Criticism focuses on language, but the result is to re-energise the broader critical debate. But not just that. The effect of New Criticism is to unsettle old ways of reading texts and their contexts. It is in this sense that New Criticism might have helped bring about the new radical criticism of the 1970s. After New Criticism there could never be a return to the old, unselfconscious ways of looking at texts, contexts or at criticism. Within New Criticism, with its stress on the plurality of meaning and the instability of language, we can begin to detect a move towards poststructuralism and the whole rethinking of criticism.

CHAPTER SEVEN

Recent Criticism

Introduction

CRITICISM OF Shakespeare has changed radically since the early 1970s. What has caused the change has been the introduction of new approaches and new ways of reading the plays. More specifically, Shakespearean criticism, like literary studies as a whole, has been changed by new models of theoretical thinking, in particular by feminism, cultural materialism, psychoanalysis, New Historicism and deconstruction.[1] The most obvious sign of this change is the different kind of critical language often used in contemporary criticism, which is sometimes described under the broad heading of poststructuralism or poststructuralist criticism.

While there are a large number of different critical approaches employed today, and a rich diversity of critical thinking, it is, none the less, possible to point to common links between recent approaches. First, nearly all the new ways of reading are concerned with questions of politics, especially questions of gender, language and power. Second, nearly all recent approaches historicise their approach. This is in sharp contrast to the New Criticism of the previous chapter, with its principal stress on the text alone. But current criticism also challenges the kind of historical approach adopted by Tillyard: instead of seeing texts as a product or reflection of a history outside the text, recent criticism sees both texts and history as part of culture and ideology. Thirdly, there is, in poststructuralist criticism, a stress on the plurality of texts, on the idea that meaning is always plural. Finally, recent criticism returns again and again to the text as something contradictory, unresolved and unresolvable, with critics always conscious of how criticism itself imposes patterns upon the text.

There is, however, a danger in summing up recent criticism in this way, as if it were a set of formulae. As in all critical movements, the best critics are constantly shifting and refining their approach. Some of the most interesting recent work on Shakespeare, for example, has been concerned with the implications of textual editing, drawing together ideas from cultural history and politics rather than following the traditional set approach to such matters.[2] Recent criticism is, then, a criticism which presents itself as always in process. In this it is the very antithesis of eighteenth-century Neo-Classical criticism with its rules, but also perhaps at odds with all previous criticism, particularly in its emphasis on different ways of reading and the role of the reader in producing the meanings of the text. This is not the same as saying that the text can mean anything we want it to mean. Meaning, recent criticism argues, is not subjective in this way because language is always public and conventional. The business of criticism is 'to release possible meanings',[3] but also, it has to be said, to intervene in the critical debate.

In the case of *Richard II* this means that contemporary criticism inevitably finds itself re-examining many of the issues raised by Tillyard. There have, in fact, been a number of major studies of the histories in recent years, most notably by Graham Holderness and Phyllis Rackin, which mark a distinct shift in our understanding of the plays.[4] I have included extracts from both of these critics in this chapter. In addition, I have selected two essays – by Catherine Belsey and Christopher Pye – which not only illustrate some of the ways in which critical theory has made a difference to our reading of the texts but also to the nature of criticism itself. A brief note sets each piece in context, but the thrust of the chapter is to encourage readers to think about the extracts for themselves, testing them against the text and their own reading of the play.

I. History

Graham Holderness is perhaps the most prolific critic writing about the histories from a contemporary standpoint. In his analysis of the play below he sets out to challenge the Tillyard assumption that what is dramatised is a simple clash between Richard's medievalism and Bolingbroke's Machiavellian modernism. Rather, Holderness contends, the history plays are themselves a form of historiography, of historical writing. What they construct is a feudal world and society represented by Bolingbroke and the lords. Richard seeks to curb their power through a policy of absolutism; it is only when this policy fails that we hear the language of royal tragedy and prophecy. Holderness's argument offers a strong counter to the traditional, sentimental royalist reading; his contention is that the play, far from endorsing absolutism, presents the divine right of kings as a myth emerging from the declining power of the monarchy.

From Graham Holderness, 'Shakespeare's History: *Richard II*' (1981)

■ The conventional understanding of the 'history' dramatized by [*Richard II*] . . . is well known: it is thought to portray a medieval society (that which John of Gaunt looks back on), which was a harmonious, organic community, dominated by kings, bound together by order, hierarchy, degree; an order which is mismanaged by Richard, and therefore falls prey to the civil conflict which deposes him. But the nature of that old society guaranteed that Richard's deposition could not be a mere change of regime; Bolingbroke's usurpation destroyed a traditional, divinely ordained and divinely sanctioned monarchy, and thereby destroyed the old medieval 'order' irrevocably. The break ushers in civil war, which divides the realm until the Tudor reconciliation.

If, as I am proposing, Shakespeare developed his own understanding of history from his historical sources – rather than simply interpreting the past by the concepts and images of Tudor political and historical philosophy – then he would have known the Middle Ages, *not* as a period dominated by order and legitimacy, the undisputed sovereignty of a monarchy sanctioned by Divine Right; but as a turbulent period dominated by a great and fundamental conflict . . . between the power of the Crown, and the power of the feudal barons. . . .

. . . The quarrel between the Earls is an appropriate inception for the action of *Richard II*, as all the succeeding events can be seen to flow from it. But this incident also links the play indissolubly to precedent history, as Shakespeare read it in Holinshed: the appeal is the climax of that conflict between monarchy and feudalism which had been actively fought out throughout Richard's reign. . . .

The King, the fount of justice, presides over this legal process: legally his authority is absolute; in practice (in the drama as in actual history), his control is somewhat tenuous. In the first scene he restricts himself carefully to the role of mediating authority, 'chairman'. But the scene resolves itself into an assertion by the Barons of a code of values which is actually antagonistic to royal power, *hostile* to Richard's authority as sovereign; and the ceremony and pageantry of the proceedings are *connected more closely* with *that* code of values, than with the courtly culture of the Crown. It is in recognition of this fact that Richard seeks to remain ostensibly neutral (a position which symbolizes very precisely the predicament of a King in a still largely feudal society). The conflict which ultimately leads to the King's deposition is not a conflict between old and new, between absolute medieval monarchy and new Machiavellian power-politics. It is a conflict between the King's sovereignty and the ancient code of chivalry; which is here firmly located in the older and more primitive tribal and family code of blood-vengeance. Richard initially acquiesces in this code . . . [but] subsequently attempts to affirm a policy of royal absolutism, which insists on the King's prerogative overriding the procedures of chivalric law. Richard's political response to this constant clamouring for power on the part of the feudal lords, is to impose a policy of *absolutism*. . . .

Richard's decision to stop the combat is another open question for which various explanations have been offered, and various motives supplied. If we presuppose the stated historical context, listen carefully to Richard's speech at I.iii (124–138), and understand his behaviour in I.iv, the implications of the decision become clearer.

The speech itself is an impressive homily against civil war, and the disorganizing militaristic feudalism which has precipitated that danger. It also gives us a sense of Richard's own image of his kingdom. Running through the speech is an underlying pattern of images creating a strong positive sense of the realm as it should be:

> Our kingdom's earth . . . : plough'd up . . . our peace,
> sweet infant, . . . till twice five summers
> have enrich'd our fields.   (I.iii.125–143)

The pastoral imagery of rural peace, fecundity, new life, is violated by the language of bloodshed, civil wounds, swords; the assertive arrogance of feudal pride; 'the grating shock of wrathful iron arms'. If feudalism has become a real threat to the stability and harmony of the realm, then Richard is clearly attempting not just to banish two quarrelling Earls, but to dismantle the very structures of feudal power.

Though absolutist, Richard's solution combines authority with diplomatic concession: the unequal banishments tacitly acknowledge Mowbray's guilt, and endeavour to appease the Lancastrian interest. . . .

Gaunt and York, the older generation of barons, are both loyal but now reluctant supporters of the Crown. Gaunt's famous speech . . . is clearly one of the strongest incentives to accept the conventional ideas of 'medieval kingship'. His language is uncompromisingly royalist: the realm is (or rather has been – the speech is an elegy) properly defined in terms of its monarchy, its history distinguished by the quality of its kings. Gaunt, unlike Bolingbroke, identifies kingship and chivalry, and looks back nostalgically to a time when England united the two. That identification, and the role Gaunt adopts towards Richard (that of sage counsellor) imply a kingdom in which a careful and diplomatic balancing of forces synthesized Crown and nobility into a united 'Happy breed of men' – a situation which prevailed in the reign of Edward III. The appropriate image for this marriage of Crown and aristocracy, of Christian monarchy and 'true chivalry', is that of the crusade. Though Gaunt's language is that of royalism and Divine Right, he is certainly no absolutist: his Golden Age is that of a feudalism given cohesion and structure by the central authority of a king, bound to his subjects by the reciprocal bonds of fealty.

The climax of Gaunt's speech draws the attack on Richard's economic policies into a powerful image of the dissolution of traditional social bonds: England, formerly united in itself and against other nations, is now bound together by economic contracts:

> England, bound in with the triumphant sea
> ... is now bound in with shame
> With inky blots and rotten parchment bonds. (II.i.61–4)

Gaunt's elegy is no panegyric of absolutism: it is a lament for the dissolution of a society in which King and nobility were organically bound together into a strong and unified nation: the King is now a mere 'Landlord'. . . .

The Duke of York presents a different point of view: and I think it is important to understand and to acknowledge the seriousness of his position. York's ideas are usually compromised by attention to his very obvious self-division – on stage the role is usually played as that of a fussy and indecisive senior civil servant. But we have seen the same self-division in Gaunt as well, resolved only by his death; York has to live with the difficulty of carrying his divided allegiance into the new conditions:

> Oh my liege
> Pardon me, if you please; if not, I pleas'd
> Not to be pardoned, am content withal.
> Seek you to seize and gripe into your hands,
> The royalties and rights of banished Herford?
> Is not Gaunt dead? and doth not Herford live?
> Take Herford's rights away, and take from time
> His charters, and his customary rights;
> Let not tomorrow then exceed today:
> Be not thyself. For how art thou a King
> But by fair sequence and succession? (II.i.187–208)

The spirit underlying this speech is that of Magna Carta. Richard is demanding *obedience* rather than *fealty*: fealty being a reciprocal relationship which guarantees the lord certain constitutional rights in exchange for his service and loyalty. Fealty binds subject and ruler: Bolingbroke's homage to Richard is no mere subjection but the entry into a reciprocal social bond. York's image of society is that of a social contract: the king, by violating the contract, inevitably raises the spectre of rebellion even in the most 'well-disposed' hearts. There is even a touch in York's speech of the early medieval view that rebellion could be justified against a monarch who violated his own side of the 'fealty' contract. York's self-division is clearly expressed again at II.ii. . . .

By the end of this scene rebellion is a reality. Northumberland (Shakespeare's classic Machiavellian) makes it plain here, despite his covert and non-committal speech, that he is proposing to rescue the Crown from its present incumbent: to reclaim the throne on behalf of the nobility. The barons are preparing to replace the dynastically legitimate King with one of their own choice and approval.

The loyalist and baronial ideologies are brought into direct collision, in the meeting between York and the newly-returned Bolingbroke (II.iii). Within the language of royalism ('Cam'st thou because the anointed king is hence?') Bolingbroke's actions receive their automatic valuation as 'gross rebellion and detested treason'. Bolingbroke's case however is also reasonable and valid, within its limits – he restricts his thinking to feudal terms, and does not imagine or conceptualize the consequences of his pushing at the balance of power . . .

By this stage the political and military battles are really over: and in the speech of Salisbury at II.iv we hear the first stirrings of the language and imagery of royal tragedy, divine right and apocalyptic prophecy which will dominate the rest of the play.

Act III opens with Bolingbroke in a commanding position. . . . His speech defines very precisely his specific relationship with England: it is the solid, proprietary language of a nobleman talking about his estate: it contrasts with Gaunt's impersonal conception of the realm as a feudal nation; and even more sharply with Richard's image of England, as it is revealed in the next scene. Like the charges against Mowbray, those against the favourites are no more than a gesture towards public justice: and just as those charges collapsed into the fundamental accusation of Gloucester's murder, so the allegations of treason carry very little weight by comparison with the *personal* injury sustained by Bolingbroke himself – *that* part of the speech carries an accent of personal grudge and recrimination, the response to an offence against the aristocratic class:

> Myself – a prince by fortune of my birth,
> Near to the King in blood, and near in love,
> Till you did make him misinterpret me –
> Have stooped my neck under your injuries,
> And sigh'd my English breath in foreign clouds,
> Eating the bitter bread of banishment,
> Whilst you have fed upon my signories,
> Dispark'd my parks and fell'd my forest woods,

From my own windows torn my household coat,
Rac'd out my imprese, leaving me no sign,
Save men's opinions and my living blood,
To show the world I am a gentleman   (III.i.16–27)

The 'caterpillars' have fed on Bolingbroke's *property*, his *estates*, concepts defined very precisely by his clear, concrete images of parks, forests, emblazoned windows, coats-of-arms, personal heraldic symbols – the concrete social identity of a 'gentleman'. Bolingbroke's consciousness is still that of a rebellious baron rather than the incipient King: although in fact he has already pushed the policy of opposition beyond the point of balance; the whole realm of England is about to become the baron's property.

That solid, possessive sense of England as private property contrasts sharply with Richard's feelings about his kingdom on his return from Ireland, in the next scene (III.ii). For the first time, Richard's speech moves towards the language and imagery of Divine Right – though there is no explicit affirmation of this doctrine for almost forty lines. In the preceding lines we see a fantastic reduction of Divine Right to a kind of childish superstition: the strong and bitter masculinity of Bolingbroke's relation to his estate, gives way to Richard's intimate, sentimental, physical cherishing of 'my Kingdom'. The conjuration is that of a child, who invokes the supernatural to combat the apparent omnipotence of parents: it is the voice of an imagination already beginning to experience defeat. . . .

For it is here, at the point where his defeat is imminent, that Richard's mind begins to split king and man, divine power and practical authority. 'Divine Right' is not seriously offered by the play as an unquestionably valid understanding of Plantagenet England: it is shown as a historical myth, emerging with its full imaginative force and splendour in the alienation of Richard's consciousness, as it responds to specific conditions of military and political defeat. . . .

The state itself ready to fall into Bolingbroke's hands, Richard's imagination is released to a vivid realization of the difference between effective power and 'mere' legitimacy; between the power of the man and the authority of the royal office; between the man who can rule a state and the King who has only the charisma of 'Divine Right'. He feels that he has reached death, and has nothing to bequeath to his heirs, no property in the realm. The only substance of his kingship is now the experience of royal tragedy: the only thing he can bequeath is his own tragic myth: 'sad stories of the death of Kings'. This speech [III.ii.144–77] is a penetrating tragic insight into the hollowness of 'Power' without power – the imagery of hollowness runs from the hollow grave, to the hollow crown, to the 'wall of flesh' encircling the mortal life, which seems as impregnable as a castle, but contains only a vulnerable, isolated life. . . .

It should be clear by now that *Richard II* is far from being a simple redaction of some 'official' Elizabethan ideology; a play designed to support and confirm that ideology by reducing the complexities of medieval history to a dogmatic orthodoxy – substantiating the Divine Right of Kings, condemning the deposition of a King as a crime against God, nature and humanity, and demonstrating the inevitable providential consequences of deposition, in discord, rebellion and civil war. On the contrary the play *challenges* that ideology of Divine Kingship: showing that society is a social contract which can easily be broken, and that the historical myth of Divine Right, for all its power, can never effectively heal the breach from which it is generated. . . .

This argument does not seek to invalidate the concept of divinely-sanctioned kingship, which is clearly central to the play; but to suggest a different view of its *status*. The play does not tell us that this conception represents Shakespeare's understanding of the structure and quality of medieval society before the deposition of Richard II. On the contrary, the precedent past, the 'pre-history of the present' is dramatized as a social contract held together by the mutual agreement of powerful forces. The older generation of barons, sons of Edward III, are committed (though in different ways) to the concept of monarchy; but they see this operating *only* within a conception of commonwealth, a union of Crown and nobility, and independence or absolutism on the part of the King distresses them deeply. Richard himself does not describe his rule as sanctioned by Divine Right until his defeat is well under way.

The idea of Divine Right is actually presented in the play as a historical myth (not a mystifying fiction, but a real and powerful form of human consciousness) which develops and emerges from the defeat of the monarchy. Richard dramatizes that myth as the monarchy itself dissolves; he affirms it most powerfully as his power disappears; and as his effective rule declines, his tragic myth exerts ever more powerful pressures on the imaginations of those responsible for his defeat. It is a matter of critical commonplace that Richard is not only a tragic role on the stage, but a 'tragic actor' like Charles I in Marvell's poem, conscious of the role he is playing; and that he is not only a mouthpiece for tragic poetry, but a poet, composing his own 'lamentable tale'. We can now add to these a third role: Richard is also a historian, constructing and creating the myth of his own tragic history.

Once created, that myth becomes a powerful ideology: and the play reveals it to be precisely that. Like the ideology of monarchic feudalism, which was both organic order *and* battleground of historical forces, the myth of Richard's tragedy (in its twin form of martyr king and deposed tyrant) continues to haunt the civil conflicts of his successors, who are thus, in T. S. Eliot's words, 'united in the strife which divided them'; *and* determines the shape and form of the ultimate reconciliation. When Richmond at the end of *Richard III* unites the red rose and the white, his action is subsumed into the powerful mythology created by his predecessor, 'that sweet lovely rose' Richard II.[5] □

The essence of Holderness's case is that Shakespeare, in *Richard II*, creates a feudal world in which Bolingbroke and the other lords operate by a code of chivalric loyalty. Richard seeks to dismantle this structure through a policy of absolutism, of arbitrary monarchical rule with unrestricted power and without reference to law or parliament. It is only when this policy fails, Holdernesss contends, that we hear the language of the divine right of kings: Richard's claim to be God's deputy is born out of defeat as a myth to counter the stark reality of his loss of power. That claim seeks to naturalise itself through the use of pastoral imagery of England and through Richard's construction of himself as a Christ-figure betrayed by his followers. The significance of Holderness's argument is that it reverses the traditional Tillyard reading: it is not Richard who is the representative of feudalism but Bolingbroke; it is not Bolingbroke who violates the divine right of kings but rather Richard who invokes it as a political strategy. Far from endorsing 'order', the play opens up the implications of the political struggle against the growing threat in the Renaissance of absolutist government.

II. Power

The next essay is perhaps the most difficult in this book. It combines a number of topics common in recent criticism: the relationship of power to theatrical spectacle; human subjectivity and the gaze or looking, epitomised in Richard's mirror sequence in Act IV scene i. A way to read the essay is to see how it complements Holderness's argument above: that where Holderness reverses the traditional critical assumption that the play depicts Richard as a medieval king protected by divine right, here Pye contests the idea that authority can ever be absolute.

In this first section from the essay Pye takes up Stephen Greenblatt's argument that power always involves mastery though subversion. Richard's deposition speech seems to prove the case – that even as he is deposed so his royal power is asserted. Pye suggests, however, that Richard cannot master subversion because his undoing has always already underwritten his power: the two cannot be separated so easily. This is a characteristic move of deconstructive criticism, to suggest that apparent opposites – here subversion and royal power – are part of each other. The effect of such a move is to undermine any fixity of meaning or absolutes.

From Christopher Pye, 'The Betrayal of the Gaze: Theatricality and Power in Shakespeare's *Richard II*' (1988)

■ The concerns I touch on here – authority, subversion, theatricality – have been elegantly drawn together in the recent work of Stephen Greenblatt. In the Renaissance, Greenblatt argues, 'power . . . not only produces its own subversion but is actively built upon it'. In reference to Shakespeare's sovereigns he writes that the 'ideal image [of the king] involves as its positive condition the constant production of its own radical subversion and the powerful containment of that subversion . . . order is neither possible nor fully convincing without the presence and perception of betrayal.' A power thus engaged in staging and overcoming its own subversion depends upon a mobile, improvisatory, and vicarious structure such as theatre to realize itself, Greenblatt suggests.[6] Greenblatt's account of the aims of Renaissance power is both accurate and contradictory. If subversion is the 'positive condition' of power – if it enables the possibility of power – how can power be said to 'create' that subversion? The contradiction should not be too quickly resolved, either in the direction of authority or subversiveness, for it suggests the possibility of a theatre which exceeds the power that institutes it, one which, like the traitor's equivocal glass, betrays the very authority it reflects and confirms. The apparent indeterminacy of such a structure does not at all place it beyond the politics of representation. Insofar as it catches up the subject in its resolutely specular snares, theatre sustains the dread that sustains the monarch.

––––

Richard II certainly lends itself to Greenblatt's theory of power, for the central question in the drama is whether sovereignty can prove itself absolute by mastering its own subversion. That formulation is severe, particularly since Richard often seems drawn more to the pathos of his fall than to any affirmation of his glory. Yet Richard's rule does assume its most irrefutable form through negation. 'Now mark me how I will undo myself,' Richard says, as if announcing a sleight of hand:

> I give this heavy weight from off my head,
> And this unwieldly sceptre from my hand,
> The pride of kingly sway from out my heart;
> With mine own tears I wash away my balm,
> With mine own hands I give away my crown,
> With mine own tongue deny my sacred state,

> With mine own breath release all duteous oaths;
> All pomp and majesty I do forswear;
> My manors, rents, revenues, I forgo;
> My acts, decrees, and statutes I deny.   (IV.i.203–13)

As Bolingbroke knows, if power is to be transferred legitimately only the king may unking himself. And that is an impossible act. Pompously forswearing all pomp, decreeing the end of all decrees, the king speaks an oath that can't affirm itself except by refuting itself – that can only be spoken in endless self-mockery. At this thoroughly performative moment, Richard's power cannot be denied.

The cunning performativeness of the king's self-subverting oath suggests the grounds of the ancient claim that the king's words have the power to enact what they signify. The speech also suggests that, for all its elaborate hysteria, Richard's more overtly theatrical deposition of himself – his mirror game – reflects some of the serious requirements of absolutism. In the mirror scene, too, the king seems to defy his onlookers to read the moment of his undoing. 'Mark,' he says again, after dashing the mirror to the ground, 'How soon my sorrow hath destroy'd my face' (IV.i.290–91). The scene is, of course, an overt bit of theatrics; Richard shatters only the 'shadow of [his] face', as the remote and knowing Bolingbroke calmly remarks (IV.i.293). But the king's sport beguiles nonetheless.

> Give me that glass, and therein will I read.
> No deeper wrinkles yet? . . .
>   . . . O flatt'ring glass,
> Like to my followers in prosperity,
> Thou dost beguile me. Was this face the face
> That every day under his household roof
> Did keep ten thousand men? Was this the face
> That like the sun did make beholders wink?
> Is this the face which fac'd so many follies,
> That was at last out-fac'd by Bolingbroke?
> A brittle glory shineth in this face;
> As brittle as the glory is the face,
> [*Dashes the glass to the ground*]
> For there it is, crack'd in an hundred shivers.
>
> (IV.i.276–77, 279–89)

Richard's melodramatic finale merely confirms his cool mastery of this mirror game. Absorbed perhaps more than the king himself in the specular play of his rhetoric, we had not caught the moment the 'flatt'ring' and concealing glass became the brittle face itself. As a result, shattering the fragile glass merely serves to affirm its deceptive powers. The problem for the onlooker is not that Richard's sport seems real, but that its theatrical illusion seems limitless.

The deception is not easily undone. If shattering the hollow glass merely seems to extend its domain, it is because the mirror never was separable from the response it elicited. Conflating the king's glorious face and its effacement, sovereignty and its negation, the radically indeterminate glass reflects back from the outset nothing more than the marking of it. And as a fathomless mirror of reading, the regal glass proves the king's powers to be unassailable. Richard had set out to 'read . . . the very book indeed/Where all [his] sins are writ' (IV.i.274–75). Through his self-reading, Richard does indeed mark his cardinal sin – 'undeck[ing] the pompous body of a king' – but only by way of an elusive reenactment that erodes all distinction between the king's reading and the event it laments. Through his limitlessly theatrical sport, Richard shows himself still king of his griefs, and still irrefutable master of his own demise.

While all this makes perfect sense in theory, and follows a certain implacable logic, Richard's theatricalizing nevertheless continues to feel diversionary, a desperate antic set against a larger political drama over which he has no command. In fact, the king's claim that he 'will read enough' by reading himself, that he is 'the very book indeed where all [his] sins are writ,' is in itself a disavowal. At all costs, the king would avoid reading his crimes in another text, the paper recounting his transgression against the state that Northumberland has been insistently pressing upon him. Richard's self-deposition satisfied all demands but that one. 'What more remains,' the king asks. 'No more,' Northumberland replies, 'but that you read/These accusations, and these grievous crimes/Committed by your person and your followers/Against the state and profit of this land' (IV.i.222–25). Richard's reluctance seems understandable enough. If through his spectacular self-reading Richard can elude all who 'stand and look upon [him]', the formal writ would separate the crime from the punishment and thus expose the king indeed.

Still, in seeking to deny his real condition, the king unmasks the more fundamental truth of his theatrical one. For here too Richard confronts a text of his sins that cannot be marked, but whose performative effects even the sovereign now cannot escape. 'Gentle Northumberland,' Richard says,

> If thy offences were upon record,
> Would it not shame thee, in so fair a troop,
> To read a lecture of them? If thou wouldst,
> There shouldst thou find one heinous article,

Containing the deposing of a king,
And cracking the strong warrant of an oath,
Mark'd with a blot, damn'd in the book of heaven.
Nay, all of you, that stand and look upon me
Whilst that my wretchedness doth bait myself,
Though some of you, with Pilate, wash your hands,
Showing an outward pity – yet you Pilates
Have here deliver'd me to my sour cross,
And water cannot wash away your sin.
Northumb.: My lord, dispatch, read o'er these articles.
Richard: Mine eyes are full of tears, I cannot see.
And yet salt water blinds them not so much
But they can see a sort of traitors here.
Nay, if I turn mine eyes upon myself,
I find myself a traitor with the rest.
For I have given here my soul's consent
T'undeck the pompous body of a king.   (IV.i.229–50)

Richard's teary-eyed blindness feels like an evasion, a means of turning a blind eye to the articles being forced on him and of turning from the inscribed history of his crimes against the state to the present occasion of his self-betrayal. Yet Richard's self-protective tears betray him more than he knows. His assertion that his tear-soaked eyes blind him to the text of his crimes directly follows his pronouncement that 'water cannot wash away [the] sin' of those who, 'with Pilate, wash [their] hands,/Showing an outward pity.' Richard's tears do indeed show him to be 'a traitor with the rest', but they expose him in spite of himself; the king betrays himself even as he seeks to know himself for the self-betrayer he is.

The curious redundancy of Richard's response inheres in the nature of the crime itself. Richard's tears may blind him to the text of his sins, but in doing so they mimic the 'heinous article/Containing the deposition of a king'. For that crime is itself 'marked' only with a 'blot', only by its effacement. In *Richard II* and Elizabethan culture generally the most unspeakable of crimes is always marked in that unmarked form. 'If ever I were traitor,' Mowbray exclaims, 'My name be blotted from the book of life' (I.i.201–2). When York makes Bolingbroke read the 'heinous . . . conspiracy' he cannot describe – 'Peruse this writing here, and thou shalt know/The treason that my haste forbids me show' – the new king discovers a crime that can be pardoned but still not shown: 'thy abundant goodness shall excuse/This deadly blot in thy digressing son' (V.iii.47–48, 63–64). The digressing son's own attempt to answer to the sin committed against Richard is doomed to errancy and self-contradiction by the nature of the transgression he would amend. 'Is there no plot / To rid the realm of this pernicious blot?' Aumerle asks, after viewing the 'woeful pageant' of the king's deposition (IV.i.324–25). To 'rid' the realm of this 'blot' would be to erase it, and to erase a blot is of course to renew it once again. The unmasterable persistence of treason's blot suggests that the mark of the king's undoing had always underwritten his absolute power; when Richard insists that 'water cannot wash away' the sins of his betrayers, and that 'salt water' blinds his own eyes, he unwittingly echoes his earlier pronouncement, 'Not all the water in the rough rude sea / Can wash the balm off from an anointed king' (III.ii.54–55).

Ultimately, Richard cannot be the master of his subversion because the crime is inscribed from the outset in his attempt to know it. Richard's tear-blinded sight is intimately bound up with the divisive and self-eluding gesture through which he would see himself for the traitor he is. Self-reflection once again reenacts the loss it would mark, but now the king's response to the text of his sins opens the more extravagant possibility that his grief, and his crime, are not his own. Yet despite the apparent political risks, *Richard II* gravitates toward the galvanizing pathos of these moments when inscription and specula-tion intersect.[7] □

We might see Pye's reading as exploring those theatrical moments in the text when it confronts the paradoxes and ambiguities that inhere in the action and language: that Richard's self-deposition seems to reinscribe his power as king; that the imagery of treason as blots in the play seems to suggest that treason will not only persist but is a condition of power; that the mirror does not reflect Richard's true state so much as the radical indeterminacy of all readings, that neither he nor we can separate his treason from that of the other characters. Pye's method is to examine in close detail the contradictions and tensions he sees in the play's language, particularly the images of sight and eyes, all the time moving towards a reading that stresses equivocation and slippage of meaning.

III. Language and politics

Catherine Belsey in the following essay combines ideas from Marxism and more generally from poststructuralism. Central to the essay, as in Pye's essay above, is the point that meaning is unstable: there is no necessary link between words and their signifieds or between names and their referents. In the first part of the essay (not included here), Belsey argues that there is an alternative to Tillyard's master narrative of history, his reading of the histories as telling a single story from Richard II to Henry Tudor. Rejecting the postmodern idea that we should abandon the notion of history and simply see the past as a construct, she goes on in the rest of the essay to reread the history plays as posing questions about power and its proper location, and questions about how to gain power. These questions begin in *Richard II*.

From Catherine Belsey, 'Making Histories Then and Now: Shakespeare from *Richard II* to *Henry V*' (1991)

■ It is possible to read Shakespeare's history plays otherwise, in ways which have explicit resonances for us now. The second tetralogy tells a story of change which begins in nostalgia for a lost golden world and ends in indeterminacy. Early in *Richard II* John of Gaunt speaks wistfully of a time when kings were kings and went on crusades (II.i.51–6), but by the end of *Henry V* the legitimacy of kingship itself is in question. The issue is power. Similarly, the beginning of *Richard II* seems rooted in the simple unity of names and things, but the plays chart a fall into differance which generates a world of uncertainties.[8] The issue is meaning. And the texts themselves bear witness to the difference within textuality. Read from a postmodern perspective, they reveal marks of the struggle to fix meaning, and simultaneously of the excess which necessarily renders meaning unstable.

The vanishing world to which the opening of *Richard II* alludes is an imaginary realm of transparency, plenitude and truth, where the essential link between signifier and referent has not yet been broken. Names, their meanings and the condition they name are apparently one:

> *Rich.* What comfort, man? How is't with aged Gaunt?
> *Gaunt.* O, how that name befits my composition!
> Old Gaunt, indeed; and gaunt in being old.
> Within me grief hath kept a tedious fast;
> And who abstains from meat that is not gaunt?
> For sleeping England long time have I watch'd;
> Watching breeds leanness, leanness is all gaunt.
> The pleasure that some fathers feed upon
> Is my strict fast – I mean my children's looks;
> And therein fasting, hast thou made me gaunt.
> Gaunt am I for the grave, gaunt as a grave,
> Whose hollow womb inherits nought but bones.
> (II.i.72–83)

For Richard this reiteration of Gaunt's name, specifying in a series of figures its meaning and its cause, is no more than an instance of the play of the signifier: 'Can sick men play so nicely with their names?' (II.i.84). But from the point of view of the audience, the sequence has the effect of producing a convergence on a single truth, identifying a unified state of being, gaunt by name and gaunt by nature.

Ironically, this affirmation of plenitude, of the fullness of truth in the signifier, is also an assertion of absence, of leanness, fasting, the hollow womb of the grave. Its occasion is the absence Richard has made in the political and the symbolic order. John of Gaunt is dying of grief for a land which has no heirs, a realm whose lineage is coming to an end as Richard fails to *live* the true and single meaning of sovereignty: 'Landlord of England art thou now, not King' (II.i.113). Richard divorces the name of the king from the condition, leasing out the realm and banishing Bolingbroke.

Gaunt's grief is also for his own heir. The name of Duke of Lancaster has a material existence: it is a title, an entitlement, meaning land, a position, an army, power. By sending his son into exile, Gaunt protests, 'thou dost seek to kill my name in me' (II.i.86), to end the dynasty and expropriate the land. Thus Richard, already identified as the murderer of Gloucester, is now represented as causing the death of Lancaster.

It is not, of course, to be done by fiat. Lancaster is not merely a name but a material presence. Since the title is precisely an entitlement – to property and to power in the realm – the inscription of power in the symbolic order cannot be created or destroyed by an act of individual will, not even the sovereign's. In the opening scene of the play Bolingbroke, Duke of Hereford, nephew of the dead Gloucester, challenges the king in Mowbray. In Act II Bolingbroke, his identity transformed by his father's death, returns to challenge the king again by reclaiming his title, in all its materiality: 'As I was banish'd, I was banished Hereford; / But as I come, I come for Lancaster' (II.iii.113–14); 'I am come to seek that *name* in England' (II.iii.71, my emphasis).

But as in Gaunt's sequence of figures, here too the names of England and Lancaster are linked as elements in a system of differences where meanings are interdependent. All names are authorised by inheritance, as fathers are authors of their children. The inscription of authority in a name is reciprocal and differential, not individual, and it is specified by blood. In consequence Bolingbroke is entitled to argue, 'If that my cousin king be King in England, / It must be granted I am Duke of Lancaster' (II.iii.123–4). It is not granted, of course. In the event, the king's repudiation of the symbolic order, which also guarantees his own succession, impels civil war to manure the ground with English blood in another but, of course, related sense of the word 'blood'.

There is thus only a brief moment in Act I when the truth of things is perceived to reside in names, when the grand simplicities appear to be in place, or when the (royal) sentence seems absolute. By naming

the banishment of Mowbray and Bolingbroke the king is able to bring
it about – or to repeal it. Richard sees Gaunt's grief signified in his
tears and reduces the term of Bolingbroke's exile. Bolingbroke draws
attention to the inscription of power in the signifier:

> How long a time lies in one little word!
> Four lagging winters and four wanton springs
> End in a word: such is the breath of Kings.   (I.iii.213–15)

But within the system of differences which gives meaning to kingship,
inscribes the power in royal utterances, kings are only the location of
authority, not its origin. In practice Richard cannot give meaning to his
sentences or deny meaning to the names of his subjects. His words are
absolute only on condition that they remain within the existing system
of differences. He, like his subjects, is subject to the symbolic order,
which allots meaning to the orders he gives.

Richard transgresses this system of differences when he tries to
remake the meaning of kingship in the image of his own desires. His
predecessors lived the regality of their name, Gaunt complains. Their
sovereignty was thus synonymous with England's, and the realm was
a *'scepter'd* isle', an 'earth of *majesty*' (II.i.40–1, my emphasis). But this
world of unity and plenitude is already lost. Richard-as-England has
consumed England's material wealth in riot, misusing his sovereignty
to mortgage the land, devouring in the name of his title his own entitlement. He has thus turned the sceptre against the isle, majesty against
the earth itself, and in consequence fragmented the singleness of the
realm. The 'teeming womb of royal kings' (II.i.51) is now, according to
the logic of Gaunt's rhetoric, empty, and it is this absence of heirs
which propels one of its few remaining denizens towards the grave,
'Whose hollow womb inherits nought but bones' (II.i.83). Richard
violates the symbolic order, and in consequence his words lose their
sovereignty: Bolingbroke returns, repudiating the royal sentence of
banishment.

Richard makes a gap between names and things, between kingship and its referent, majesty, and Gaunt cannot live in the new world
he makes. But Bolingbroke belongs there already, and thus prolepti-
cally identifies himself as Richard's heir even more surely than he is
his father's. Gaunt offers consolation for exile in the supremacy of
the signifier:

> Go, say I sent thee forth to purchase honour,
> And not the King exil'd thee; or suppose
> Devouring pestilence hangs in our air
> And thou art flying to a fresher clime.

> Look what thy soul holds dear, imagine it
> To lie that way thou goest . . .   (I.iii.282–7)

But his son recognises the power to remake the referent in accordance with the signifier as precisely imaginary:

> O, who can hold a fire in his hand
> By thinking on the frosty Caucasus?
> Or cloy the hungry edge of appetite
> By bare imagination of a feast?
> Or wallow naked in December snow
> By thinking on fantastic summer's heat?   (I.iii.294–9)

But if Bolingbroke recognises the differance that Richard has made, or has made evident, the difference and the distance between the signifier and what it re-presents, Richard himself is tragically unable to do so. This is the dramatic irony of what follows, as Richard, deserted by 12,000 Welshmen, clings to the imaginary sovereignty of the signifier:

> Is not the King's name twenty thousand names?
> Arm, arm, my name! a puny subject strikes
> At thy great glory.   (III.ii.85–7)

In practice, we are to understand, the unity of the king's name and kingship itself have fallen apart. The realm has deserted him for Bolingbroke, and Richard is king precisely in name only.

Meanwhile, the new and silent sovereign says nothing, uses few words, or none (IV.i.290). It is Richard himself who employs the breath of kings to strip away the signifier of his own monarchy: 'What must the King do now? . . . Must he lose / The name of king? A God's name, let it go' (III.iii.143–6). But like Gaunt, he cannot survive in the world of differance, where if he is not king he has no identity at all: 'I must nothing be' (IV.i.201). 'What says King Bolingbroke? Will his Majesty / Give Richard leave to live till Richard die?' (III.iii.173–4). As Marjorie Garber points out, the king performs an act of erasure, as differance thus invades his identity, enters into the selfhood of Richard:[9]

> I have no name, no title –
> No, not that name was given me at the font –
> But 'tis usurp'd. Alack the heavy day,
> That I have worn so many winters out,
> And know not now what name to call myself!

> O that I were a mockery king of snow,
> Standing before the sun of Bolingbroke
> To melt myself away in water drops.   (IV.i.255–62)

He is already a mockery king, other than himself, figured here as insubstantial, a snowman visibly melting away, though it is worth remembering, of course, that his name, his entitlement, will return to haunt the remainder of the second tetralogy.

———

Richard fails to find a means of holding the signified in place, guaranteeing his title. The Bishop of Carlisle proffers the grandest of all grand narratives:

> Fear not, my lord; that Power that made you king
> Hath power to keep you king in spite of all. (III.ii.27–8)

And Richard reiterates it (III.ii.54–62). But the play at once subjects the master-narrative of divine protection for divine right to ironic scrutiny, as first Salisbury and then Scroop deliver their *petits récits* of desertions and defeats.[10] If God has the power, he signally fails in a fallen world to exercise it on behalf of his anointed deputy. The only power on earth that supports the materiality of titles is the law of succession, and Richard breaks it by seizing Bolingbroke's title (II.i.195–208).

Bolingbroke's regime becomes in consequence one of bitter uncertainties, of conflicts for meaning which are simultaneously conflicts for power. These constitute the story of the reign of Henry IV, but the uncertainty begins in the deposition scene in *Richard II*, when it becomes apparent that the word is no longer anchored in the referent, no longer names a single, consensual object. The Bishop of Carlisle defends Richard's sovereignty in the name of the transcendental signified: the king is 'the figure of God's majesty' (IV.i.125). In consequence, he argues, 'My Lord of Hereford here, whom you call king,/Is a foul traitor to proud Hereford's king' (IV.i. 134–5). As he concludes his argument, Northumberland steps forward on behalf of Hereford (now Lancaster; now England?) and turns the verbal and political tables on Carlisle: 'Well have you argued, sir; and for your pains,/Of capital treason we arrest you here' (IV.i.150–1).

In a world of differance who is the traitor? who is the king? When in Act I Mowbray and Bolingbroke accuse each other of treason, the truth is available: in the following scene the exchanges between Gaunt and the Duchess of Gloucester make clear to the audience that Richard is responsible for Gloucester's murder. But in the new world of differance who can be sure? If Richard is king, Bolingbroke is a traitor. But is he? If Bolingbroke is king, Carlisle is a traitor. But is he? Richard's breach of the symbolic order has divorced the name of king from the power, laying bare a world of political struggle for possession of meaning, property and sovereignty. In this new world it is not a name but the allegiance of the Duke of York and of 12,000 Welshmen which proves decisive. The orders of the mockery King are now subject to confirmation by Bolingbroke:

> For do we must what force will have us do.
> Set on towards London. Cousin, is it so?
> *Bol.* Yea, my good Lord.
> *K. Rich.* Then I must not say no.   (III.iii.207–9)

Bolingbroke comes back to claim his title in the name of law, but his victory, the play makes clear, is an effect of force, not legality. Nevertheless, the repressed law of succession returns to disrupt the reign of Henry IV. It is Mortimer's legal title as Richard's heir which cements the quarrel between Hotspur and the king (*1 King Henry IV*, I.iii.77ff., 145–59), and if Mortimer is not the motive, he is none the less the legitimating occasion of the rebellion which constitutes the main plot of the *Henry IV* plays.[11] □

Belsey's argument is that Richard's utterances initially have authority precisely because they are part of the 'symbolic order', the order of language and culture. His words do not have power on their own to fashion the world. His action of taking Gaunt's land and repudiating Bolingbroke's titles, however, disrupts the system of difference which holds meaning in place: in the new world Richard has created it is no longer clear who is a traitor and who is king. The struggle that follows is both about control of the country and control of meaning. The histories, then, do not, as Tillyard proposed, tell a master-narrative endorsing kingship and condemning rebellion. Rather, they raise questions and the possibility of other kinds of thinking.

IV. Gender

As Jean E. Howard and Phyllis Rackin point out in the introduction to their book *Engendering A Nation*, there have been relatively few feminist readings of *Richard II*.[12] This may be because, in its early stages, feminist criticism was more concerned with the comedies where women have prominent roles. 'What is important about the histories', they continue (p. 20) 'is not primarily the images of women they construct . . . but the impact on the ways we imagine gender and sexual difference'. Here we might include the sort of impact the history plays (but not just the histories) have had over the centuries on the thinking about what constitutes the nation, manliness, heroism and the position of women in a military society. The extract below, however, analyses the way in which women are presented in *Richard II*, and how the play undermines simple gender oppositions.

From Jean E. Howard and Phyllis Rackin, *Engendering A Nation* (1997)

■ From a feminist standpoint, one of the most striking features of the second tetralogy is the restriction of women's roles. We have already seen how the formidable power of the women warriors in the Henry VI plays and *King John* was replaced in *Richard III* by the pathetic laments of mourning widows and bereaved mothers. In the second tetralogy, women's roles are further constricted. There are fewer female characters; they have less time on stage and less to say when they get there. Moreover, virtually all the women we see in these plays are enclosed in domestic settings and confined to domestic roles. . . .

In the plays of the second tetralogy, as in *Richard III*, female sexuality no longer threatens to disrupt legitimate authority. When Bullingbrook charges in *Richard II* that Bushy and Green 'have in manner with [their] sinful hours/Made a divorce betwixt his queen and him,/Broke the possession of a royal bed' (III.i.11–13), the sexual culprits are the king and his male favourites: it is not even clear that any women are involved. The only reference to the queen's sexuality is purely metaphorical – the 'unborn sorrow, ripe in fortune's womb' her feminine intuition detects (II.ii.10). The sorrow, moreover, is a fully legitimate conception: caused by a premonition of her husband's impending fall, it is implicitly designated as the offspring of her lawful marriage. The other women in the play – the Duchess of Gloucester and the Duchess of York – are too old to pose a sexual threat. The Duke and Duchess of York, in fact, make this point explicit. In V.ii the duchess reminds her husband that her 'teeming date' is 'drunk up with time' (91); and in V.iii, York opposes her attempt to plead for her son's life by reminding her how preposterous it would be if her 'old dugs' should 'once more a traitor rear' (90).

Barbara Hodgdon's observation about *Henry IV, Part I* – that the play is 'unlike Shakespeare's earlier histories, where conflict centres on genealogical descent in a struggle for the crown's rightful ownership'[13] – is applicable to the entire second tetralogy. . . . In *Richard II* York gives his allegiance to Bullingbrook despite his knowledge that Richard is the legitimate heir of Edward III. Because patrilineal inheritance is no longer sufficient to guarantee patriarchal authority, female sexual transgression no longer threatens to subvert it. The issues of bastardy and adultery arise only briefly and only in Act V, when the action degenerates from the historical tragedy of Richard's fall to the farcical domestic quarrel between the Duke and Duchess of York about their son. Terrified by her husband's threat to report Aumerle's treason to the new king, the duchess assumes, wrongly, that he is motivated by doubts about his son's paternity:

> But now I know thy mind, thou dost suspect
> That I have been disloyal to thy bed,
> And that he is a bastard, not thy son.
> Sweet York, sweet husband, be not of that mind,
> He is as like thee as a man may be
> Not like to me, or any of my kin. (V.ii.104–9)

Neither York nor the audience has any reason to doubt what the duchess says. In fact, her anxious suspicion that York doubts his son's paternity is expressed in terms that render it ludicrous. Instead of empowering the duchess as a sexual threat to the authority of her husband and the legitimacy of her son, her reference to the possibility of her adultery is designed to elicit dismissive laughter.

Here, as in *Richard III*, the constriction of women's roles represents a movement into modernity, the division of labour and the cultural restrictions that accompanied the production of the household as a private place, separated from the public arenas of economic and political endeavour. To move from the first tetralogy to the second is to move backward to the time of Richard II, but it is also to move forward from a story of warring feudal families to one of the consolidation of the English nation under the power of a great king. In the first tetralogy, virtue and military power like Talbot's are inherited along with the patrilineal titles of nobility; in the second, they are the personal assets that enable the son of an enterprising upstart like Henry Bullingbrook to achieve the status of the mirror of all Christian kings and the aspiring men in the theatre audience to earn their places in the commonwealth.

In *Richard II* the contradictions between those two models of personal and royal legitimacy are personalized in the opposition between Richard and Bullingbrook; but they are also framed as abstract issues, the subjects for repeated debate by male characters in the play, the motives and rationalizations for their acts and decisions. The dynastic loyalties that motivate much of the action in the first tetralogy typically make political action the product of filial devotion, but in *Richard II* the private affective bonds that unite fathers and sons are opposed to and superseded by the demands of political principle and civic duty. Gaunt agrees to the banishment of his own son because, as he tells King Richard, 'You urg'd me as a judge' and not 'like a father' (I.iii.237–8). The Duke of York, discovering that his son has joined a conspiracy to kill the new king, Henry IV, pleads that his son *not* be pardoned because, he explains, 'If thou do pardon, whosoever pray, / More sins for this forgiveness prosper may. / This fest'red joint cut off, the rest rest sound, / This let alone will all the rest confound' (V.iii.83–6). Even the instructions the gardener gives his helpers take the form of a lesson in political theory:

> Go thou, and like an executioner
> Cut off the heads of [too] fast growing sprays,
> That look too lofty in our commonwealth:
> All must be even in our government.   (III.iv.33–36)

The concern for the commonwealth that unites the lowly gardeners with their betters at court also separates men from women. All of the female characters in *Richard II* come from the top of the social and political hierarchy, but their interests are delimited by the private affective bonds of family loyalty, and the women are entirely preoccupied by concerns for their male relations. These concerns differ significantly from the strong genealogical ties that bind fathers to sons in the Henry VI plays. Those ties, while they often include an affective dimension, as in Talbot's concern for his son, also have a public political and economic dimension: the defense and consolidation of dynastic power and its transmission from one generation to the next. Gaunt shares the Duchess of Gloucester's grief for her murdered husband, who was his own brother, but when the duchess tries to persuade him to avenge Gloucester's death, Gaunt refuses because his loyalty to the principle of divine right takes precedence over his personal loyalty to his brother: Richard, he explains, is God's 'deputy', and 'I may never lift / An angry arm against His minister' (I.ii.38–41). The same gendered difference distinguishes the gardener and his helper from the queen. The common men lament Richard's bad government and its effects upon the commonwealth as well as his downfall; the royal woman responds to the news as a personal catastrophe for herself and her husband. Intensified to the point of caricature, the opposition between masculine political considerations and feminine affective loyalty is reiterated in Act V when the Duke and Duchess of York wrangle over whether their son should be punished or pardoned for his part in the conspiracy to assassinate the new king.

Like the bereaved and grieving women in *Richard III*, the Duchess of Gloucester and the queen in *Richard II* dramatize the private emotional costs of the men's public, political conflicts; and, like the women in *Richard III*, they are powerless to affect the outcome of those conflicts. When Gaunt refuses to avenge her husband's murder, the Duchess of Gloucester leaves the stage to die of grief. The queen does not even learn that Richard is to be deposed until she eavesdrops on the gardeners' conversation. When Bullingbrook pardons Aumerle, the Duchess of York becomes the only woman in the play who manages to influence the action, but her farcical wrangling with her husband also reinforces the separation between the public, political concerns of men and the private, affective loyalties of women. The bickering between the duke and duchess – and with it the lowering of the dramatic register – begins in V.ii when York struggles frantically to get his boots so he can ride off to warn the king about Aumerle's participation in a conspiracy to assassinate him, while the duchess, equally frantic, struggles to prevent him. In the following scene the domestic quarrel resumes in the royal presence, and this time the humour is explicitly identified with the inappropriateness of the duchess's intervention. Her demand to be admitted to the royal presence initiates a telling remark from the new king: 'Speak with me, pity me, open the door!', she cries, 'A beggar begs that never begg'd before.' In a comment probably meant to be addressed to the audience, the king responds, 'Our scene is alt'red from a serious thing, / And now changed to "The Beggar and the King"' (V.iii.77–80), signalling that the historical 'Tragedy of Richard II' is being interrupted by the low comic farce of 'The Beggar and the King'. Significantly, it is the woman who is blamed for initiating both the generic lowering of the drama and the social lowering of the action. The solemn dignity of the court (and of the history play) has no place for domestic quarrels or the shrill-voiced supplications of an anxious mother.

The gendering of excessive emotion as feminine has unsettling effects on the gender position – and the authority – of Richard II, perhaps the most emotive of all Shakespeare's kings. While masculinity and femininity are never the exclusive properties of male and female persons, aspects of English culture in the late sixteenth and early seventeenth centuries made the performative and constructed nature of gender difference disturbingly visible. In the theatres, boys played women's roles and many kinds of social distinctions were indicated by a semiotics of dress and gesture. On the throne, there was a female monarch who claimed masculine authority by referring to herself as a 'prince'. In the streets of London, women paraded in masculine dress. An increasingly urbanized and performative culture destabilized traditional status distinctions, including the distinctions between men and women, and produced a wide variety of anxious attempts to re-establish them. For the literate, increasing concern with the need to observe masculine and feminine roles was expressed in satiric writing that made the 'womanish' man and the 'mannish' woman stock objects of invective. In villages, failure to abide by the codes of gendered behaviour was punished by court prosecutions of scolds and witches and community shaming rituals such as charivaris.

All these efforts to enforce gender difference can be seen as responses to an emergent culture of personal achievement. If a man's place in the social hierarchy had to be achieved and secured by his own efforts, any claims to authority required that both social status and gender status had to be sustained in performance. In *Richard II*, the king's patrilineal authority is vitiated by his womanish tears and his effeminate behaviour: he has no taste for foreign wars, he talks when he should act, and he wastes his kingdom's treasure by indulging in excessive luxuries. Bullingbrook, who has no hereditary right to the crown, acquires it by the successful performance of masculine virtues.

Many critics have remarked that the conflict between Richard and Bullingbrook is framed as a conflict between two models of royal authority, Richard associated with a nostalgic image of medieval royalty, grounded in heredity and expressed in ceremonial ritual, Bullingbrook with the emergence of an authority achieved by personal performance and expressed in the politically motivated theatrical self-presentation of a modern ruler. What is less frequently noted is how thoroughly the binary opposition personalized in the conflict between Bullingbrook and Richard is implicated in an early modern ideology of 'masculine' and 'feminine'. Deborah Warner's 1995 production of the play, which starred Fiona Shaw as Richard, exploited this gendered opposition to brilliant dramatic effect. Shaw, in the words of one reviewer, 'simply played Richard as a woman'. Although Shakespeare does not literalize the gendered opposition between the two antagonists, his Bullingbrook, like Warner's, plays the 'man' to Richard's 'woman'. A master of military and political strategy, Bullingbrook is shown in company with a noble father, and he alludes to the existence of an 'unthrifty' son (V.iii.1); but we hear nothing of his wife or mother, and he is never represented in association with women. Richard, by contrast, has a wife but no son. Although our own gender ideology privileges male heterosexual passion as an expression of virility, this was not yet the case in Shakespeare's time. Richard is characterized as 'effeminate', but this does not mean that he is 'homosexual': indeed, the terms 'homosexual' and 'heterosexual', along with the conceptions of gendered personal identity they denote, are post-Shakespearean inventions. Richard is effeminate because he prefers words to deeds, has no taste for battle, and is addicted to luxurious pleasures. His rapid fluctuations from overweening confidence to the depth of despair (III.ii) recall early modern misogynist denunciations of feminine instability, but even his virtues are represented in feminine terms: York's sympathetic description of Richard's behaviour in adversity – his 'gentle sorrow' and 'His face still combating with tears and smiles,/The badges of his grief and patience' (V.ii.31–3) – draws on the . . . discourse of suffering feminine virtue. . . . Bullingbrook speaks few words but raises a large army. Richard is a master of poetic eloquence, unsurpassed in what Mowbray calls 'a woman's war . . . of . . . tongues' (I.i.48–9), but he surrenders to Bullingbrook without waging a single battle. His viceroy is the super-annuated York, who appears 'weak with age', 'with signs of war about his aged neck' (II.ii.83, 74); confronted by Bullingbrook's military challenge, York immediately capitulates, declaring that he will 'remain as neuter' (II.iii.159).

The gendered opposition between Richard and Bullingbrook takes much of its force from the predicament of the English aristocracy at the time the play was produced. The noblemen who support Bullingbrook's rebellion are motivated by what they perceive as monarchial threats to their traditional power and authority, threats which are explicitly identified as emasculation when Ross charges that Richard's appropriation of Bullingbrook's inheritance has left him 'bereft and gelded of his patrimony' (II.i.237). As Richard Halpern points out, 'the aristocracy felt emasculated by conversion from a militarized to a consuming class'. This anxiety was heightened during Elizabeth's reign by the presence of a female monarch and by the queen's transformation of the medieval culture of aristocratic honour from martial service to courtly display.[14] Richard's possession of the throne, like Elizabeth's, is authorized by the old warrant of patrilineal inheritance, but his loss of it is defined in terms of the new anxieties that Halpern describes. . . .

Confronted by rapid cultural change, Shakespeare's contemporaries often idealized the past as a time of stable values and national glory, when social status was firmly rooted in patrilineal inheritance and expressed in chivalric virtue. In Shakespeare's representation of Richard II, however, the schematic oppositions between an idealized masculine past and a degraded effeminate present give way to expose the cultural contradictions that lay at the heart of Elizabethan nostalgia for the medieval past. In Richard's characterization – as in the case of Elizabeth herself – the polluting forces of effeminate modernity are embodied in the same person who represents the patrilineal royal authority they threaten to subvert.[15] □

Howard and Rackin suggest that women's roles in *Richard II* and the second tetralogy are much more restricted than in the earlier history plays (*Henry VI, Richard III*). They are, essentially, confined to the domestic rather than public sphere. Again, women throughout *Richard II* are powerless to change things. At the same time female sexuality is no longer seen as a threat because 'patrilineal inheritance' – the inheritance of sons from fathers – has been disrupted by Richard. Richard himself, however, 'is characterised as "effeminate"', so that his challenge to the feudal aristocracy is also a threat to their masculinity. In effect, Richard simultaneously embodies an 'effeminate modernity' and 'patrilineal royal authority' and so acts as a site of the play's anxieties and contradictions.

What we might notice about Howard and Rackin's essay is how it takes a familiar topic in criticism of *Richard II* – in this case, Richard's so-called effeminacy – but interprets it in a larger political and cultural context. This is true of all the essays in this final chapter. Recent criticism has not abandoned the themes and issues that traditional criticism has identified in the play, but it has interpreted them in a new way, so changing our perception of those themes and issues and of the play itself. That work is likely to continue into the future, generating new insights into the texts and new readings of them. *Richard II* is at the centre of that process because it is a play that, perhaps more than any other of Shakespeare's histories, lends itself to each new wave of criticism, provoking critical debate about every aspect of itself, including its own critical history.

NOTES

INTRODUCTION

1 Josephine A. Roberts, 'Richard II': An Annotated Bibliography, 2 vols. (New York: Garland Press, 1988).

2 Quoted in Margaret Shewring, King Richard II, Shakespeare in Performance series (Manchester: Manchester University Press, 1996), p.191.

3 Samuel Taylor Coleridge, in Thomas Middleton Raysor (ed.), Coleridge's Shakespearean Criticism, 2 vols. (London: Constable & Co., 1930), II, p.186.

4 E.M.W. Tillyard, Shakespeare's History Plays (London: Chatto & Windus, 1948), pp.259, 261.

5 Roland Barthes, 'The Death of the Author', in Image–Music–Text, trans. Stephen Heath (New York: Hill and Wang, 1977), p.148.

6 Cf. Diane Elam, 'Why Read?', 'CCUE News' (The Council for College and University English), 8 (1977), pp.10–13.

7 Regenia Gagnier, 'The Disturbances Overseas: A Comparative Report on the Future of English Studies', 'CCUE News', 8 (1997), p.8.

8 Peter Ure (ed.), King Richard II, The Arden Shakespeare (London: Methuen, 1991); Stanley Wells (ed.), King Richard The Second, New Penguin Shakespeare (Harmondsworth: Penguin, 1969); Andrew Gurr (ed.), King Richard II, The New Cambridge Shakespeare (Cambridge: Cambridge University Press, 1984).

9 Alexander Pope, preface to his edition of The Works of Shakespeare, Collated and Collected (1725), reprinted in Brian Vickers (ed.), Shakespeare: The Critical Heritage, 6 vols (London: Routledge and Kegan Paul, 1974), II, p.414.

10 Margaret Shewring, King Richard II, Shakespeare in Performance series (Manchester: Manchester University Press, 1996).

CHAPTER ONE

1 See Peter Ure (ed.), Richard II, Arden edition, p.xiii.

2 E.K. Chambers, William Shakespeare: A Study of Facts and Problems, 2 vols. (Oxford: Clarendon Press, 1930), I, p.353.

3 Andrew Gurr (ed.), King Richard II, New Cambridge edition, p.182.

4 Peter Ure (ed.), Richard II, Arden edition, p.xiv.

5 Stanley Wells (ed.), King Richard The Second, Penguin edition, p.269.

6 Graham Holderness, Shakespeare's History (Dublin: Gill and Macmillan, 1985), p.132.

7 Margaret Shewring, King Richard II (Manchester: Manchester University Press, 1996), pp.23–4. All further references are given in parentheses in the text. Shewring's account of the early staging of the play is essential reading.

8 See further Janet Clare, 'Art made tongue-tied by authority': Elizabethan and Jacobean Dramatic Censorship (Manchester: Manchester University Press, 1990), and Mervyn James, Society, Politics, Culture: Studies in Early Modern England (Cambridge: Cambridge University Press, 1986).

9 See James, pp.448–9 (quoted in Shewring, p.26).

10 Quoted in the Arden edition, p.lviii.

11 Cf. Evelyn May Albright, 'Shakespeare's Richard II and the Essex Conspiracy', PMLA, 42 (1927), p.695.

12 E.W. Ives, 'Shakespeare and History: Divergences and Agreements', Shakespeare Survey, 38 (1985), p.22.

13 For E.M.W. Tillyard, see Chapter Five.

14 Ernst H. Kantorowicz, The King's Two Bodies: A Study in Medieval Political Theology (Princeton: Princeton University Press, 1957), pp.40, 28 n.15. An extract from Kantorowicz appears in Chapter Six. For Walter Pater, see Chapter Four.

15 For a brief discussion of New Historicism, see the extract from Christopher Pye in Chapter Seven. New Historicism is most often associated with the American critic Stephen Greenblatt.

See the 'Introduction' to his *The Power of Forms in the English Renaissance* (Norman, Oklahoma: Pilgrim Books, 1982) for a brief discussion of *Richard II*.

16 David Norbrook, '"A Liberal Tongue": Language and Rebellion in *Richard II*', in John M. Mucciolo *et al.* (eds), *Shakespeare's Universe: Renaissance Ideas and Conventions* (Aldershot: Scolar Press, 1996), pp. 37–51.

17 See, for example, Leeds Barroll, 'A New History for Shakespeare and his Time', *Shakespeare Quarterly*, 39 (1988), pp. 441–64.

18 Phyllis Rackin, *Stages of History: Shakespeare's English Chronicles* (London: Routledge, 1991), p. 110ff.

19 Rackin, p. 118.

CHAPTER TWO

1 Reprinted in Brian Vickers (ed.), *Shakespeare: The Critical Heritage, 1623–1801*, 6 vols. (London and Boston: Routledge and Kegan Paul, 1974–1981), I, 4. Vickers is an invaluable source of criticism for the period 1623–1801. All further references are given in parentheses in the text by volume and page number. Charles Forker (ed.), *Shakespeare: The Critical Tradition: 'Richard II'* (London and Atlantic Highlands: Athlone, 1998) is an important supplement to Vickers, and covers the years 1780–1920.

2 See Terence Hawkes, *Meaning By Shakespeare* (London and New York: Routledge, 1992), and Gary Taylor, *Reinventing Shakespeare: A Cultural History from the Restoration to the Present* (London: Hogarth Press, 1989).

3 See Oswald LeWinter (ed.), *Shakespeare in Europe* (Harmondsworth: Penguin, 1963), pp. 18–19.

4 Margaret Shewring, *King Richard II* (Manchester: Manchester University Press, 1996), p. 53. All further references are given in parentheses in the text.

5 Nicholas Brooke (ed.), *Shakespeare: 'Richard II'*, Casebook Series (London: Macmillan, 1973), p. 13.

6 The reference to *King Lear* in Tate's Preface suggests that he was working on a formula basis, that having had a hit with changing that play he sought to achieve the same effect with his version of *Richard II*.

7 Brooke (Casebook), p. 13.

8 I have benefited greatly from Susan Bruce's lucid discussion of Dryden and Neo-Classicism in her *William Shakespeare: King Lear*, Icon Critical Guides (Cambridge: Icon, 1997).

9 See Shewring, p. 41, quoting James G. McManaway, 'Richard II at Covent Garden', *Shakespeare Quarterly*, 15 (1964), p. 163.

CHAPTER THREE

1 Jonathan Bate (ed.) *The Romantics on Shakespeare* (Harmondsworth: Penguin, 1992), p. 2. All further references are given in parentheses in the text. I have made extensive use of Bate's excellent introduction for this chapter.

2 L. C. Knights is best known for his books *Explorations* (London: Chatto and Windus, 1946) and *Some Shakespearean Themes and An Approach to Hamlet* (Harmondsworth: Penguin, 1966). G. Wilson Knight is perhaps best known for his book *The Wheel of Fire: Interpretations of Shakespearian Tragedy* (London: Methuen, 1930), though this is only one of several on Shakespeare. For political approaches to Shakespeare, see Jonathan Dollimore and Alan Sinfield (eds), *Political Shakespeare* (Manchester: Manchester University Press, 1985); John Drakakis (ed.), *Alternative Shakespeares* (London: Methuen, 1985); Terence Hawkes (ed.), *Alternative Shakespeares: Volume 2* (London: Routledge, 1996).

3 Oswald LeWinter (ed.), *Shakespeare in Europe* (Harmondsworth: Penguin, 1970), p. 27, notes the mixture in Voltaire's criticism of Shakespeare of admiration and antagonism.

4 I owe this point to Susan Bruce (ed.), *William Shakespeare: King Lear*, Icon Critical Guides (Cambridge: Icon, 1997), pp. 49–50.

5 Victor Hugo, *William Shakespeare*, trans. Melville B. Anderson (London: George Routledge and Sons, n.d.), p. 289.

6 Hugo, p. 294.

7 See Bate, p. 9 ff. Herder also vigorously challenged the unities.

8 Augustus William Schlegel, *A Course of Lectures on Dramatic Art and Literature*, trans. John Black (London: Henry G. Bohn, 1846), p. 340. All further references are given in parentheses in the text.

9 See Bate's introduction for a full discussion.

10 Samuel Taylor Coleridge, in Thomas Middleton Raysor (ed.), *Coleridge's Shakespearean Criticism* (London: Constable & Co, 1930), I, pp. 223–4. All further references are given in parentheses in the text.

11 See Margaret Shewring, *King Richard II* (Manchester: Manchester University Press, 1996), p. 38 for details.

12 For Tillyard, see Chapter Five.

13 Coleridge begins his lecture by defending Shakespeare's use of puns, a feature of his language which had been singled out for attack by eighteenth-century critics.

14 See Charles Lamb, 'On the Tragedies of Shakespeare, considered with reference to their fitness for stage representation', in Edmund D. Jones (ed.), *English Critical Essays: Nineteenth Century* (London: Oxford University Press, 1950), pp. 81–96.

15 William Hazlitt, in W. E. Henley (ed.), *The Collected Works of William Hazlitt*, 12 vols (London: J.M. Dent and Sons, 1903), VIII, pp. 278–84.

16 Nicholas Brooke (ed.), *Shakespeare: 'Richard II'*, Casebook Series (London: Macmillan, 1973), pp. 13–14.

17 Hazlitt, I, pp. 272–6.

CHAPTER FOUR

1 A.C. Bradley, *Shakespearean Tragedy* (London: Macmillan, 1904).

2 Margaret Shewring, *King Richard II* (Manchester: Manchester University Press, 1996), p. xi. All further references are given in parentheses in the text.

3 A.C. Sprague, *Shakespeare's Histories: Plays for the Stage* (London: The Society for Theatre Research, 1964), p. 31.

4 Ralph Berry, *On Directing Shakespeare: Interviews with Contemporary Directors* (London: Croom Helm, 1977), p. 16 (quoted in Shewring, p. 2). As Shewring notes (p. 58), in 1903 Beerbohm Tree went even further, using live horses for the tournament scene.

5 Edward Dowden, *Shakespeare: A Critical Study of His Mind and Art* (1875; London: Routledge & Kegan Paul, 1967), pp. 193–202.

6 Walter Pater, *Appreciations: with an Essay on Style* (London: Macmillan, 1910), pp. 193–204.

7 C.E. Montague, 'F.R. Benson's *Richard II*', in *The Manchester Guardian*, 4 December 1899, reprinted in Nicholas Brooke (ed.), *Shakespeare: 'Richard II'*, Casebook Series (London: Macmillan, 1973). Brooke's introduction, though brief, provides a perceptive summary of the play's critical history.

8 W.B. Yeats, *Ideas of Good and Evil* (London: A.H. Bullen, 1903), pp. 142–67, reprinted in W.B. Yeats, *Essays and Introductions* (London: Macmillan, 1961), pp. 96–109.

9 E.K. Chambers (ed.), 'Introduction' to *King Richard II* (London and New York: Longmans, Green & Co., 1891), pp. vii–xxvii, reprinted in Jeanne T. Newlin (ed.), *'Richard II': Critical Essays* (New York: Garland & Co., 1984), pp. 207–16.

CHAPTER FIVE

1 David M. Bergeron, *Shakespeare: A Study and Research Guide* (London: Macmillan, 1975, p. 56, quoted in Graham Holderness, *Shakespeare's History* (Dublin: Gill and Macmillan, 1985), p. 192.

2 Richard Dutton, 'The Second Tetralogy', in Stanley Wells (ed.), *Shakespeare: A Bibliographic Guide* (Oxford:

Clarendon Press, 1990), p. 349.

3 Margaret Shewring, *King Richard II* (Manchester: Manchester University Press, 1996), pp. 71–2.

4 Caroline Spurgeon, *Shakespeare's Imagery and What it Tells Us* (New York: Macmillan, 1935).

5 Dutton, pp. 339, 340.

6 E. M. W. Tillyard, *The Elizabethan World Picture* (1943; London: Peregrine Books, 1963), pp. 18–27.

7 Irving Ribner, *The English History Play in the Age of Shakespeare* (Princeton: Princeton University Press, 1957), pp. 12–13.

8 E. M. W. Tillyard, *Shakespeare's History Plays* (1944; Harmondworth: Penguin, 1964), pp. 245–63. With Tillyard also compare M. M. Reese, *The Cease of Majesty: A Study of Shakespeare's History Plays* (London: Edward Arnold, 1961), and D.A. Traversi, *Shakespeare from 'Richard II' to 'Henry V'* (London: Hollis & Carter, 1957).

9 Holderness, pp. 194, 195.

10 Holderness, p.17.

11 John Dover Wilson (ed.), 'Introduction' to *King Richard II* (1939; Cambridge: Cambridge University Press, 1951), pp. xvi–xxxviii.

12 Lily B. Campbell, *Shakespeare's "Histories": Mirrors of Elizabethan Policy* (1947; London: Methuen, 1964), pp. 194–212.

CHAPTER SIX

1 New Criticism is primarily associated with the American academic Cleanth Brooks and the poet John Crowe Ransom, but it owed much of its thinking to T. S. Eliot and I. A. Richards, the inventor of modern practical criticism. Although he would have denied the label, F. R. Leavis, the foremost influence on literary criticism in Britain in the 1960s, was, in some senses, also a New Critic. The term in this way becomes something of a catch-all. See M. H. Abrams, *A Glossary of Literary Terms*, sixth edition (Orlando: Harcourt Brace Jovanovich, 1993).

2 See Catherine Belsey, *Critical Practice* (1980; London: Routledge, 1994), p.15 ff.

3 A.P. Rossiter, *Angel With Horns* (London: Longmans, Green and Co, 1961), pp. 36, 37.

4 Robert Ornstein, *A Kingdom for a Stage* (Cambridge: Harvard University Press, 1972), pp. 105, 113. Similar challenges to Tillyard include Moody E. Prior, *The Drama of Power* (Evanston, Illinois: Northwestern University Press, 1973), and Wilbur Sanders, *The Dramatist and the Received Idea: Studies in the Plays of Marlowe and Shakespeare* (Cambridge: Cambridge University Press, 1968).

5 Norman Rabkin, *Shakespeare and the Common Understanding* (New York: Free Press, 1967), pp. 80–90.

6 Richard Altick, 'Symphonic Imagery in *Richard II*', *PMLA*, 62 (1947), pp. 339–65, reprinted in Nicholas Brooke (ed.), *Shakespeare: 'Richard II'*, Casebook Series (London: Macmillan, 1973), and Jeanne T. Newlin (ed.) *'Richard II': Critical Essays* (New York: Garland & Co., 1984).

7 M.M. Mahood, *Shakespeare's Wordplay* (London: Methuen, 1957), pp. 73–82.

8 Ernst H. Kantorowicz, *The King's Two Bodies: A Study in Medieval Political Theology* (Princeton: Princeton University Press, 1957), pp. 24–40.

9 Jan Kott, *Shakespeare Our Contemporary* (1965; London: Methuen, 1967), pp. 5–13.

10 Alvin Kernan, 'The Henriad: Shakespeare's Major History Plays', *Yale Review*, 59 (1969), pp. 3–13.

CHAPTER SEVEN

1 For the impact of critical theory, see Terry Eagleton, *William Shakespeare* (Oxford: Basil Blackwell, 1986); Kiernan Ryan, *Shakespeare* (Hemel Hempstead: Harvester-Wheatsheaf, 1989); John Drakakis (ed.), *Alternative Shakespeares* (London: Methuen, 1985); Terence Hawkes (ed.), *Alternative Shakespeares: Volume 2* (London: Routledge, 1996); Patricia Parker and Geoffrey Hartman

(eds), *Shakespeare and the Question of Theory* (New York and London: Methuen, 1985). Useful books on theory include Terry Eagleton, *Literary Theory: An Introduction* (Oxford: Basil Blackwell, 1983); Catherine Belsey, *Critical Practice* (1980; London: Routledge, 1994); Ann Jefferson and David Robey (eds), *Modern Literary Theory: A Comparative Introduction* (London: Batsford, 1986); Andrew Bennett and Nicholas Royle, *An Introduction to Literature, Criticism and Theory* (Hemel Hempstead: Harvester, 1995).

2 See, for example, Leah Marcus, *Unediting the Renaissance: Shakespeare, Marlowe, Milton* (New York: Routledge, 1996), and the series *Shakespeare Originals*, edited by Graham Holderness and Bryan Loughrey (Hemel Hempstead: Harvester-Wheatsheaf, 1992).

3 Belsey, *Critical Practice*, p.144.

4 Graham Holderness, *Shakespeare's History* (Gill and Macmillan, 1985); *William Shakespeare: Richard II* (Penguin, 1989); with Nick Potter and John Turner, *Shakespeare: The Play of History* (University of Iowa Press, 1988). Phyllis Rackin is the author of *Stages of History: Shakespeare's English Chronicles* (London: Routledge, 1990), and, with Jean E. Howard, *Engendering a Nation: A feminist account of Shakespeare's English Histories* (London: Routledge, 1997).

5 Graham Holderness, 'Shakespeare's History: *Richard II*', *Literature and History*, 7 (1981), pp.2–24.

6 See Stephen Greenblatt, 'Invisible Bullets: Renaissance Authority and Its Subversion', in *Political Shakespeare*, ed. Jonathan Dollimore and Alan Sinfield (Manchester: Manchester University Press, 1985), pp.24, 30.

7 Christopher Pye, 'The Betrayal of the Gaze: Theatricality and Power in Shakespeare's *Richard II*', *ELH*, 55 (1988), pp.575–98. On power in the histories and the tragedies, see also Jonathan Dollimore, *Radical Tragedy: Religion, Ideology and Power in the Drama of Shakespeare and his Contemporaries*

(Brighton: Harvester-Wheatsheaf, 1984), and Leonard Tennenhouse, *Power on Display* (London: Methuen, 1986).

8 *Différance* (sometimes Anglicised as here) is an important term in modern critical vocabulary. Coined by Jacques Derrida, it suggests both the difference between meanings and how meaning is constantly deferred. It is so because meaning involves the process of referring to other meanings; the result is that meaning constantly slides. The notion of *différance* lies at the heart of deconstruction criticism. For a fuller discussion, see Belsey, *Critical Practice*, and Abrams, *A Glossary of Literary Terms*.

9 Marjorie Garber, *Shakespeare's ghost writers: literature as uncanny causality* (London: Methuen, 1987), pp.20–1.

10 *Petits récits* are literally 'little narratives'; the term is used to suggest a story that does not claim to be master narrative but a more modest form of narrative that challenges limits or offers a different meaning. The term is from Jean-François Lyotard's *The postmodern condition: a report on knowledge*, trans. Geoff Bennington and Brian Massumi (1979; Manchester: Manchester University Press, 1984).

11 Catherine Belsey, 'Making Histories Then and Now: Shakespeare from *Richard II* to *Henry V*', in Francis Barker, Peter Hulme and Margaret Iversen (eds), *Uses of History: Marxism, Postmodernism and the Renaissance* (Manchester: Manchester University Press, 1991), pp.24–46. For a different approach to language in the play, see James L. Calderwood, *Metadrama in Shakespeare's 'Henriad'* (Berkeley: University of California Press, 1979), reprinted in Graham Holderness (ed.), *Shakespeare's History Plays: 'Richard II' to 'Henry V'*, New Casebooks (London: Macmillan, 1992).

12 Two important exceptions are Linda Bamber, *Comic Women, Tragic Men: A Study of Gender and Genre in Shakespeare* (Stanford: Stanford University Press, 1981), and Coppélia Kahn, *Man's Estate: Masculine Identity in Shakespeare* (Berkeley: University of California Press,

1981). Both are reprinted in Holderness (New Casebooks).

13 Barbara Hodgdon, *The End Crowns All: Closure and Contradiction in Shakespeare's History* (Princeton: Princeton University Press, 1991), p. 155.

14 Richard Halpern, *The Poetics of Primitive Accumulation: English Renaissance Culture and the Genealogy of Capital* (Ithaca: Cornell University Press, 1991), p. 245.

15 Jean E. Howard and Phyllis Rackin, *Engendering a Nation: A feminist account of Shakespeare's English Histories* (London and New York: Routledge, 1997), pp. 137–47. Useful introductions to feminist theory and criticism include Toril Moi, *Sexual/Textual Politics: Feminist Literary Theory* (London: Methuen, 1985); Catherine Belsey and Jane Moore (eds), *The Feminist Reader: Essays in Gender and the Politics of Literary Criticism* (London: Macmillan, 1989). See also Valerie Wayne (ed.), *The Matter of Difference: Materialist Feminist Criticism of Shakespeare* (Hemel Hempstead: Harvester-Wheatsheaf, 1991), and Kathleen McKluskie, *Renaissance Dramatists* (Hemel Hempstead: Harvester-Wheatsheaf, 1989).

BIBLIOGRAPHY

Abrams, M. H., *A Glossary of Literary Terms*, sixth edition (Orlando: Harcourt Brace Jovanovich, 1993).

Albright, Evelyn May, 'Shakespeare's *Richard II* and the Essex Conspiracy', *PMLA*, 42 (1927), 686–720.

Richard Altick, 'Symphonic Imagery in *Richard II*', *PMLA*, 62 (1947), 339–65, reprinted in Brooke (Casebook).

Atkins, G. Douglas and David M. Bergeron (eds), *Shakespeare and Deconstruction* (New York: Peter Lang, 1988).

Bamber, Linda, *Comic Women, Tragic Men: a Study of Gender and Genre in Shakespeare* (Stanford: Stanford University Press, 1981).

Barroll, Leeds, 'A New History for Shakespeare and his Time', *Shakespeare Quarterly*, 39 (1988), 441–64.

Barthes, Roland, 'The Death of the Author', in *Image–Music–Text*, trans. Stephen Heath (New York: Hill and Wang, 1977).

Bate, Jonathan (ed.), *The Romantics on Shakespeare* (Harmondsworth and New York: Penguin, 1992).

Belsey, Catherine, *Critical Practice* (1980; London and New York: Routledge, 1994).

Belsey, Catherine, 'Making Histories Then and Now: Shakespeare from *Richard II* to *Henry V*', in Francis Barker, Peter Hulme and Margaret Iversen (eds), *Uses of History: Marxism, Postmodernism and the Renaissance* (New York: Blackwell, 1989; Manchester: Manchester University Press, 1991).

Belsey, Catherine, *The Subject of Tragedy: Identity and Difference in Renaissance Drama* (London and New York: Methuen, 1985).

Belsey, Catherine and Jane Moore (eds), *The Feminist Reader: Essays in Gender and the Politics of Literary Criticism* (London: Macmillan, 1989).

Bennett, Andrew and Nicholas Royle, *An Introduction to Literature, Criticism and Theory* (Hemel Hempstead and New York: Harvester, 1995).

Bradley, A. C., *Shakespearean Tragedy: Lectures on Hamlet, Othello, King Lear, Macbeth* (London: Macmillan, 1904).

Brooke, Nicholas (ed.), *Shakespeare: 'Richard II'*, Casebook Series (London: Macmillan, 1973).

Brooke, Nicholas, *Shakespeare's Early Tragedies* (London: Methuen, 1968).

Bruce, Susan, *William Shakespeare: King Lear*, Icon Critical Guides (Cambridge: Icon, 1997).

Calderwood, James L., *Metadrama in Shakespeare's 'Henriad'* (Berkeley: University of California Press, 1979).

Campbell, Lily B., *Shakespeare's 'Histories': Mirrors of Elizabethan Policy* (1947; London: Methuen, 1964).

Chambers, E. K., *William Shakespeare: A Study of Facts and Problems*, 2 vols (Oxford: Clarendon Press, 1930).

Chambers, E.K. (ed.), 'Introduction' to *King Richard II* (London and New York: Longmans, Green & Co., 1891), reprinted in Newlin.

Clare, Janet, *'Art made tongue-tied by authority': Elizabethan and Jacobean Dramatic Censorship* (Manchester: Manchester University Press, 1990).

Cohen, Walter, *Drama of a Nation: Public Theatre in Renaissance England and Spain* (Ithaca: Cornell University Press, 1985).

Coleridge, Samuel Taylor, in Thomas Middleton Raysor (ed.), *Coleridge's Shakespearean Criticism*, 2 vols (London: Constable, 1930).

Dollimore, Jonathan, *Radical Tragedy: Religion, Ideology and Power in the Drama of Shakespeare and his Contemporaries* (Brighton: Harvester-Wheatsheaf, 1984).

Dollimore, Jonathan and Alan Sinfield (eds), *Political Shakespeare: New Essays in Cultural Materialism* (Manchester: Manchester University Press, 1986).

Dowden, Edward, *Shakespeare: A Critical Study of His Mind and Art* (1875; London: Routledge & Kegan Paul, 1967).

Drakakis, John (ed.), *Alternative Shakespeares* (London: Methuen, 1985).

Dutton, Richard, 'The Second Tetralogy', in Stanley Wells (ed.), *Shakespeare: A Bibliographic Guide* (Oxford: Clarendon Press, 1990).

Eagleton, Terry, *Literary Theory: An Introduction* (Oxford: Basil Blackwell, 1983).

Eagleton, Terry, *William Shakespeare* (Oxford: Basil Blackwell, 1986).

Forker, Charles (ed.), *Shakespeare: The Critical Tradition: 'Richard II'* (London and Atlantic Highlands: Athlone, 1998).

Greenblatt, Stephen, 'Invisible Bullets: Renaissance Authority and Its Subversion', in Dollimore and Sinfield.

Greenblatt, Stephen, *The Power of Forms in the English Renaissance* (Norman: Pilgrim Books, 1982).

Gurr, Andrew (ed.), *King Richard II, The New Cambridge Shakespeare* (Cambridge: Cambridge University Press, 1984).

Hawkes, Terence (ed.), *Alternative Shakespeares: Volume 2* (London: Routledge, 1996).

Hawkes, Terence, *Meaning By Shakespeare* (London and New York: Routledge, 1992).

Hazlitt, William, in W. E. Henley (ed.), *The Collected Works of William Hazlitt*, 12 vols (London: J. M. Dent and Sons, 1903).

Hodgdon, Barbara, *The End Crowns All: Closure and Contradiction in Shakespeare's History* (Princeton: Princeton University Press, 1991).

Holderness, Graham, *Shakespeare's History* (Dublin: Gill and Macmillan, 1985).

Holderness, Graham (ed.), *Shakespeare's History Plays: 'Richard II' to 'Henry V'*, New Casebooks (London: Macmillan, 1992).

Holderness, Graham, 'Shakespeare's History: *Richard II*', *Literature and History*, 7 (1981), 2–24.

Holderness, Graham, *William Shakespeare: Richard II* (Harmondsworth: Penguin, 1989).

Holderness, Graham, Nick Potter and John Turner, *Shakespeare: The Play of History* (Iowa City: University of Iowa Press, 1987).

Howard, Jean E. and Phyllis Rackin, *Engendering a Nation: A feminist account of Shakespeare's English Histories* (London and Boston: Routledge, 1997).

Hugo, Victor, *William Shakespeare*, trans. Meville B. Anderson (London: George Routledge and Sons, n.d.).

Ives, E. W., 'Shakespeare and History: Divergences and Agreements', *Shakespeare Survey*, 38 (1985) 19–35.

James, Mervyn, *Society, Politics, Culture: Studies in Early Modern England* (Cambridge and New York: Cambridge University Press, 1986).

Jefferson, Ann and David Robey (eds), *Modern Literary Theory: A Comparative Introduction* (London: Batsford, 1986).

Kahn, Coppélia, *Man's Estate: Masculine Identity in Shakespeare* (Berkeley: University of California Press, 1981).

Kamps, Ivo, *Materialist Shakespeare: A History* (London: Verso, 1995).

Kamps, Ivo and Deborah E. Barker (eds), *Shakespeare and Gender: A History* (London: Verso, 1995).

Kantorowicz, Ernst H., *The King's Two Bodies: A Study in Medieval Political Theology* (Princeton: Princeton University Press, 1957).

Kernan, Alvin, 'The Henriad: Shakespeare's Major History Plays', *Yale Review*, 59 (1969), 3–32.

Knight, G. Wilson, *The Wheel of Fire: Interpretations of Shakespearian Tragedy* (London: Methuen, 1930).

Knights, L. C., *Some Shakespearean Themes and an Approach to Hamlet* (Harmondsworth: Penguin, 1966).

Knights, L. C., *Explorations* (London: Chatto and Windus, 1946).

Kott, Jan, *Shakespeare Our Contemporary* (1965; London: Methuen, 1967).

LeWinter, Oswald (ed.), *Shakespeare in Europe* (Harmondsworth: Penguin, 1963).

Mahood, M. M., *Shakespeare's Wordplay* (London: Methuen, 1957).

Marcus, Leah, *Unediting the Renaissance: Shakespeare, Marlowe, Milton* (New York: Routledge, 1996).

McKluskie, Kathleen, *Renaissance Dramatists* (Hemel Hempstead and New York: Harvester-Wheatsheaf, 1989).

Moi, Toril, *Sexual/Textual Politics: Feminist Literary Theory* (London: Methuen, 1985).

Montague, C.E., 'F.R. Benson's *Richard II*', in *The Manchester Guardian*, 4 December 1899, reprinted in Brooke (Casebook).

Newlin, Jeanne T. (ed.), *'Richard II': Critical Essays* (New York: Garland & Co., 1984).

Norbrook, David, '"A Liberal Tongue": Language and Rebellion in *Richard II*', in John M. Mucciolo *et al.* (eds), *Shakespeare's Universe: Renaissance Ideas and Conventions* (Aldershot: Scolar Press, 1996), pp. 37–51.

Ornstein, Robert, *A Kingdom for a Stage* (Cambridge: Harvard University Press, 1972).

Parker, Patricia and Geoffrey Hartman (eds), *Shakespeare and the Question of Theory* (New York and London: Methuen, 1985).

Pater, Walter, *Appreciations: with an Essay on Style* (London: Macmillan, 1910).

Prior, Moody E., *The Drama of Power* (Evanston, Illinois: Northwestern University Press, 1973).

Pye, Christopher, 'The Betrayal of the Gaze: Theatricality and Power in Shakespeare's *Richard II*', *ELH*, 55 (1988), 575–98.

Rabkin, Norman, *Shakespeare and the Common Understanding* (New York: Free Press, 1967).

Rackin, Phyllis, *Stages of History: Shakespeare's English Chronicles* (London: Routledge, 1991).

Reese, M. M., *The Cease of Majesty: A Study of Shakespeare's History Plays* (London: Edward Arnold, 1961).

Ribner, Irving, *The English History Play in the Age of Shakespeare* (Princeton: Princeton University Press, 1957).

Roberts, Josephine A. *'Richard II': An Annotated Bibliography*, 2 vols (New York: Garland Press, 1988).

Rossiter, A. P., *Angel With Horns* (London: Longmans, Green and Co, 1961).

Ryan, Kiernan, *Shakespeare* (Hemel Hempstead: Harvester Wheatsheaf, 1989).

Sanders, Wilbur, *The Dramatist and the Received Idea: Studies in the Plays of Marlowe and Shakespeare* (Cambridge: Cambridge University Press, 1968).

Schlegel, Augustus William, *A Course of Lectures on Dramatic Art and Literature*, trans. John Black (London: Henry G. Bohn, 1846).

Shewring, Margaret, *King Richard II*, Shakespeare in Performance series (Manchester: Manchester University Press, 1996).

Sprague, A. C., *Shakespeare's Histories: Plays for the Stage* (London: The Society for Theatre Research, 1964).

Spurgeon, Caroline, *Shakespeare's Imagery and What it Tells Us* (New York: Macmillan, 1935).

Taylor, Gary, *Reinventing Shakespeare: A Cultural History from the Restoration to the Present* (New York: Weidenfeld & Nicholson, 1989; London: The Hogarth Press, 1990).

Tennenhouse, Leonard, *Power on Display* (London: Methuen, 1986).

Tillyard, E. M. W., *The Elizabethan World Picture* (1943; London: Peregrine Books, 1963).

Tillyard, E. M. W., *Shakespeare's History Plays* (London: Chatto & Windus, 1948).

Traversi, D. A., *Shakespeare from 'Richard II' to 'Henry V'* (London: Hollis & Carter, 1957).

Ure, Peter (ed.), *King Richard II*, The Arden Shakespeare (London and New York: Methuen, 1991).

Vickers, Brian (ed.), *Shakespeare: The Critical Heritage*, 6 vols (London: Routledge, 1974–1981).

Wayne, Valerie (ed.), *The Matter of Difference: Materialist Feminist Criticism of Shakespeare* (Hemel Hempstead: Harvester-Wheatsheaf, 1991).

Wells, Stanley (ed.), *King Richard The Second*, New Penguin Shakespeare (Harmondsworth: Penguin, 1969).

Wilson, John Dover (ed.), 'Introduction' to *King Richard II* (1939; Cambridge: Cambridge University Press, 1951).

Yeats, W. B. *Ideas of Good and Evil* (London: A. H. Bullen, 1903), pp. 142–67, reprinted in W. B. Yeats, *Essays and Introductions* (London: Macmillan, 1961).

A Note on Further Reading

The bibliography above lists the essays extracted in this book as well as criticism of the history plays in general. A useful place to start further reading on *Richard II* is with the recent books by Graham Holderness and Phyllis Rackin. Equally rewarding is Margaret Shewring's analysis of the politics and reception of the play's production in the theatre.

Jonathan Bate's *The Romantics on Shakespeare* has a fine introduction and provides the obvious starting point for work on that area. Similarly, Brian Vickers' volumes in *The Critical Heritage* series are invaluable to anyone who wishes to explore the critical reception of the play from 1623 to 1800. A helpful anthology covering earlier twentieth-century criticism is Nicholas Brooke, *Shakespeare: 'Richard II'* (Casebook Series). Richard Dutton's essay in Stanley Wells' *Shakespeare: A Bibliographic Guide* provides an incisive survey of criticism of the play and a substantial reading list of items up to 1990. A more recent list of criticism can be found in Jean E. Howard and Phyllis Rackin's *Engendering A Nation*. For the way in which critical theory has changed the study of Shakespeare, a good place to begin is with Kiernan Ryan's book and with the collection of essays edited by John Drakakis in *Alternative Shakespeares*. The best introduction to modern critical theory remains Catherine Belsey's *Critical Practice*. Graham Holderness's excellent New Casebook on *Shakespeare's History Plays* discusses contemporary critical approaches to the plays and has an annotated reading list.

ACKNOWLEDGEMENTS

The editor and publishers wish to thank the following for their permission to reprint copyright material: Manchester University Press (for material from *King Richard II* and *Uses of History: Marxism, Postmodernism and the Renaissance*); Scolar Press (for material from *Shakespeare's Universe: Renaissance Ideas and Conventions*); Peregrine Books (for material from *The Elizabethan World Picture*); Cambridge University Press (for material from *King Richard II*); Penguin Books (for material from *Shakespeare's History Plays*); Methuen (for material from *Shakespeare's 'Histories': Mirrors of Elizabethan Policy* and *Shakespeare's Wordplay*); Free Press (for material from *Shakespeare and the Common Understanding*); Princeton University Press (for material from *The King's Two Bodies: A Study in Medieval Political Theology*); Yale University Press (for material from *Yale Review*); *Literature and History* (for material from 'Shakespeare's History: *Richard II*'); Routledge (for material from *Engendering a Nation: A Feminist Account of Shakespeare's English Histories*).

Every effort has been made to contact the holders of any copyrights applying to the material quoted in this book. The publishers would be grateful if any such copyright holders whom they have not been able to contact, would write to them.

The editor would like to thank John Peck, of the School of English, Communication, and Philosophy at Cardiff, for his generous help and invaluable comments in the preparation of this volume.

Martin Coyle is Senior Lecturer in English at the University of Wales, Cardiff. He is the editor of the Macmillan New Casebook on *Hamlet*, and joint author (with John Peck) of the Macmillan volumes *Literary Terms and Criticism* and *Practical Criticism*.